A BARN IN
NEW ENGLAND

A BARN IN

making a home on three acres

NEW ENGLAND

Joseph Monninger

CHRONICLE BOOKS

SAN FRANCISCO

Library of Congress Cataloging-in-Publication Data available.

ISBN: 0-8118-2974-X

Printed in the United States
Designed by A. Galperin

Distributed in Canada by Raincoast Books
9050 Shaughnessy Street
Vancouver, British Columbia V6P 6E5

10 9 8 7 6 5 4 3 2 1

Chronicle Books LLC
85 Second Street
San Francisco, California 94105
www.chroniclebooks.com

for PIE

My heart was a habitation large enough for many
guests, but lonely and chill, and without a household fire.
I longed to kindle one! It seemed not so wild a dream.

The Scarlet Letter
Nathaniel Hawthorne

Remember that you ought to behave in life as you would at a banquet. As something is being passed around it comes back to you: Stretch out your hand, take a portion politely. It passes on; do not detain it. Or it has not come to you yet; do not project your desire to meet it, but wait until it comes in front of you.

The Encheiridion
Epictetus c. 50-120

winter

W e saw the pine trees first. A hundred years before we arrived, someone had planted a row of pines as a windbreak to the north of the barn. They were spectacular, tall, green masts reaching up two hundred feet. Their southern branches extended toward the barn, reaching across the plowed drive. Two low limbs brushed the top of our Dodge pickup as we parked. When we turned off the engine, we heard nothing at all.

I looked up through the windshield at the barn, the white barn, four stories tall. I could not quite believe the size of the building, the thought that I could own such a thing. It might have been drawn by a child: straight lines, a cupola on top, wide, welcoming doors overlooking a broad meadow. Surely we had drawn this building ourselves, imagined it a thousand times in our secret hearts, added a strand of chimney smoke above it, a bright, smiling sun in the sky. Brown crayon wedges for birds. More wedges, impaled by a brown trunk, to form pines. A stick figure dog beside a stick figure mom and dad.

"Well, what do you think?" Wendy asked, her eyes locked on the building.

"It's huge," I said.

"It's enormous. It really is a barn."

"That's what the prospectus said."

"I know, but it's strange to see it here. In wood and stone, I mean. It's a barn. We could live in a barn. It hasn't quite sunk in yet."

"I know what you mean," I said, and I thought I did.

We leaned closer to the windshield to get better views. I wanted to get out, to walk around, but something held me back. Maybe it was the worry of rushing toward some good thing you knew would happen. It was like savoring the moment before you open a letter from someone you miss or who you knew was sending you excellent news. We continued bending back and forth, trying to get our vision around the height of the building, the wide ship of it as it lay in the white meadow. As we looked, the truck clicked and began losing heat. A few dollops of snow fell softly out of the pines whenever the wind blew, depositing white egg cups on the hood of the truck.

"Ready?" Wendy asked.

It had been her idea to come early in order to look at the place before we had to talk it away. Our appointment was for ten, and we had twenty minutes to walk around. She grabbed the prospectus and slid the roll of papers up the sleeve of her ski parka and then she was out the door. I climbed out, too, and stood for a second beneath the enormous pines. It was rare to see a pine so large; to see ten, maybe fifteen all in a line, all of them limned with snow, was a remarkable sight. All the air to reach the barn, summer or winter, was first filtered by the green needles.

We circled around back, away from the road and the pines. The backyard opened onto a wide, white meadow. An oak hedgerow marked the northern border of the property; just beyond the hedgerow, a fishpond, perhaps an acre wide, pulled the snow into a volcano crater of ice and more snow. And far beyond the meadow, like the V of a goose's wing, Mt. Moosilauke cut a pyramid in the sky. Clouds and mist rolled over the mountaintop, arching slowly into the western horizon and joining again with the white snow.

When we turned and faced the barn, this time from the southeast, I could still hardly believe the size of it. It was a true barn set on a north-south angle in a flat meadow. An enormous farmer's porch, roofed by a slope of rafters and supported by five beams, covered the entire rear of the barn. Beneath the snow the porch appeared to be fieldstone, gray rocks, mortar. Two sets of French doors, both equally spaced in the east wall, took the morning sun, what there was of it, directly on their surfaces. The glass in each door was old enough to have settled, the mottled glaze of antique glass trying to return to sand and liquid.

Wind came off the meadow behind us. We heard it pass through the pines and saw it raise a snow devil from the field. The devil hung for a moment in the air like a genie, like a question mark, then disappeared. We stepped onto the porch. The snow here, beneath the porch roof, reached halfway up the legs of the three Adirondack chairs left by the former owners. The barn helped to block some of the wind, but it was still cold, bitterly so, and my hands felt numb. I looked at Wendy. She stood on the porch, her eyes moving quickly to take in every element of the structure. We had talked for months about this day, about finding a building like this one. It needed work and devotion, but anyone could see it would be worth the effort. It was a building with character. No amount of work would be wasted on it.

Wind pushed at us again, and this time Wendy let it push her toward the building, toward the French doors. I followed. Like children looking through a screen door on a summer day, we put our hands up to shade our eyes and looked through the glass. Blinded for a moment by the white field behind us, I couldn't see anything in the dimness of the interior. I pressed my hand more tightly to the glass, adjusted to give myself more shade, then squinted to see.

At about that instant Wendy's hand found mine. She did not want to hold my hand, exactly, but wanted to steady herself in the face of what we had glimpsed. Through the glass, in the dimness, we saw an enormous keeping room. It contained an open space the size of a backyard whiffleball stadium, and only beams interrupted the clear run of open flooring. A nine-foot-wide granite fireplace took up one side of the barn; a twelve-foot Irish wake table halved the room. A jigsaw puzzle lay three quarters formed on the table, and a bowl of cut hydrangea, dried to flakes, had turned into a tired corn broom. Bending to one side, my free hand still in place, I saw the southern wall, the gable end of the barn. Here, I realized, animals had once passed into the barn, the lumbering walk of the cattle across the ancient threshing floor a dull, sonorous business. Someone had removed the sliding track barn door on the southern end and had installed in its place a two-story-tall bank of windows. The glass transom above the southern door—the old farmer's transom—still held glass a century old. Charlotte had spun her web in such a barn. Cattle had once munched their evening feed in lines on either side of the barn, their heads like black and white compass needles stretching from hand-hewn stalls.

The interior still held every feature of the original barn. Wood beams, huge beams that ran up three stories, pushed the roof to twenty or thirty feet. I had never seen a room so spacious, so tall, in a private home. Five skylights let sunshine in from above, the milky rays drifting down through the cathedral roof, through the rafters and purlins. Pegged beams, original barn boards, an enormous threshing floor. Former animal stalls on each corner of the building, from what I could see, had been converted into bedrooms. One stall served as a kitchen. A ladder, made of rough-cut lumber—more tree than lumber, actually—climbed to the roof of the kitchen where, presumably, another bedroom was located. The ladder lent the barn a tree-house feeling, a place for fun and romance.

"All this land, too," Wendy said.

She had already turned away from the house. Standing on the porch, we could look out across a meadow of snow. White drifts had piled against the hedgerow, some as high as basketball rims. I slipped off my gloves and pulled a copy of the realtor's sheet from the pouch of my anorak. Three acres came with the barn, flat land running roughly toward the northeast. This had been a farm once. I had known that, of course, given the presence of the barn, but I really saw it now looking across the land. The fishpond, attached to the northern end of the property, lay under snow, invisible. Only the dent in the snow and the legend of the map confirmed its presence.

Wind tried to take the map out of my hands. Wendy grabbed the other corner. She studied the map for a second, took in what she needed, then nodded. She got it; the barn had finally stepped out of the prospectus. We stared for a little longer at the land, then back at the barn, as if we had to connect to the two things with our vision. I knew she would recall details later that I had neglected or forgotten altogether.

I folded the map and put it back in my pouch. My fingers had begun to sting. A crow flapped across the meadow, a black kite of a bird in a white day. It landed in a pine and snow tickled down the skin of the tree.

Wendy and I walked to the other end of the porch, the southern end. When we rounded the corner we spotted a garden. Defined by a white picket fence and a trellis arch at the entrance, the garden consisted of a white bed of snow. The owners had placed the garden outside the bank of windows on the southern end, making it the logical destination through the third and last set of French doors. Morning light would find it. In the evening it would be pale and quiet.

"I didn't see the garden listed on the prospectus," Wendy said. "It's a lovely garden."

"It's a lot of house," I said, not quite knowing what I meant.

Or rather, not quite knowing why the appearance of the garden should make me see the barn as a lot of house.

"It will keep you busy weeding."

Wendy and I kissed then. It was a cold and silly kind of kiss. We pushed into the front yard. Here, at last, we could gain some perspective on the barn, its clean, classic lines, the lovely white façade. Far above, a weather vane with the letter G turned quietly in the wind. Hydrangea bushes occupied the two corners of the building—the source, obviously, of the cut flowers inside. The grayed heads of the desiccated flowers held small fields of snow. Snow sat on the picket fence of the garden and on the steep pitch of the roof.

Standing in the center of the front yard, we decided to buy this house, to move in, to put everything we could into this building. With little talk, we made our decision before the realtor ever arrived.

❄

Dick Gowen, an ex-football coach, is a broad, gentle fellow whose voice sounds like hay falling from a wagon. He is truly a good guy, a fair, honest man, whose sales pitch consists primarily of opening doors. He honked his horn and waved when he pulled into the driveway. Then he handed us more information about the barn along with some vintage photos the former owners had photocopied. The cold didn't seem to bother him.

"It's unique, isn't it?" he said as he trudged through the snow in front of us. "I saw a show on television about extreme housing. It talked about people who buy old fire stations and barns and things. I guess it's a trend."

"So are you saying we could be on TV?" I asked.

"Maybe," he said.

We went in through the basement directly off the driveway, passing first under an overhang—a lip, an open grin of wood and beams, used for outside storage. Someone had backed a motor boat into the overhang, the tail swallowed by the hollow of the barn, the bow covered by a tarp. Dick looked at the boat and told us the owners hadn't been up in some years; the boat belonged to another neighbor who used the overhang for storage. We nodded. We wanted to be inside. But I saw, too, how useful the overhang could be. It was an ideal place to keep wood, a barbecue grill, the three kayaks we had purchased over the years.

Then we were inside. Cement covered the basement floor, but I hardly noticed it next to the massive fieldstone foundation. Stones the size of liquor boxes or larger stood eight feet tall around us. It was like standing in a fort. Nineteenth-century barns are not anchored by metal spikes to sills the way residential houses are, but are set on top of the foundation like a cap propped on a rectangle of stone. The sheer size of the supporting beams and floor joists astonished me. The beams measured nine by nine, sometimes larger, and ran in thirty- or forty-foot lengths. I could not imagine the trees that provided such beams. I had never entered a house that appeared so permanent.

On our right, a small family room had been framed out of rough-sawn pine. A Franklin woodstove stood against the stone base of the enormous fireplace we had seen on the main floor. Here was where you would sit on a cold day. Heat would push up through the floor and keep the next room warm as well. Farther on, beneath the southeastern quarter of the building, someone had located the hot water heater and septic outlet pipe. On the other side of the building, a dark jumble of a room—storage and a bare dirt floor—lay dank and ugly as our worst fear of basements. Spider country, Wendy said. We barely glanced at it, although we could not pretend it didn't shake us.

We followed Dick upstairs and into the light, because around him, flowing down from windows we had already seen, light suffused the air. Dick didn't say anything. He stepped aside and smiled and waited for our reaction. He knew, as anyone who entered the barn must know, that few people consider owning a house like this.

Here at last was the interior. What we had glimpsed before could not compare to the impact of standing in the keeping room. I later learned that barns had been built as churches had been built. The Greek word *nave,* which I understood to mean aisle of a cathedral, also meant ship. A church, like a barn, is a ship turned over.

Our eyes ran up and down the beams. Wendy took my hand for a second, but then she had to pull it away so that she could look freely. The main room, the keeping room, ranged thirty by thirty and twenty feet high. Above us, the haymow, from which the farmer had forked hay to the cattle below, ran like a dark tongue through the building. A dry log, ten feet long and flattened on one side, served as a mantel. The beams themselves, all entirely exposed, ran like ribbons of cattail-colored wood, dividing first one perspective, then the next. The skylights let the morning light sift down and through the barn and dust rose to meet it and twirled there, like memory, until the light spent itself on the threshing-room floor. In the course of a minute the light shifted and changed. Standing in the barn, we watched clouds nosing over the roof.

"Feel free to look around," Dick said, and it was only after he spoke that I realized we hadn't actually moved beyond the top of the stairway from the basement.

Wendy, her eyes, I knew, taking in the floor plan, the possibilities, walked forward. The owners had decorated with country touches: a wagon-wheel light fixture, a grain bin for a sideboard, moose antlers on the fireplace, a hay fork nailed high to one wall. A rope hammock dangled between two beams, the ends braided like a game of cat's cradle. The Irish wake table gave the fireplace area a sense of enclosure. Although the barn had been decorated in keeping with its nature, the owners had evidently seen it as a summer place. A few snack tables stood beside the couch; a TV, with snaggled rabbit ears, eyed the room from a place near the fireplace. The arrangement seemed temporary.

Looking around, Dick explained that the owners had used the place when their children were young. It had been a summer retreat from Boston. In winter, they occasionally came up to ski, but when they did they stayed in the downstairs room, close to the woodstove. Otherwise no one had occupied the place during the winter. Snowmobilers used the fields outside; a hired man mowed the meadow each summer. For all intents and purposes, the barn had been empty too long for its own good.

We listened, but only halfheartedly, because we had begun to picture ourselves here. Now and then, after spotting a new element of the barn we caught each other's eye. *This too?* We looked at the kitchen. It was rough. An aluminum sink rested on wooden legs carved from jack pine. The oven—which would remain with the house—was an unknown brand from the 1940s. The fridge, which resembled a black casket set up on end, stayed too. Its sides rounded back and away, art deco, or an artillery shell designed for a warship. Only after staring at it for several moments did I realize it was the exact model as our basement refrigerator had been thirty years before—our childhood refrigerator that had held the milk for seven children and the blanched carcass of the Thanksgiving turkey when no room could be made in the more modern, upstairs fridge. I pulled open the door and half expected to see a tent of aluminum foil over a desiccated turkey, a jellied, quivering plate of cranberries beside it. Instead only a yellow box of baking soda remained behind, its base surrounded by a drift of white powder. A squirrel had been at the box, its claws leaving footprints across the black roof of the fridge.

After the kitchen, we climbed. A catwalk rimmed the northern face, taking us past shelves and shelves of books. It had been a long-standing dream of mine to have a wall covered with books, a ladder to slide back and forth across it. The barn went one better: The catwalk allowed you to browse for books and to take in the downstairs seating arrangements from an aerial perspective. I had never seen anything quite like it in a house. We stood for a long time on the catwalk, trying to gobble the house up with our eyes. From our vantage point we could at last see the configuration of the stable rooms. The bathroom and kitchen, both converted from stables, straddled the large bank of windows and occupied the southern ends. That was why, I understood, the plumbing had been beneath them in the basement. On the northern end, two stables had been transformed into bedrooms. A second floor—essentially the roofs of the ground-floor stables—had been given over to two additional bedrooms. The stables worked like building blocks. If the barn had been a conventional house, it would have been three stories tall without counting the basement.

Then higher. We climbed a wooden staircase and worked our way out onto the hayloft. Twenty feet off the ground, we stared down at the keeping room. Dick, who stayed below, laughed and waved. We waved back, then climbed the last set of stairs to the cupola. Sea ropes, acting as banisters, ran from the cupola to the hayloft. The sense of being on a ship came back to me. Going up the final staging to the cupola, both of us slightly nervous at the height, it felt as though we had climbed a cargo ladder.

We climbed through a hatch and into a tiny, six-by-six birdcage atop the roof. Snow and whiteness pushed away from the barn, ran up into the hills and across the meadow. Trees, below us now, resembled brushes clogged by old plaster. Tracks of birds ran in miniature necklaces across the fresh snow on the roof. The weather vane, knotted into the roof of the cupola, twisted quietly in the wind. We could see for miles in every direction. Now and then a gust pushed against the house and we watched snow rise from the roof ridge, ghosts riding into bright, cold sunshine.

At dinner in Wendy's apartment, Pie, her eight-year-old son, asked if the barn cost more than a hundred dollars. He ate a bowl of spaghetti by twirling it on his fork, then lifting the squirrely noodles to his mouth. He had taken off the coonskin cap he wore during the day, but he wore a light saber through his belt. Archer and Slam Fist, two rubberized action figures, stood beside his plate, both of them muscled and glaring at each forkful. He listened when I told him the house cost a lot more than one hundred dollars, though I knew he couldn't quite take it in. His grandfather had once given him one hundred dollars on his birthday and that represented the outer limits of his financial universe.

"Houses cost thousands and thousands of dollars," Wendy said, pulling apart a piece of garlic bread. "You usually pay them off over years. You also pay interest."

"What do you mean, pay them off?" Pie asked.

"A little bit at a time. The interest is what the bank gets paid for lending you the money. That's why they lend it in the first place."

Pie nodded. He ate more spaghetti. I had found that he didn't always reveal that he comprehended things on the first go-around, but he often revisited the subject a day or week later and showed that he had in fact understood it perfectly. For now he had established that the house cost more than his hundred dollars. He would have to chew on that a while.

After dinner we played Dino-Zoo, a board game that he loved. Each player had a spaceship, and the object was to travel back in time to capture dinosaurs. Pie was a very big fan of dinosaurs. He made a beeline for T. Rex, his favorite, while Wendy and I captured the relatively insignificant Brontosaurus and Triceratops. Capturing the minor dinosaurs added up, but Pie didn't care as long as he could trot T. Rex off the board while making T. Rex roars. He took the T. Rex to bed with him, loping the dinosaur across his covers as we turned off the light.

Wendy and I sat on the couch afterward and drank tea and talked about the barn. We wanted it; that much was clear. We had fallen in love with the barn, the setting, the white meadow stretching away from the farmer's porch. The asking price was $129,000, but we didn't take that number seriously. We knew the owners had paid $30,000 for the barn sometime in the mid-1980s. The barn needed insulation; it needed to be modernized; a few beams required work. Portions of the electrical wiring were outdated and potentially dangerous. The sill on the southern end of the building seemed soft and worn and would probably need to be replaced. The septic tank had not been pumped in fifteen years, primarily because the Rogerses, the current owners, could not find it. It was probably substandard and would need to be replaced. The asphalt roof, although serviceable, appeared to be about midway through its useful life. To replace a barn roof, we guessed, would be expensive as hell. We had also spotted some evidence of powder post beetles, an insect that bores into wood and eats away until the wood becomes porous and weak. In a structure made of old beams, the beetles could be devastating.

On a scratch pad we drew an estimate of renovation costs. We planned to do as much of the work as possible ourselves. Still, in no time the figures put a knot in our throats. We tried not to be conservative in the guesses so that we would have a frank appraisal of what the building might cost to fix. In some instances we placed a question mark beside the figure. We imagined the cost could go up or down, depending on labor and materials. The wiring job, for example, was impossible to estimate. We had no idea what it might require or how much electricians charged these days. We came up with the following figures.

Roof	$ 10,000
Septic	$ 10–30,000
Wiring	$ 4,000 ?
Replace sill	$ 5,000 ?
Insulation	$ 10,000
Kitchen renovation	$ 10,000
Surprises	$ 5,000
TOTAL	**$ 54,000 plus or minus**

That left a lot of wiggle room. With luck we could reduce it to around $30,000, but we didn't figure we could go much lower than that. It was equally possible that the figures could go up to $60,000. For tax purposes, the building had been appraised at $75,000. In another location—in southern Vermont, for example—a barn like this one might be worth a quarter of a million dollars. But in Warren, New Hampshire, a town with a depressed economy, $100,000 should carry the day. We decided to subtract $30,000 from what we thought the house was worth, thereby accounting for the renovation costs, and make an offer on the barn for $70,000.

"That doesn't seem like enough," Wendy said after we kicked it around for a while. "They want one hundred and thirty."

"All they can do is say no. Besides, we have to figure the costs of owning the property. Heat's going to cost a bundle. It's going to be a lot of work."

"The Rogerses may decide to wait a while and see what happens."

"It's just an offer," I said. "I'll make it seventy-five thousand just to even it out, but that's as high as we'll go."

The next morning I called Dick Gowen. I listened carefully to determine if Dick thought the offer was too low, but he didn't let on one way or the other. He said he'd call the Rogerses and let them know they had an offer in hand. We talked for a while about selling my cottage in Bridgewater, New Hampshire, a small, single-story building I had lived in for the past five years. I asked Dick if he thought it would stay on the market long and he said it was an attractive package for a young couple starting out. But you never knew, he said. One thing at a time.

That afternoon I dressed warmly and took D Dog, my six-year-old black Lab, for a long walk, a pair of snowshoes on my back in case I needed them. We walked beside Clay Brook, a small stream now stiff with cold. We followed the stream up current, skirting it when necessary, occasionally tiptoeing across the quieter sections. We had as our destination a waterfall several miles north of my cottage. We had visited it hundreds of times, mostly in spring when the runoff turned it into a white paddle slapping against the black rocks, but in winter it still gave purpose to a good walk. D Dog knew the route and followed it with her nose down, her chest plowing a furrow in the snow.

We found the waterfall after clumping up an arching walk over a particularly deep portion of the stream. Ice had grabbed the waterfall and squeezed it into a glazed pillar. I sat on a wide flat rock we often used for picnics. The rock presented a good view of the waterfall and farther down, through the trees, to the spill of forest running out to the west. D Dog came to sit beside me. I gave her a biscuit and told her she was a good girl. She leaned against me. The afternoon turned gray between the tree boles. Snow lay everywhere.

I thought about the barn, about Wendy and Pie, and about what the move would mean. What we planned to do would change the course of our lives. To people who asked, we said we were throwing our hats in together, but the truth seemed more serious than that. For my part, by joining forces on the house I was consenting to help raise Pie. That remained foremost in my mind. I loved Pie as I had never loved anyone else in my life. I had loved friends and family and women, but this love, the love of a man for a son, was unlike anything I had experienced. Although

I was not his biological father, Pie was the boy I would have chosen from a thousand boys. It excited me to consider watching him grow to adulthood. But once I committed to this, I wanted to stand by my word. In that quiet late afternoon, I asked myself if I was certain.

I didn't have any great revelation, but when I stood to return to my cottage I knew my mind. I would make a home with Wendy and Pie and fill up our days with as much kindness as I could. We would buy the barn and hope that it shaped things for us. We would have a home.

A little sentimental, I knew, but it was true nonetheless. I whistled to D Dog to get her started. She bounded off the rock and sank in the snow. Her leap touched against a beech tree and started the brown leaves shaking. She led me down through the snow, the late afternoon sun occasionally landing on her back and placing a gold coin there.

On Friday night I cooked dinner for Wendy and Pie. Wendy liked a dish I made called Russian Peasant Pie. It was a simple dinner that used up leftovers, cabbage, and hard-boiled eggs. Baked in a pastry shell, it was a sort of chicken potpie without the chicken. Our own Pie hated it and opted for Kraft macaroni and cheese, a glowing orange puddle of noodles that he ate with ravenous delight.

We had just finished dinner when the phone rang. I went into the kitchen and picked it up without giving it a thought. Dick Gowen was on the line saying he had some good news. The Rogerses had been out of town so they hadn't reacted to our offer, but after giving it some thought they had now decided to accept it. Wendy must have heard something in my voice, because she came out and stared at me. She went back and got our wine glasses from the table. Behind her, I heard Pie's fork chasing noodles around his plate.

I wrote down a bunch of phrases on a chalkboard beside the phone, but they didn't really make any sense. I did write, however, the word *yes* on the side of the board and Wendy came over and tucked beneath my arm as I finished the conversation. I thanked Dick and asked him what happened next. He said we should come by the office Saturday afternoon and sign papers, make arrangements, talk about what to do with the Bridgewater cottage. Wendy rented, so it was a simple matter to terminate her lease. Dick congratulated us. He said the Rogerses were pleased that people who loved the barn as much as they did would be moving in.

I hung up. Wendy and I kissed for a while. Then we pushed away from each other and stood for a moment staring at each other. I told her everything I could remember about the conversation, even insignificant details that couldn't possibly have any bearing on the outcome. She didn't care; she wanted everything. I told her that the Rogerses had accepted the offer. We could probably close in about three months. Call it May or June. That would give us the whole summer to insulate the house, to winterize it, to make it snug. It had worked out perfectly. The Rogerses hadn't vacillated. Seventy-five thousand constituted a fair price.

Then we kissed again, a good, wild kiss full of the future, happiness, and things to come. Pie carried his plate into the kitchen and we broke off to tell him that our offer on the barn had been accepted. He said that was great, then picked up D Dog's front legs and did a mambo with her. I doubted the whole thing made much sense to him, but he was happy to celebrate. He danced D Dog in a circle, making her follow on her back legs, her claws clicking on the kitchen slate, her paws on his shoulders.

Afterward we roasted some marshmallows, our traditional Friday-night fare. Pie ate half a bag, his mouth turning into a white hole. He gave D Dog anything that dropped or spilled over, which was a good deal for D Dog. Wendy and I roasted the marshmallows more slowly, then pulled them off and ate the crackling rind. We talked about where furniture might go, what we would do first in terms of renovation. Pie asked about the school. What about Chris and Ryan, a pair of twins with whom he buddied around? It hit him that he wouldn't be going to the same elementary school any longer and that his friends would change. That information caused a moment of gloominess, but then we told him he would be living near the Baker River, close to the White Mountain National Forest, and that D Dog would be entirely his. That brightened things a good deal, and he spent the rest of the marshmallow session asking about what tricks he thought it was possible to teach D Dog. He felt, obviously, that she had been underemployed in my company.

The next morning we woke early to go sledding. In the garage, Pie faced a dilemma. He had received a new Flexible Flyer for Christmas—the new boards almost yellow, the runners barn red—though his old sled, one we nicknamed Arrow, remained perfectly sound. Watching him inspect both sleds as they hung on the garage wall, I appreciated his struggle. He wanted to be loyal to the old sled, a short-bed Flexible Flyer I had bought in a yard sale for ten dollars two years before, but the appeal of the new sled was undeniable. Wendy came out and told him to make up his mind.

"Rocket," he said, which was the name of the new sled, and he looked at me to see if I disapproved. We had been sledding together before and he knew I liked old sleds, the ones that have turned the color of horse harness. I collected them the way some people collect tools or duck decoys, and I've always had five or six around the place. I liked the way they look and I liked the way the front assemblage could bend and twist, a calf's neck being bulled by a cowboy. I hoisted mine from the wall, a sled named Thunder Boy, while Wendy lifted down Mustang.

"Maybe I'll take Arrow," he said, referring to the old sled.

"No, use Rocket," I said. "It needs to be broken in."

He stared up at me, uncertain. After we broke our stare, he nodded and helped me lift Rocket off the wall. He scooted it down the driveway and lifted it into the back of my pickup, where D Dog already waited.

Fifteen minutes later we stood at the top of a long run, one packed solid by snowmobiles the night before. But today the snowmobiles were gone and now the forest was quiet except for an occasional chickadee calling from winter branches. Pie didn't wait. He folded the rope of his sled back, squared it so it wouldn't dangle, then made a short, rump-high run, his legs churning behind. His snowsuit made a whistling sound as he ran. Then he grunted and lunged forward, his belly umphing a bit when he hit the bed of the sled. As he turned the corner of the first section, his arms steering perfectly, he yelled back over his shoulder, "To infinity and beyond," one of his favorite lines from the *Toy Story* movies. D Dog tore after him, her paws flicking up snow, her fur covered by a glistening frost. She ran head down, flat out, chasing Pie as he whooped down the half-mile run.

"We have the barn," I said to Wendy as we listened to him going down the hill.

She nodded, then she charged forward and glided off into the middle distance, her shouts equally aimed at Pie and at me. I waited a ten count, then jumped forward, landing with a krumph on the slatted boards, the runners hissing underneath me. For a moment the world still came at me slowly. My vision filled with mounded snowbanks and pine boughs trapped by late-night storms, but little by little my speed increased. When I rounded the first bend I saw Wendy in front of me, D Dog bobbing around her. Then suddenly I knew I was going fast, flicking along the ground, covering ice and snow, wind grinding against my cheeks. "To infinity and beyond," I yelled, because it was what Pie liked us all to yell and because it seemed like a sensible thing to yell on a sled. And I glimpsed Pie down at the bottom of the run, climbing onto the snowbank, looking uphill to see us coming.

A classic catch-22: Though we had excellent credit, no bank wanted to accept our mortgage because the barn wasn't heated. Was it an unheated summer residence? Was that what we proposed? Because, in that case, they might be able to work something out. If it was a year-round residence, didn't it have a heating system? And if not, how in the world were we going to last through a winter? Did we have any idea how cold it got in New Hampshire in January?

We had this conversation a dozen times. The holders of my small mortgage on the Bridgewater cottage had problems with the barn mortgage. One bank official, a short, nervous man who seemed to live in fear of dress-down Fridays, explained it this way:

"The way we operate is the way most banks operate. We extend a mortgage to you, but then we don't hold on to it. We sell the mortgage to a bigger company. The bigger companies have a policy. They won't accept a mortgage on a structure with no heating system. Let's say the worst happens and you can't meet payments. Then that bank is stuck with an unheated house. They can't sell an unheated house."

"But we can't heat it until we occupy it," I said. "Surely you can see that's a rub. And we can't live in it without heat. So in order to buy the house, we have to heat it. But we can't heat it without buying it."

This fellow appeared sympathetic, but he didn't see a way to do it. Ironically, mortgage rates stood at an all-time low—6.7 percent was not uncommon. Even the fattest mortgages ran somewhere in the low 7-percent range. Most banks eagerly lent money to any applicant. Money was cheap, if you could get it.

But we couldn't. The barn, as we had explained to us a dozen times, fit no known profile. Sitting together one night after we put Pie to bed, Wendy and I despaired. Maybe we couldn't get the barn after all. February had settled on New England, licking the streets and trees into a white glaze. It did not seem a time for new or inventive thinking. Pot-roast days, in other words, when night comes quickly and you don't range too far from shelter. The delight we took in talking about where we would place our furniture in the barn, what we would do with this or that room, how we would get a fire going on a certain evening, suddenly turned hollow. I suspected there must be a way to establish a mortgage, but I didn't know how to go about it. Dick Gowen's employer and partner, Al Ports, an avid birder with a lifetime list somewhere in the thousands, had intervened and made one more overture to a tiny local bank called Community Guaranty Savings. Al explained that Community Guaranty often held mortgages on summer camps—the lakeside cottages that existed all over New Hampshire. Many of those properties had been in families for generations, but occasionally they were bought and sold and frequently they had no heat other than a woodstove. Al informed us that the barn we hoped to buy was now officially a camp—a 6,000-square-foot camp. Al said Shakespeare was wrong: a rose isn't necessarily a rose by any other name. A camp was a camp and a house was a house and to banks that made all the difference.

Meanwhile, we continued our daily routines. Classes where I taught had resumed after Christmas break. Wendy began working as a ski instructor on the weekends. Growing up in New Hampshire, Wendy had never paid for a day's skiing. As an instructor at Tenney Mountain, she received free passes for Pie and me. We went skiing every Saturday and Sunday, leaving early from the Bridgewater cottage and spending the day on the mountain. Pie skied like a mongoose, loose-limbed and sure. He skied absolutely without fear and in the space of a few weekends was so far superior to me that I couldn't entertain him. I watched him pass by with his pack of eight-year-old gangsters, all of them dressed in navy snowsuits, all of them skiing without poles, his pack deliberately finding jumps and moguls, his shouts to me over his shoulder containing the pity young people must feel for their dinosaur parents.

After lunch on a particularly clear day in late February, I called home to check messages and heard Dick Gowen's voice pop over the line to say he had some good news. The Community Guaranty Savings Bank had offered a mortgage. They saw no problem with the transaction, we could proceed quickly, the Rogerses had been notified, and the barn was as good as ours. He offered a few more details, but I hardly listened. I headed back to the lunch table where I found Pie suiting up for another afternoon skiing, his Inca fleece hat pulled tight over his ears. I sat next to Wendy and whispered the news to her and she hugged me. Pie demanded to know what was going on and I told him. "Awesome," he said, though I wasn't quite sure he knew what had happened. He stood looking at us, his earflaps down, his goggles like a pair of pale yellow turtles strapped to his head.

peepers

P ie tells the story this way: The first night we moved into the barn, he lay in the small trundle bed built into the wall of his room, listening to spring peepers. It was May. Winter had melted and the ice had floated, like white time, down the Baker River. Now the peepers called so loudly that he could not fall asleep. He had never lived near a pond, never heard frogs croaking at such close range, so the sound of their inflating and deflating lungs unnerved him. He watched the playground swing—suspended from the beams in his room—for a long time, hoping the peepers would stop. He wasn't sure he could live in a place where the animals made so much noise. Finally, he called to his mother and said he was having trouble sleeping. His room was level with the catwalk and he could watch our movements beneath him. From her place near the open boxes, the inside of her elbow licked by a carton top, Wendy paused and asked, "What it is, sweetie?" The French doors to the porch stood open, and the breeze, a spring breeze, came and went through the house, a pant, the smell of meadow and soil riding with it. Only a few lamps pushed light out against the darkness, and the house, the barn, had settled into itself, comfortable on an easy spring night. Pie wondered about bats, he said, in such a large house, but when his mom answered that everything was okay, just hush sweetheart, he remained quiet even though he didn't sleep. He listened for a while, heard the boxes rasping his mother's arms, then later, to our voices out on the porch. He listened to us talking, heard our voices find new, unexpected angles, as if they were coming from the boxes, or from holes in the floor, deep, quiet murmuring. But our voices caught the dots of the frogs' calls, connected them, quieted them. His swing rocked easily in the moving air. Around him, at eight, he still kept his army of stuffed animals. Hobbes, Teddy, Stinky, Reggie. On the beam above his bed, action figures stared down at him: Slam Fist, GI Joe, Superman, Batman, Archer, Woody. Half asleep, he heard the slow cadence of D Dog climbing the steps toward him. "D Dog, here, come here," he whispered, and she did. Climbing the last few steps to the trundle bed, she put her front paws up, then her back, curled once, twice, and sighed as she balled into the covers beside him. With D Dog in bed, the peepers did not seem so loud. No monster, he says, could get past D Dog. He lay back with his arm tucked under her, an arm that would turn to stone in the middle of the night, the pins and needles so sharp that he had to sit up and shake it, but for now he smelled her fur, the muddy scatter of her paws. When she grunted in satisfaction, he grunted too. And the wind pushed our voices up to him, past the boxes, past the swing, past the dark beams that ran like wishes to the ceiling.

Near midnight that first night in the barn, I made the final rounds to turn out lights. Nothing about it came naturally, because in the first hours of our habitation I didn't know where the switches were. We had turned on lights throughout the day, plugging in lamps haphazardly to have illumination where a box needed unpacking, flicking on switches of other lights with the dull, suspicious snap of a chicken pecking sideways at an insect, but my mood by the end of the day was not sharp and angular. Wendy had just gone to bed and Pie had been asleep for hours. The house stood quiet and I was alone in it for the first time.

I started in the basement, the cool cement under my bare feet, and found the switch to the family room on my first grab. A click and the room ceased to exist. The darkness forced me to put my hands forward, my feet searching while my arms waved in front like Frankenstein, ready to fend off unfamiliar beams or cords. Going slowly, I found the stairs—the same stairs we had climbed with Dick Gowen months before—and went up them with foot rising to meet foot, a bride marching. Light found me at the top of the stairs, and I went around the room clicking off one lamp after another, more capable now in the illumination. Each light extinguished sharpened the cut of the next; the darkness became more and more exact. When I clicked off the final lamp, leaving the large keeping room in darkness, I realized for the first time that we could see the stars through the southern bank of windows.

The stars. We could stand in the center of our living room and look up at the sky, watch the moon and stars make their way across the transom. We'd never seen the house at night. Our inspections had all been accomplished during the day, but now the sky pressed in and fell through the windows. Standing still, I let my eyes adjust. In time I saw the tops of the pine trees, the branches sometimes holding out white, blinking stars. The eastern edge of the pines shone white and pale, moonbeams cut by the broom of their needles. When I was certain of my eyesight, I walked to the French doors looking out on the meadow. The Big Dipper scooped the fishpond next to our land; in an hour, I knew, or maybe two, it would shift and spin, spilling its contents onto the summer grass. I had watched the Dipper any number of nights on camping trips, on late-night swims, and now I realized the North Star pointed past the corner of my house. I would never be able to see the Big Dipper again without believing it emptied itself each night on our meadow. It struck me that something like luck was at work here.

Then for a little longer I simply stood and listened. The old beams, cut from trees a century and a half ago, creaked in the summer breeze. I heard D Dog shake her collar—her foot rattling in an ear scratch—then nothing afterward. A minute later Pie turned in his bed. The peepers wiggled sound through the screen. When I closed the French door, their sound moved and wandered to our open bedroom window. I followed it inside. A cool, pale knife of wind tucked over the bed.

I undressed, then slipped under the down comforter. Wendy, exhausted, didn't move. I pulled close to her, spooning, her body warm and quiet. As I lay beside her, I thought that maybe I would be here, in this bed, for the rest of my life. In the course of a single day, that had become possible. I lay quietly, listening to the peepers, to D Dog's occasional movement. I wanted morning to come quickly, and for night, sleep, to remain as well.

fence

B acon. Our first Sunday morning, our first full day in the barn, our first breakfast. At five-thirty I woke and took D Dog for a walk along the perimeter of the land. Fog grazed the grass, and when she chased the tennis ball I tossed in front of us, she became a ghostly apparition, a black Lab strung with kelps of mist. A few times she abandoned the ball altogether and rolled on her back, crazy to have the scratch of grass and sticks. We finished our walk by skirting the fishpond. She waded in up to her elbows and lapped the water for a long time. Apart from bird song, her tongue made the only sound for miles.

I whistled her into our Dodge pickup and she sat beside me as we drove to the Warren Village Market, a mile away. The market is the only store in town, the place to get coffee, a paper, a loaf of bread, and a powdered doughnut. On moving day I had been in once or twice for soft drinks and bottled water, but now I stepped inside as a townsman, someone who belonged to the community. I bought a paper and a pound of local slab bacon, a dozen farm eggs, and a chocolate-covered doughnut for Pie. It was Sunday and I felt easy and comfortable, as happy as I had been in a long time. I bought orange juice and a quart of strawberries. I bought a tank of gas and I bought a balsa-wood glider, just for the hell of it.

I drove back with D Dog beside me, her nose busy sniffing the open barrel of the paper bag. The fog had curled and lifted, pried up from the earth by the sun that now used the mountains as a fulcrum. The mountains, on the shady side, were as definite and dark as rhinos. I told D Dog to look, but she couldn't pull her attention away from the groceries. We listened to the radio. *Darling, you send me.* Sam Cooke. I sang softly to D Dog, rolled down the windows, and hung my arm out.

Back home, I carried the groceries inside, set them on the breakfast bar, then lit a fire in the hearth. I burned birch logs first, letting the paper skin sizzle and crack until they built enough heat to eat oak. The heat felt good. I threw on two more logs, then went to the kitchen to start the bacon. D Dog sat against the refrigerator and watched as I pulled down our largest skillet, a black iron magnet, then pieced the chubby bacon in. When the bacon began to bubble, I made a pot of coffee in our old percolator, the wheezy pot like an old man tied to the counter. I flicked on National Public Radio, keeping the volume low. As I cooked I watched the sun find different corners of the barn. It flowed in as spring sunlight, carrying green and white, pulsing lazily over the tumble of boxes, the stacks of books, the homeless clothing. I walked to the French doors and watched the sun dig at the garden, the white picket fence quiet as teeth, old stalks of chives and rose hips rising up in a stretch of spring suppleness. A chickadee landed on the garden fence and preened for a while. I watched it until I heard the bacon move in the pan, then I returned to my post. Light followed me, turning the barn interior into a golden cake of a building.

I spread out the *Boston Globe Sunday* sports section and read the baseball scores. I kept looking up to see something new in the way the sun found the beams and I couldn't concentrate on the paper. I leaned over the breakfast bar and watched morning break on the meadow. Then I watched where the sun struck the gray granite of the hearth. The birch and oak snapped and popped. I walked around and stood for a long time warming my back by the fire. I tried to picture how the light would strike the house in winter, fall, and late summer. For five minutes I watched sunlight climb the black tangle of a pile of hangers. It would be possible to chart the change of seasons by where the sun struck a chair, a lamp, a potted plant. A sundial of furniture.

The bacon finally woke Pie. He came down from his upstairs bedroom, hair bushed out from his pillow, eyes still sleepy. He said he felt as hungry as two bears. He kissed me on the lips and then poured himself orange juice. He climbed onto a stool and read the comics, again explaining to me that he wasn't sure if he wanted to be a veterinarian, a movie actor, or a cartoonist. He said this every Sunday morning when he read the cartoons.

Wendy came out a few minutes later. She's a night owl who can stay up until dawn but who doesn't like hitting the ground running first thing in the morning. I gave her the crossword. She went to sit by the fire and wake up.

"Eggs?" I asked Wendy.

"Just coffee," she said.

I poured her a cup and sent it with Pie. I watched him return. He stopped to bomb a partially assembled Lego town he had transported from Wendy's apartment. I made him some scrambled eggs and toast. I cracked the bright eggs into a bowl, whisked them, added pepper, then poured them into the skillet. As they cooked, Pie quizzed me on fun facts from the newspaper. Where was the world's largest ranch? (Canada.) Where was the world's largest skating rink? (Moscow.) Would you wear a water moccasin? (No.) He answered the questions before I could try. Finished with me, he began quizzing his mother on the same questions, but she'd already heard all the answers. He returned to reading the comics, his hand sometimes shooting off into the air with a Lego missile. He made rocket sounds in his cheek and his lips sometimes moved in imagined radio transmissions.

Wendy set up a card table next to the fire and helped me carry the food. Bacon, toast, eggs, strawberry jam. It took five minutes to find forks and knives. The heat from the wood fire hit us at the knees and thighs. I threw on a few cedar scraps for scent. In minutes the house smelled like fresh shoe trees and the dried ends of fir limbs. By the time the cedar burned off, I knew, we would be pulled outside by light and the cool mist lingering still on the meadow.

We had snacked in the house before, but this was our first true meal. We clicked coffee cups with Pie's milk glass, toasted the House of Frankenstein. We owned this now. Pile fifty Cadillacs in ten stacks each five high, and you would have the dimension of the room. Picture a rope swing in the best tree on the best lake in New Hampshire and the arc of the rope would lick like a pendulum across only half the room. Had the barn doors been capable of opening wider, we might have driven the U-Haul into the barn and unloaded it directly into our dressers and closets. We tucked into the eggs. I wondered if we needed a little ceremony, but that seemed superfluous. The sun stretching inside, the welcome heat of the fire glimmering at our knees, the reedy click of knife and glass, served us well enough. I caught Wendy's eyes repeatedly. We both felt the same thing— the good gladness at what we had done, the joy of sitting, at last, in a home together. This home, this barn. So much lay before us we could not sit still easily. Like field spaniels we wanted to be up and poring over the house, discovering each nuance. At the same time, the anticipation of what we would discover seemed worth prolonging.

When Pie had sawed his way through half his breakfast I gave him the balsa glider, and we put it together as we ate. Our construction project brought about a discussion of paper planes, and Wendy and I realized that he did not have plane folding as a solid part of his education. We grabbed a few sheets of loose-leaf paper and folded them in half lengthwise, folded the wings, folded again to give them a crease, then notched the pilot's seat by tearing a tiny tab in the downward keel. A plane. Pie had seen paper planes, of course, but he didn't have the memory of them in his fingers. We gave him three sheets of paper and supervised until he got it right. Then he took a marker and inscribed his plane the U.S.S. *D Dog,* said he might be a vet after all, and challenged me to fly my plane against his from the catwalk. I made him finish his breakfast first.

Up on the catwalk I stood beside him. He had brought the balsa glider as a backup. We inspected the flight lanes. Thirty feet away and ten feet below us, Wendy remained by the fire. The size of the room—the great brown sweep of the beams up and down my vision, the dangling wagon wheel candelabra, the white glass doors everywhere, the pyramid of granite stones in the hearth—astonished me.

"Count to three, then throw it," Pie said.

"Okay."

"No cheating," he said, because he thinks if I win at something I must have cheated.

"Okay. No cheating."

We cocked our arms while he counted. I wasn't sure about the nature of the competition, but I suspected we were going for distance. Wendy stood by the fire, her back warming, and declared herself official judge. At three we launched. The planes glided up in air currents, then fell in a long, easy run toward the breakfast table and fireplace. His plane glanced off the large table and crashed on the floor. Mine went a little farther, making a smooth landing on a stack of magazines we had emptied from a box. Before I could ask him who had won he had already dismissed the results of the contest as aberrant, a fluke, and he put his frustration into winging the balsa glider nearly straight at the ceiling. Here, he seemed to say, was a real plane. It flew up and looped in a wide circle, banked to the left, swooped down, and arced up before stalling and diving straight down. It crashed nose first smack on the birch floor. The pilot had just cost the government a couple million dollars and probably lost a few lives in the bargain. All of that and it was only eight-thirty in the morning.

"Awesome," Pie said.

By the time he had thrown the planes through four more flights, the sun had reached the fieldstone porch. Wendy and I carried our coffee outside and sat on the edge, our legs dangling. Pie came out with a tennis racket and whacked a ball for D Dog, who chased it through the meadow and returned it at a trot, the ball a dandelion color in her mouth.

"We have to get a table for the porch," Wendy said. "A big table."

"A big table," I agreed. "I hate those little fussy tables. The wrought iron ones."

"They make some good ones that are big enough."

"And we'll plant berries and eat those."

"Blueberries," she said.

"And blackberries."

"And everything," she said, which was how we both felt.

We drank coffee and watched Pie. The meadow flickered in the early sunlight, moisture escaping and turning the air into glimpses of imperfect, glimmering mirrors.

We worked that first full morning with the doors open, with the westerly breezes forming cool brooms of air that charged through the screened doors. Boxes stood everywhere. Heaps of clothes, tennis rackets, winter coats, boots, shoes, fly rods, bed frames, framed paintings, framed photographs, a bread box, a plant stand, an ironing board, clay pots. Wendy wore shorts and sandals and worked with fierce concentration, dismantling boxes as soon as she had emptied them. We piled the flattened boxes, like a deck of bloated playing cards, on the porch. Pie floated around yanking things haphazardly out of boxes, holding them up so we would notice, then losing interest in the items once we acknowledged them. Because he hadn't helped with the packing, he seemed to think that something miraculous had happened: that we had moved and, abracadabra, his toys and clothes and games had followed him. Better still, he often found toys that he had forgotten altogether, so that moving took on for him the air of Christmas morning. Around the barn we heard shouts of "Awesome!" then listened to the ratty dig of him going deeper into a box. He found a Fisher-Price dragon attack tower, a Robin Hood tree fort, a few yo-yos, a radio-controlled car. He ran the car in the obstacle course of boxes, weaving around the wide birch threshing floor. The car spooked D Dog, who backed away whenever she saw it. Eventually she climbed the stairs and rested on Pie's bed, her eyebrows rising and dipping at the electric whine of the car.

Altogether the boxes formed a happy scatter of activity. I stopped Wendy at one point in the morning and asked her how she might feel if this proved to be the last move she made in her life. She had been digging through a kitchen box, the plates waiting to be arranged on shelves. She said, "I never want to move from this barn," and she seemed to mean it. Then she returned to work.

We emptied boxes for an hour before I realized we didn't seem to be getting anywhere. Nearly everything still lay around us, little of it organized. Standing for a second and taking stock, the boxes seemed to have erupted like so many miniature volcanoes. Nothing had been put away. We had cleared some clutter, compressed the mess, but something felt odd.

"We don't have rooms," Wendy said. "In most houses you put one box in the dining room, one in the living room, and one in the den. This barn is mostly one big room. Plus, the building doesn't have any closet space to speak of, so that's a challenge too. See? Other than the bedrooms, there's nothing to divide out."

"I guess I hadn't thought of it like that," I said.

"I hadn't either, really. The other thing is, you have to be careful how you arrange things or you'll end up with everything dwarfed. Settling in is going to take a little while."

"You want to arrange some furniture? Maybe get that in place?"

"We can try. We'll probably have to move it again afterward, but it will get us started."

With bite-size rooms to decorate, put a lamp here, a couch there, and you run out of viable options. Wall and window space dictate much of how you arrange things. In the barn, though, the walls rose like blank shutters, brown and neutral, and the birchwood floor stretched on for miles. Our barn contained approximately 6,000 square feet. The keeping room boasted ceilings forty feet high at the ridge, with vertical rafters making it appear even higher. In such a setting, furniture can be swallowed whole. Bookcases seem insignificant. When you sit at a table and eat a meal in a barn, the size and scope of the interior can make you feel temporary, a farmhand come inside to get out of the sun.

The posts and beams, although beautiful, also sectioned the room in complicated ways, so that you could not set chairs in a number of positions without placing a beam smack in the line of sight. A guest seated in one of those chairs would suffer like the Phantom of the Opera, half his face cut off from the world. Put another way, most things in the barn—like it or not—became framed by the twelve-foot bays originally designed to house cattle. Communication from one space to the next proved a tricky business, something ignored at peril. Without aiming for the effect, one could easily wind up with tableaux vivants, little manger scenes linked by the ballooning architecture overhead. I had never been as conscious of height and perspective in arranging furniture as I was that morning.

Added to the challenge of decorating was the sensitive nature of melding two sets of furniture, kitchen plates, forks, knives, spoons. How does one suggest using this couch here without it being a statement that the other couch, her couch, isn't up to par? Sometimes the piece of furniture in question was obviously the inferior one. But at other times either piece of furniture might have fit nicely, and it required diplomacy on both our parts to make sure the other person did not feel slighted on behalf of her or his furniture. Silly, but only in retrospect.

We arranged the fireplace area first. We carried everything away from the bay that contained the hearth, then went with the most obvious choices first. We put a camel hair couch (mine) in front of the fire, a blue wing chair (hers) next to it. The fireplace reached out a stone tongue and devoured both pieces. The combination resembled a college dorm room, an attempt by a few frat boys to make ratty furniture look more studied. I glanced at Wendy. Her face appeared resolute, like a boxer who had taken a good jab on the chin but remained determined nevertheless. I said, "Holy mackerel." For the first time I had a solid notion of how large the keeping room was, and how massive the granite chimney.

We had purchased the Irish wake table from the Rogerses, and that helped anchor things. We needed one secure piece of furniture in place, and so we spent the next forty-five minutes lifting the table and moving it around like water witches. Call it the first X or O in a tic-tac-toe game. As we monkeyed it back and forth, it improved the couch and chair, which seemed braced by its presence. We settled it parallel to the hearth, so that one now had to enter the squared-off region beside the fire. We had created a room within a room, a sitting area, and that became the secret to decorating the rest of the barn.

Adding lamps was difficult, too, because the plugs did not run in standard positions. No builder had glanced at a blueprint and included electrical outlets here, one over there beside the picture window, one beside the couch coffee table. Wires ran next to the beams and dropped down their flanks or rose up from the floor below. The wires ran where the electrician could string them, and if a furniture arrangement happened to profit, hooray. When the outlet did not run where we wanted it, connecting lamps to it had the feeling of stringing outdoor Christmas lights in a prickly fir. It became evident that we would require more than an ordinary amount of extension cords.

In an hour and a half we had something. The fireplace and Irish wake table complemented each other, with the smaller features of the normal-size furniture pulling the eye in various directions. Call it harmony or feng shui, but gradually we established a soothing combination of elements. Wendy told me to stand back while she put a potted Christmas cactus on the coffee table. Then she junked the coffee table and replaced it with an old blanket trunk. Then the Christmas cactus returned, this time benefiting from the trunk's golden shine. With each new arrangement, we stepped away and tried to see it anew. Light filtering in from the skylights above reminded us both that this space could only belong to a barn. Moving furniture into new positions around the bays, I could imagine hoof steps and the smoky haunches of cows steaming from spring rain.

We moved everything food-related to the kitchen. We called Pie to help us and it became a treasure hunt. Plates, trays, knives, forks—we passed them to Wendy while she sorted things as well as she could. Suddenly, though, the floor of the keeping room began to have open spaces. The established seating area next to the fireplace invited contributions. Wendy's brown lamp; an African figurine; a stack of seven Hardy Boys books; *Stuart Little*; a postage scale; a collection of seashells in an old Hellman's mayonnaise jar. *Things need a place to be*, I remember thinking. Soon we had given the house the first good stir. As one gains momentum on a jigsaw puzzle when more and more pieces are placed, so, too, we began to see the greater design. The proportions of the barn became manageable, and knickknacks began to suggest their own destinations.

At noon I left Wendy to work on the kitchen while I mowed the lawn. The meadow had pushed up against the farmer's porch, the grass reaching to the middle of my calf. Social scientists say that as humans we prefer to control nature, to have vistas so that we might see approaching predators, and that is why dominant views command high prices in real estate markets worldwide. True or not, I cannot abide a lawn choking a house. I suspected that Wendy, too, would feel better once we had a trimmed lawn, a place to walk. We both needed to put our hands on things, and cutting the lawn was as significant as clearing boxes in the kitchen.

I cut the back lawn with our old Tecumseh-engine lawn mower, a push model, deciding in the first few swipes what would be cultivated and what would be meadow. The configuration of the land, at least on the first go around, was mine to invent. I outlined a bed of immature lupines; I cut around the large bore well, using its edge as a demarcation between lawn and meadow. From the well eastward, meadow, then forest, then the White Mountains. Already, this early in spring, the meadow had sprouted clover and timothy grass, the green leading like a runway to wilderness beyond. Closer to the farmer's porch, I clipped the grass to lawn length. Pie came out and walked in the bracket of my arms, his hands out to the mower's handle, his miniature form too light to push the mower himself. Together we marked off what would be our lawn, abandoning the rest to grow as it liked. With each stripe, I felt the pleasure of claiming land for use.

I cut the front lawn alone and more quickly. The front lawn had an obvious outline; no meadow contested with it or tried to seduce it to wilder growth. I ringed two young apple trees and cut for a while sideways on the hill that banked up to the barn. As I worked, I noted a few cars slowed—not obviously, but in the brake-tapping way we do when someone new has moved into the neighborhood—to see who this person was out in the yard cutting the lawn. We were the new kids in the neighborhood.

Warren had a population of 800, but most of the people lived pressed against the White Mountain National Forest. A new family in town was an event.

It's impossible for any man to cut a lawn without thinking of his father. As I walked behind the mower, I wondered what he would think of this barn, this huge white building that had somehow become mine. I imagined he would see the appeal of it. He liked yard work and had me, from an early age, wear my football cleats when I cut our lawn, telling me that I aerated the sod as I cut it. From the fifties, he gardened in the great chemical haze of DDT and dandelion killer, his suburban lawn an odd vestige of royalty, of English country homes, that proved, in our democratic state, his civic reliability. His lawn attached to a hundred other lawns in New Jersey and he did not intend to let his fellow suburbanites down. He would not infect his neighbor's lawn with crab grass or dandelions, nor would he shirk the responsibility of keeping it green. As I pushed the mower back and forth in front of the house, I vowed never to use a whiff of chemicals on the lawn. Nothing impure or poisonous would touch my land as long as I had anything to say about it.

When I finished, the house had benefited by the nip of the lawn. Here, the grass said, order had been imposed. I went to the barn overhang where we had stored our tools and carried a pair of garden loppers to the hydrangea bushes planted at either corner of the barn. Shoots ran wild beneath the main clump of bushes. I began cutting the saplings, again imposing order, the flex of the tool's jaws quick and definite. In no time I began to sweat, but it was a good sweat. I liked being hot and sticky and working on my own piece of land. I whacked the runners and shoots as fast as I could get to them, tossing them behind me. It was a much bigger job than I had anticipated, but the appeal of cleaning out space, of whittling it to something useful and presentable, completely absorbed me. I yanked out nettles and kept cutting in a wider circle, the main bushes nodding approval when I brushed against them. Husbandry, I thought. I piled the brush in faggots and carried them to the backyard. The hydrangea bushes had stepped out from the clutter of their reproductive shoots and suckers; they stood like green pillars at each corner of the barn, balanced and tended without being fussy.

Afterward I scavenged peanut butter sandwiches and forced Wendy to take a break. We sat on the edge of the porch and had our lunch. Pie lectured me on my peanut butter sandwich-making ability. I have never bothered to spread the ingredients very well. I was a glopper, Pie said, a guy who builds sandwiches with glops. He ate the sandwich anyway. Afterward he said he missed Chris and Ryan, and wondered if they couldn't come over. We told him we might arrange for it the following weekend, or sometime in the future. I found an old croquet set and diverted him for a while playing killer, a game I devised on the spot. Each ball had poison and the object was simply to *cobra* the other guy, which meant we hooded our hands like cobras, and hissed before we aimed at the other ball. Pie loved sharks, dinosaurs, and poisonous snakes. Before he shot, he insisted Wendy give him the cobra sign, too. Lying flat on her back on the porch, exhausted, she gave him a halfhearted cobra.

In the early afternoon I strung a hammock between two adolescent oaks that overlooked the fishpond. We had carried the hammock with us for a long time, never quite finding the right spot at the Bridgewater cottage or in Wendy's apartment complex. At last, we thought, the hammock might come to roost. I wrapped chains high up on the oaks so that the hammock carried a graceful curve close to the ground. L.L. Bean had sold the Hatteras hammock, a good make, so that resting in it did not seem the sometimes flimsy affair that constituted my usual experience with hammocks. I lay in it and felt, suddenly, the appeal of hammocks. D Dog came to lie beneath the shade I cast and I let the wind push me back and forth. A family of mallards bothered the pond water; a murder of crows called my presence from the roof of the oaks.

From the easy swing of the hammock, I studied the barn. When European immigrants arrived in this country, they brought their building traditions with them. Along the Connecticut River Valley, Scottish, German, and Dutch influences represented the three main framing styles for barns. German barns carried the general shape of the croquet wickets Pie and I had just used; the tall, vertical beams stood at the perimeter of the building, essentially part of the building's skin or, better still, a rib cage. Scottish barns, the most distinctive of the three, depended on a central tree, a huge, sprouting beam that carried the upward force of construction from one central pillar. Dutch barns, our barn, placed the vertical beams on a twelve-foot-bay system, establishing an aisle, or nave, between the vertical beams at the building's walls. As a result, Dutch barns reminded anyone who entered of a European cathedral. The interior of Notre Dame or Chartres, though obviously far grander than anything built for simple agricultural use, nevertheless held the same configuration as our Dutch, four-bay barn.

The result, as I could see from my vantage on the hammock, proved pleasantly symmetrical. The original owner of the property, James Gale, had constructed the barn. The post-and-beam technique, the exquisite joinery, the rigid permanence of the fieldstone foundation had been his doing. As things went, it was not a bad monument to a man. I imagined him erecting the barn with neighbors, standing back, maybe, to look at the shape it created against the skyline. Over a hundred years ago he had pushed the queen beams and purlins into the air by hand, notched the rafters, built the bottom of a boat that might float in heaven. He had brought his cattle in during the cruelest months and had spread their manure where I now swung on my hammock. Inside he had hung his lanterns from the wooden hooks he had fashioned, their light powered by whale oil from Nantucket or Fall River. Maybe he had sent his milk by train to Boston and Concord. Certainly he had hayed the field where I now dangled in laziness, putting the bales inside the barn. Horses, too, pulling wagons. And more people, townsmen, friends, family, helping him to load hay through the mow, hoisting it up and sprinkling salt across it to avoid combustion in the hot days of August. The cupola, after all, represented nothing more than a ventilation shaft to bring needed air to the sweltering hay. Looking up at the barn, tracing its outline with my eyes again, I decided that we would never replace the weather vane. The letter G, for Gale, belonged above the barn.

I had tried to date the barn precisely, but it proved a slippery job. I had located one picture, taken from a hillside in 1900, that captured the entire town of Warren. Our barn stood out, bright and white, more dominant even than the churches. But the interior clues did not add up to a simple picture. In most barns, lacking a firm history, the construction date is determined by the building materials. If beams show evidence of up-and-down saw marks, for instance, then they had likely been cut with a pit blade, thereby predating circular mill saws that became common at the start of the nineteenth century. The beams in our kitchen showed evidence of pit cutting, but the other beams, the larger ones, had clearly been milled. The beams throughout the barn, though, had been secured by wooden trunnels, oak pegs, that again indicated earlier construction. No metal had been employed—no metal plates, braces, or joinery—probably because metal had been harder to come by than wood. Added to that was the fact that our barn roof did not have a ridge board. In modern construction, a ridge board is a given. It runs the length of the building, a spine of sorts, with the rib-like rafters running up to it and being toenailed in place. Our barn rafters merely pressed against each other like so many fingers playing "here's the church, here's the steeple," typical of pre-1800 construction. A few of the rafters had received collar ties, a plank running from one rafter to the other, the hypotenuse to make the construction stronger. But the collar ties, probably, had been added as an afterthought.

Those elements left us with a puzzle, or at least an amalgamation of diverse building elements. Maybe some of the wood had been stolen from other barns or projects in the area. Such recycling was typical of barn construction. The fieldstone for the foundation, I knew, had been mined farther up the Baker River Valley. It had been carted downhill by draft horse and unloaded by work crews. Without cranes or motorized mechanical advantage, the work had gone on in relative silence. As hard as I tried, I could not imagine personally performing the labor involved in bringing one stone from the mountain pass to our foundation, much less the thousand or more stones needed for the entire job. Staggering, to put it mildly.

I fell asleep in the hammock and woke a few shadows later to find Pie standing near me, a rubber-band gun pointed in my general direction. The gun had a wooden clothespin on top of the barrel; squeezing the pin launched the rubber band. When I looked closer, I realized he was not aiming at me at all, but at a series of Fisher-Price medieval warriors who had risked their lives to conquer an old maple stump. One by one he had gunned them down; the king, the only figure with a moveable arm and a broadax, held the pennant of their assault high above the bloody battleground. Pie had the king in his sights. Before he could shoot, D Dog raised up from under the hammock and whipped me with her tail as she ventured out to investigate the battlefield. Dogzilla. By proportion she was indeed a monster and she nosed the king on his plastic feet, his broadax poised to retaliate.

As I watched him shoo D Dog away, I recognized that Pie had full access to me and I to him, that we were a family. That should have been obvious, but it had a different slant now. He had spent plenty of nights at the Bridgewater cottage and I had babysat

Pie hundreds of times, but this felt different. Once when we had taken D Dog out for a walk in the snow together, Pie had thrown himself on the ground and refused to get up. He is more than a bit theatrical and he spoke to me through his folded arms that I should go on, leave him, he would survive. He must have been five or six and, honestly, the snow had to be difficult for him to navigate. But I remember thinking that Wendy would return from her errand soon, that I would hand him over to her, and that would be that. That was early in our relationship and we had come miles since then. He was as close to a son as I was likely to have in this life.

I sat up in the hammock and asked him for a shot at the king. I missed the battlefield entirely. Pie ran and retrieved the rubber band, strung it on his rifle, and shot. He missed too, but I liked watching his excitement, the pleasure he took in doing something in my presence.

Few things are as definite as a fence. Without any discussion, you are on one side or the other. Long before we had purchased the barn, Wendy and I had agreed that we would fence the acreage. The land out back had long served as an extension of the elementary school baseball field, the elementary school Pie would attend, and the kids cut across the land so frequently that they had carved a dark trail in the grass. The Rogerses had told us, too, that in winter local snowmobilers used the property to turn doughnuts in the glassy meadows, and in spring neighbors taught their kids to drive on our lumpy fields, bumping their old pickups across our deforested acreage. As a result, our thinking concerning fences ran pretty straightforward: If we put one up long after we moved in, the townspeople might see the fence as a reaction to their activities. On the other hand, if we put the fence up immediately then they could take no offense. In short order the fence would become a simple fact, as dull and significant as any other obstacle in the landscape.

On a trip to my college library I grabbed a glossy coffee-table volume on fences and spent hours lingering over the various designs. Fences are expressions of their owners, and I wanted to select carefully. The photography in the book spoke to the poetry of fences, and though you could see through the various posed effects easily enough, the point about fences nevertheless came through: A fence extended the house. Positioning a fence, in some ways, was the equivalent of choosing a point of perspective in a landscape painting. Our view of the mountains, our perspective on the trees around our property, could not help but be governed by the fence we picked.

Though I never took it seriously as a viable option for us, I found the settlers' root fence the most intriguing. Constructed of tree roots dragged together in a pattern around the land, the root fence had the enduring, thick-necked quality of a bulldog. Like a stone wall, it served as a practical answer to the problem of clearing land. Rather than see the tree roots as something to dispose of, early settlers used the gnarled roots to form a solid, primitive wall. We didn't have the trees for a root fence, but the bold assertiveness of the roots, the declaration that here land was tended, appealed to me.

A standard split-rail fence did not carry enough authority. Kids could slip through the railings or poke one end out and sprain the integrity of the fence without much effort. Split-rail fencing appeared ornamental, something to cordon off a plot of suburban garden. I also worried that a split-rail fence invited sitting. The book made it clear that people leaning on fences, sitting on fences, and climbing over fences proved more destructive than animals rubbing against them or frost heaving up underneath them. To place a split-rail fence where parents watched baseball games, or where kids historically cut across land, seemed a recipe for frustration.

I examined a hundred styles of fencing—stockade fencing, picket fencing, and even live fences made from privet hedges—but the only fence I fell in love with was the Irish snake fence. Built with split rails without vertical supports, the rails become a comb, a stack of Popsicle sticks, a delicate rake to winnow the meadow grasses. Because the fence has no vertical posts, the Irish snake fence relies on a serpentine pattern to carry the mist of the meadows up onto the top rungs. Picture your fingers interlaced in a loose prayer position, end to end. That's an Irish snake fence. The photographs in the book showed the fence spanning great lengths of hilly harrows, the pale wood faded to gray wool, the grass beneath it a brilliant green. Such a fence, I thought, did not dig its heels in too deeply. It sculpted the land's contours without breaking them. It was, I decided, the fence for us, and in bed one night I showed Wendy pictures of the Irish snake fence.

"Do you want to build all that?" she said. "It seems like quite an undertaking."

"I thought so, too," I said. "But it would be beautiful."

She nodded. She understood, as I did not, that the cost of rails would prove prohibitive. For three to four thousand dollars, I found out the next day, I could fence the land with an Irish rail system, and then only after significant work. When I returned from the hardware store disappointed, she told me her father could put up a sheep fence in no time, that a sheep fence properly suited an agricultural lot, and that the cost would be well within our budget.

After a few phone calls back and forth, Wendy's father, George, arrived from Tilton, New Hampshire, in his old station wagon early one morning, ready for work. It was a Wednesday, dead square in the middle of the week. The back of his car sagged under the weight of the materials, the large coils of extruded metal fencing wound like fists in the back. As I pulled the coils out and dumped them on the ground, I recognized the fence from fishing trips I had taken. In the West, sheep fences cover miles and miles, sometimes without an apparent homestead as a source of so much labor. When streams bent toward a hedgerow and a muddy cattle crossing, I often had to climb such a fence to go after trout. Barbed wire had made settlement of the West possible, offering landowners an inexpensive means of staking out ground and containing cattle. The sheep fence, manufactured without the characteristic twist of barbed wire, is a close but gentler cousin. Squares at the bottom of the fence held a tight pattern so that no lamb could slip beneath it; at the top, where the fence rose to five feet and the danger of a sheep making escape was less likely, the squares broadened.

Wendy's dad is a slender, handsome man who does not say much. He resembles a taller, more upright Colonel Potter on the old $M^*A^*S^*H$ series. He favors jeans and flannel shirts, a red bandanna stuffed in his back pocket. His hair is thin; his blue eyes are Wendy's eyes, the pale, translucent sort that make you feel as though you are seeing deeper than usual into the owner's personality. He can turn his hand to anything. He is frugal and careful, a true Yankee.

Carrying coffee, we walked to the northeast corner of the land, a spot where I had discovered an old beehive months before, and I pointed out the property stake. George sprayed it with orange paint. Then we walked to the next property stake and sprayed that one, too. Between the stakes ran a straight line of four or five hundred feet. An easy fencing job. George suggested that we back off the line a half a dozen feet, a friendly gesture he said was common when putting up a fence. A six-foot margin allowed for any mistakes and it would demonstrate us to be generous, friendly neighbors. In agricultural circles, stringing a fence too precisely to a property line can appear a bit grabby, George said.

Using a sextant, George set the line. He communicated with Wendy, telling her to move this way, then that, until he was eventually satisfied with the transit. While they worked, I brought a brush sickle from the barn overhang and cleared brush. Swinging the sickle back and forth, watching the red thorns crack and reveal their yellow guts, I felt purposeful. Years ago I had lived in West Africa, and I recalled how clean the land had been around the various huts and longhouses. When I had inquired about it, wondering why Africans wouldn't coax a garden to grow near their doorsteps, I was reminded that brush hid snakes and scorpions. Anthropology texts suggest that we are creatures who prefer life at the edge of a meadow. Swinging the sickle and watching the tangle of grass and prickers give way to orderliness, I couldn't deny the satisfaction in such an act.

D Dog stayed close by, inspecting the swath of grass I created in passing. Meanwhile George began to set fence posts. You can set posts with a sledge, but it is far easier to use a fence post driver. A hollow metal tube with a capped end, the post driver is lowered onto the metal post, then banged up and down until the post sinks to the desired depth. In soft soil such as ours, soil that had once been cultivated, it's a fairly painless operation. George set the posts at ten-foot intervals, working rapidly, Wendy sometimes holding the bottoms of the posts with a pair of spanners so the slamming didn't cause the post to turn. Inside of an hour we had the line of posts half planted.

I liked this work and so did Wendy. The repeated procedure—set the stake, get it ready, pound it, move on—appealed to us both. Part of the satisfaction came from the purple lupine that wandered through the field and the sense that we were outside in our own meadow. The views of the barn changed throughout the morning; the sun took the southern end and washed it white; then later, when the morning advanced, the cupola cast a shadow on the broad porch roof.

At noon we picnicked on an old blanket stretched out on the grass. Wendy put out a plate of cheese, French bread, apples, pears, a few spring strawberries. Halfway finished with our work, we ate at the southeast corner of the lot, where an apple tree had pushed its white petals out into the spring air. Wendy and George talked about Wendy's sisters. Dee was in school; Sarah had returned from the Peace Corps and was now working at the John F. Kennedy Library in Boston; Shea worked for a telecommunications firm. I pushed back onto the grass and half listened. I played the old childhood game of closing one eye and watching the land jump this way, then closing the other eye and watching it go the other. Down close to the ground, my cheek flat on a balled-up sweatshirt, I studied the grass. A ladybug hoisted itself up a spear of grass and wobbled there, too heavy for the stalk. Sunlight found her carapace and turned it pumpkin colored. Her wings spread, black underneath, then tucked back to her body. The grass bent without collapsing and she bobbed there, a black speck, until finally she let go and fell out of sight in the roots.

Wendy wouldn't let me drowse. After lunch we strung the fence wire, unwrapping it carefully from its tight coil. It could spring and take off a finger, George told us, so we handled it with palms flat, fingers away from the holes. While George rigged a come-along to pull the fence tight, Wendy and I used pliers to twist metal ties around the fence posts. The tension created by the come-along and by the coiled memory of the wire made it a touchy business. My stomach fluttered with the same apprehension I get when baiting a mousetrap. You know your fingers are out of the way, yet your eyes flutter and await the dreadful snap and throw of the release.

The empty posts became a fence. *Just like that,* I remember thinking. Take a step and you were inside the fence; step away and you were out. What little doubt I may have harbored about stringing fence in the first place evaporated. Looking down the straight shot of fence, I liked having a piece of land fenced off and apportioned to us. I imagined the meadow growing dense and green to tangle the toes of the fence in roots and eager weeds. In a month the fence would claim permanence, drawing the ground up to it and growing comfortable on its posts. Outside the fence, too, grass would rim the borders of our property, in late summer growing yellow as cola fizz.

George kept us working. While I might be tempted to get pretty far along on a project but then knock off for the day—a teacher's sense of scheduling, in other words—he possessed the workman's drive to finish. In the warm afternoon we strung a second section of fence perpendicular to the first, then did a tricky piece of work as the fence meandered around the southeast corner of the property. I had to retrieve the brush sickle again to clear a tunnel of blackberry bushes so that the fence could run, unimpeded, on its closest approach to the house. As we attached the last end of the sheep fence to the white pickets that framed the garden, we had to call D Dog inside the enclosure. She came without understanding that she was now in, boxed, though free to roam three acres as she liked. The moat, metaphorically, stood ready and filled with alligators.

Wendy had simmered a beef stew most of the day and we ate it in the early evening at the Irish wake table. Pie sat beside his grandfather. The evening sun had swung to the west and now dipped cautiously through the house. We had set a fire in the large hearth, burning it hot to get the evening chill removed. As we ate, the fire popped and sizzled. Wendy had spiced the stew with chives from the garden; she had also cut sprigs of lemon thyme and folded them in the napkins before serving. Now the meal—the dry, crackling French loaf, the white bowls, the sturdy stew—carried with it garden scents.

After dinner we carried coffee around the perimeter of the property, checking our handiwork. George, a perfectionist, wasn't entirely happy, but eventually he conceded that we had done pretty well. The fence ran true and straight, the height never varying, the posts perpendicular to the ground. George advised us to tie orange ribbons on the fence during the winter so that snowmobilers could spot it in the drifts of banked snow. As we walked, Wendy and I turned frequently to see the barn. It stood at the mouth of this lake of grass, the lamplight inviting. With the fence surrounding it, the porch quiet, the barn looked like home. We caught each other's eye now and then and motioned with our heads to look at the house. The grass had turned blue in the last light of day and the house rode as if on a wave.

mermaid
tears

I n New Hampshire snow can linger all summer in the mountains and in small, shaded hollows near cold streams. Pie found the last snowball in May. We had kayaked across Lake Tarleton, four miles from the barn, keeping to the shoreline because of a choppy breeze, when he spotted the white cub of snow in a pocket of shade. While I simply enjoyed seeing the last finger of winter losing its hold, Pie immediately saw snowballs. He scrambled out of his kayak and ran up the bank of the hill and dug at the snow until he had a set of five or six snowballs lined up. I sensed immediately where this was headed and started paddling away. He smelled my fear and, running down the hill, his arms cradling the snowballs, he had already done the calculations in his caveman mind: *Snowballs would not make it home, snowballs hurt hands to hold for very long, must throw snowballs.* I got away like Old Ironsides, cannonballs dropping all around me.

He climbed back in and followed. We had bought him his own kayak for his seventh birthday, a red plastic tub of a boat that was sufficiently beamy to make it all but impossible for him to tip. Wendy and I each had a kayak, clunky Manatees, which we had picked up from a river outfitter at the end of the last two boating seasons. Wendy had remained offshore during the snowball raid. Now she paddled closer, her pink scarf flapping in the wind.

We headed to a small island we had spotted in the lake. Pie had treasure he wanted to bury. The night before, sight unseen, he had drawn a map of the island. When I had tried to explain to him that the map was generally drawn after the treasure was buried, he dismissed me as a worrywart. Somehow the notion that he could follow his own map had intrigued him—he could be the pirate and the treasure hunter simultaneously. He had scribbled on the map with charcoal from the fireplace, and had scorched the edges so that it would appear authentic. True to convention, he drew an X to mark the spot, though where the spot might be, or how one arrived at the island, he hadn't a clue. There was something wonderfully daft about venturing out to follow an imaginary map, conceived without a trace of any understanding about the location. Wendy and I had gone along without much protest.

To reach the island, we had to cross a stretch of open water. That wouldn't usually have posed a problem, but the weather had turned windy and rain hung just above the tree line. We would have to take the waves on our port sides, one- to two-foot chops that broke white at times. Wendy led us, paddling firmly. I took up the rear with Pie between us. He paddled smoothly, not fazed in the least by the waves. In ten minutes we had the island in sight: a disc of granite, topped by three or four scrub pines, its diameter something like twenty yards.

We worked to the lee side and Wendy climbed out and held us steady as we hopped ashore. I dragged the kayaks up while Pie claimed the island in the name of King Pie. He galloped around the island, touching everything—he wanted to be first, rather like licking a spoon so your little brother wouldn't want a bite of ice cream. He identified a good camping spot, a flat rock on the southern end of the island, where, he said, it would be possible to have a fire. It was, in fact, the best spot and we dragged our picnic out of the kayak and set it up out of the wind. We ate egg salad and bright pickles, chocolate cookies and a bag of chips. The air became heavy and damp and the wind that had blown since we began the trip started to abate. Rain, I thought, for the paddle home.

Where to bury the treasure? That question occupied Pie. As he ate his sandwich he studied the possibilities. He needed a landmark, preferably something ominous and possibly hideous. Lacking that, something watertight, or at least water-resistant, would be the way to go. Unfortunately the island seemed decidedly void of skull rocks or hanging trees. Winter had scoured the island, pressing it flat against the lake. Only the most gnarled and hardy trees survived the winds. Pie resolved to bury the treasure, though he lamented his stupidity in not bringing a shovel.

"What about the map?" I asked. "Doesn't the treasure have to correspond to the map?"

"Yes," Pie said, "it does."

"Then you have to bury it where the X is," Wendy said. "Isn't that the point?"

He shrugged. The point, evidently, was whatever point he decided to honor. He asked to be excused and wandered off to look for good spots. Wendy and I cleaned up lunch, then pushed back and put our heads on the rock. We held hands and looked up at the sky. Rain might be coming soon, but for now, as we stared up, the sky looked like cream spilled into coffee, the white scarf dancers active and roiling. I felt sleepy and warm. The wind hardly reached us this low to the ground. I smelled bayberry and pine.

Pie returned a minute or two later and said he had definitely found the spot, a hollow he had dug with the pointy end of a stick, and now the only thing remaining to be done was to bury the treasure. *Bingo, bango.* We forced him into resting with us for a minute. He humored us, pretending interest in the sky and the clouds that we pointed out, but obviously he wanted to be off burying treasure. He lay between us, smelling of bug spray and Band-Aids. I started to doze, but then a few raindrops came and woke me. Pie took the rain as a sign to get moving and he jumped up and came back with the treasure from the kayak.

He buried mermaid tears—the opaque pieces of beach glass that we found at Newcastle Beach, near Portsmouth, New Hampshire, whenever we went. His small bottle contained greens, whites, ambers, and reds. Somehow we had started the story that mermaids sat on the rocks and looked at the land, then cried because they could not join us at our parties and picnics. Their tears turned to glass and rolled endlessly along the bottom of the sea until they finally came ashore. Pie put the bottle of tears in the hollow and covered it with a flat rock.

Rain came faster and we hustled to be finished with the interment. We pulled the kayaks into the lake under the first strong bursts of drops. Wendy said we should make a fire when we got home. She suggested we pull the card table close to the fire and eat bread and cheese for dinner. But we didn't have time to talk about that now. The rain sheeted down and wrapped around us. I watched Pie to make sure he could handle the rain and the persistent chop. He didn't seem rattled in the least.

It took us an hour to paddle out and by that time we were all chilled. I loaded the kayaks while Wendy started the truck and got Pie warming. We drove the four miles home, left the kayaks to sort themselves out in the rain, and ran inside to get a fire started. Wendy forced Pie to take a hot shower, a task he performed only reluctantly.

I poured for Wendy and me each a tall Scotch and set about making a fire. The Rogerses had left a stack of locust, a peculiar wood I had never burned before. I had since ordered five cords of mixed hardwood from Carol Kinney, a blocky, able man who supplied most of the cord wood in the area. I had ordered it green—my thought was to dry it for the summer along the fence line—

but had supplemented the locust with downed wood from the White Mountain National Forest. My woodpile had begun to grow. I knew the shape and cut of each log I put into the fireplace; I knew the pine cones and kindling, too. I built a wood tepee over a cone of newspaper, stuck my hand up to make sure the damper was free, then lit the match. The air pressure must have been right, because the flames didn't hesitate. They rose and pulled the kindling into a warm pile; little by little I added bigger wood and in five minutes we had a crackling fire. The pine and oak twigs burned with a will. Wendy pulled a birch stump over to the fire and sat close, waiting for it to throw greater warmth. We sipped the Scotch and fed branches to the flames. Heat pushed out from the granite walls, carving a white cave out of the gray day. Far away, out on the meadow, rain fell in soft squalls. It peppered the roof and splashed against the windows. I pictured the mermaid tears resting in their hidden lair. The rain had run like water striders across the lake. Now the mermaid tears might be discovered by the moist drops.

While we waited for the heat to build, I grabbed the Master List off the coffee table. I'm not sure who had named it the Master List, but it had become a running gag between us. The Master List, boss of all minor lists either of us might make, contained our priorities for the barn. Initially we had added items randomly, jotting them down whenever they struck us, but recently we had begun the serious task of setting priorities. Although it was only May and we had been in the house less than a fortnight, heat ranked at the top of the list. This was, after all, an uninsulated barn, and it took living in it before we understood the enormity of this fact. Maybe, we worried, the banks that had refused our mortgage knew what they were doing. Even on a raw May day such as the day of our treasure hunt, the weather found the building and dug its way inside. We could not imagine what January would be like. In places—places we didn't like to look at too closely—we could see through the walls to the meadow beyond. Barns required ventilation; without adequate ventilation, the dampness from the animals rotted out the wood. But the ventilation had outlived its useful life. Now we needed to close things in, to make them snug, to *coop up,* in the New Hampshire vernacular.

D Dog came beside me and sat with her weight against my knee. I patted her softly, watching the fire and drinking my Scotch. Maybe we were grasshoppers, fiddling, while we had more important work to do on the barn. I looked at the list again:

MASTER LIST

Heat — what are we going to use?
Insulation — walls need to be insulated. Roof?
Porch stones need to be straightened
Kitchen renovation — Vermont Salvage
Roof?
Clean out dungeon
Empty all boxes
Update electrical outlets
New fuse box?
Septic?
Plantings?
Cut down maple
Fix foundation stones in southwest corner
Flooding?

Heat had been underlined several times. We had approximately five months until it would get cold. If weather patterns held, by late November temperatures would drop below freezing at night and wouldn't go significantly higher during the day. Some of the coldest continental temperatures are registered in the Presidential Range along the eastern portion of New Hampshire, directly across the state from us. The highest wind velocity recorded on earth, well above 200 miles per hour, blew across Mount Washington in the 1950s. Near hurricanes ripped down out of Canada, picked up speed across the Great Lakes, and tore through New Hampshire like the last flick of a broom that had swept the kitchen floor.

We had not advanced far in our thinking about heat, but we knew, at least, that we faced two important issues. First, heat cost money. To put in a heating system, to figure out how to configure the air flow around an old, creaky building, was not a simple matter. We interviewed everyone who came to visit, picking their brains for new approaches, but few had solid ideas about how to proceed. With all the money in the world, it would have been an easy call. Stick in a huge boiler, run hot-water heating registers around the entire building, and you're all set. Cost? Somewhere around $20,000. We didn't have $20,000 to spare, but it was nice to think about. Other people suggested we put in a floor heating system. Again, use a boiler, run plastic hosing through the floor joists, then let the heat transfer into the floor so that the first eight feet of air are warmed on the main living floor. The floor conducts the heat and remains warm, thereby making the house warm. This technique, though efficient, would have been more expensive than heating water registers around the barn. One contractor quoted us a price of $30,000.

Wendy's father had suggested a different approach. He recommended a Home Heater, a huge coal stove, manufactured in Bennington, Vermont. Put one in the basement, one in the living room, and we'd be warm no matter what. We had the chimney for it; four thimbles connected to the huge fieldstone hearth. George's recommendation fit our notion about independent north-country living. You had to heat with what nature provided and you refused to depend on the oil or electric companies. But coal? Who had ever heated with coal? Coal equaled carbon. Carbon, as school children knew, came from plants. Like wood, coal was sunlight. It had merely remained in the ground longer.

Coal also had strange, slightly malevolent associations. Coal gave off arsenic, I thought. And coal contributed to acid rain. I had gone to university in Pennsylvania, and certainly they mined it there. Strip mines. They ripped the tops of mountains, bulldozed the rubble down slope, then hauled the black scatter off with trucks.

All true, I discovered, but coal also provided half of America's energy. Industrial furnaces across the United States churned out coal gas, primarily because it produced more BTUs per dollar than any other fuel source. We knew that we needed something large, something that churned out heat, and something we could stand beside and be warm. But even before that, we had to decide how to insulate the barn walls. Winter would climb through our single barn board construction and make any form of heat academic.

The next day we took the old Dodge pickup to Home Depot in Concord, New Hampshire. Our shopping list extended through a page and a half on a legal pad. We needed extension cords, a shop vacuum, a new power drill, assorted screws, assorted nails, picture wire, a set of wrenches, saw blades, lightbulbs, and on and on. We had taken some pleasure in writing out the list. Lists are the blueprints of ideas and yet they require little work. As we loaded Pie into the middle of the truck, I grabbed the mail from the street-side box. Among the usual clutter, I opened our first mortgage bill. The sum came to just under $500, due in three weeks' time. That set me in a good mood. Not only was it reasonable—I had once paid $2,500 a month to rent a one-bedroom flat on Central Park West—but it also represented the final outcome of so much financial calculation on our part. Here it was in black and white. We could handle the payments without difficulty, and we hoped this boded that the rest of our calculations for renovations might be roughly on the mark.

On the drive to Concord, Pie resumed his ongoing intergalactic battle against the Dark Lord, Volkswagen Beetles, and all other alien spaceships, using a pair of sunglasses dangling from the rearview mirror to shoot anything that moved. His cheek filled again and again with bullets, while we talked around the spatter of his ray guns.

Wendy and I discussed Reflectix, a new insulating sheet that we planned using as wall insulation. Formed like fancy bubble wrap with a foil backing, it was simple to apply. Wendy had already planned to cover the walls with shiplap pine, maintaining the barn feel of the building while adding substance to the structure, but we needed to insulate beneath the boards. Although we had considered several options—the pink fluffy stuff was too cumbersome; stiff, flaky Styrofoam too easily broken—we had narrowed in on Reflectix. It was astonishing, actually, to realize how passionate we had become on the subject. During our short tenure in the barn, we had become obsessed with a product we hadn't known existed two weeks before. Now we preached the virtues of Reflectix to anyone who would listen, probably trying to reassure ourselves that we had selected the correct product for our barn. If we had gone into the early stages of renovation believing there existed a right and wrong way to do something, we had quickly lost that naive belief. It was conceivable to come up with twenty or thirty plans, all of them bestowing some benefit. We yearned for a *This Old House* crew to arrive, a competent Larry or Bob in neat flannel shirts to direct us. Instead we seemed locked on a course of trial and error, tempered by financial restraints, that might conceivably work out in the end.

It was a Wednesday, not busy, and we parked a short walk from the entrance. Wendy collected our lists while Pie asked if he could drive the cart and maybe later see what kind of plans they might have for tree houses. We said we'd see about everything, meaning, of course, in that daily treachery employed by parents, that we intended to honor none of his requests. Meanwhile we grabbed a huge shopping cart and pushed into Home Depot. The electric doors clapped open.

A store like Home Depot is attractive for many reasons. It's hard to resist the limitless tools and materials and the designs they suggest, but even more attractive to the home renovator is the sense that inside a Home Depot the world at last becomes orderly. It is the ultimate garage workshop, the shelves metal and well braced, the place for every tool clearly demarcated. Weighed against the relative chaos at home, the parceled shelves soothe the homeowner as little else can. Pie stood on the front of the shopping cart and swayed with me as I wheeled him to light-bulbs, past lawn mowers, past splitting mauls, post diggers, hand trucks, hoes, shovels, picks, work gloves. Wendy walked ahead, list ready, pencil stabbed through her ponytail.

We loaded the first cart in no time. Pie hopped off repeatedly, glad to be helpful. Wendy picked through everything, efficiently sorting what we would need immediately and what could wait for another day. We paused for a long time in front of the water faucets. We needed to replace the kitchen sink and we both wanted to select a faucet swan-necked enough to fill a spaghetti pot. The high-range faucets cost a few hundred dollars, but we found something for just under fifty dollars. Pie put the new hardware in the basket in front of him. Farther down the same aisle we picked a window shade, a box of drawer pulls, a caulking gun. We bought duct tape and electric tape, and a tool belt, complete with a hammer holster, for Wendy. We bought paint scrapers and safety goggles, razor blades and wooden dowels. Everything went into the basket, Pie riding backward through the store.

We loaded two carts with Reflectix, the foil cylinders set inside like the pipes of a carnival organ. Two cartloads wouldn't amount to much on the barn, but it was a start. After checking through the register, I drove the pickup around and met Wendy at the front door. Together we loaded in the foil cylinders, each one dry and light. The rolls felt insubstantial; I could not believe only this material would stand between us and the cold New Hampshire winters. How much better, maybe, to put our trust in lumpy, fluffy pink fiberglass, a down comforter for a house. But instead we relied on science. Like a leftover lasagna, our barn would be wrapped in foil.

On our trip home we purchased a bag lunch and then spent an hour trying to find a large granite boulder beside the Baker River where, according to the Warren Historical Society, Native Americans had once cleaned their salmon catches. Joseph Patch, Warren's first white settler, lived in a hut beside the Baker River, fishing and hunting, much as the Pemigewassett Indians had done centuries before him. The Pemigewassett, part of the Algonquin peoples who inhabited the Atlantic seaboard, had named the Baker River, where we searched for the salmon rock, Asquamchumauke. Its name changed in 1709 when Lieutenant Baker led an excursion against the Pemigewassetts, killing the women and children who had been planting their fields while the men hunted. When the Pemigewassetts mounted a retalia-tory excursion, Lieutenant Baker played a trick on them. To fool the hunting party into thinking he had more men than he did, Lieutenant Baker had his own men cut their evening meal in many pieces and prepare it with three or four times the usual number of cooking forks. When the trailing Pemigewassett party discovered the forks, they mistakenly concluded the lieu-tenant's party was large. For his foxiness and cowardly attack on a peaceful village, Lieutenant Baker's name was given to the river that marked the Indians' demise.

We found a rock that suggested something of what a salmon rock might resemble. The boulder extended twenty feet out of the water and might have made a useful slaughtering table if one wanted to clean a large quantity of fish. The rock had a shelf to hold offal while the rest of the salmon lay open its fillets. The same might have been said about twenty other rocks in the stream, so we didn't have much confidence in the choice. Pie had faith that we had discovered an honest artifact. Indians and cavemen existed in roughly the same time period to him; the important matter from his point of view was hunting and sneaking up on things. He became inspired by the life he imagined Indians living in the Baker Valley. Wendy and I watched him dart around the stream, perching on rocks and spearing shadows. A pair of mergansers flew low over the river, their wings beating so rapidly the motion became a skirt of darkness encircling their iridescent bodies. Ballet tutus, Wendy said.

An hour later we unloaded the Reflectix at the barn, the rolls stacking like hair curlers. We arranged the shop vacuum downstairs, setting up a workshop space. Then we carried everything else inside. I felt a momentary sag; this was work, and a lot of it, that we had purchased for ourselves. But Wendy sounded confident and eager to begin. When we ate grilled cheese sandwiches with garlic pickles that night, she read us a Five-Minute Mystery from a book that required Pie and I to guess repeatedly, narrowing the possibilities down until we solved the story's riddle.

For one of the few times since moving into the barn, I did not sleep well that night. I imagined winter coming quickly, the mergansers pushing their black tutus south through the river valleys. Math gnawed at me; we had expenses and work, and the barn, at least that night, loomed as a cavernous, unwieldy shell. Why had I left the simple comfort of the Bridgewater cottage? Wasn't leisure the greatest comfort in the end? We should have converted the garage, I decided, and finished a porch off the back. The cottage might have been small, but at least it did not require the rolls of foil now stacked in the basement. Misgivings pressed on me and I slept fitfully, computing reparations until early light.

From bed I watched the sun rise behind Carr Mountain, the sky turning peach long before the sun cleared the rounded dorsal of the ridges. Light walked across the meadow and turned the grass to winter white. Snow, I thought, then realized that was impossible. The sun had merely become tangled in the dew.

In the 1940s—so the local story goes—Ira Morse, the first true shoe baron in New Hampshire, a man made rich by the Merrimac mills, built a museum next to our barn. He built of river stone, mortared and stacked like bowling balls, until the building climbed four stories tall. On the outside of the building he inscribed: AFRICAN BIG GAME TROPHIES, never flinching at how extraordinarily out of place the building might appear in such a small country hamlet. This was the age of the steamship, and Morse traveled the world collecting curios and transporting them back to Warren, New Hampshire. In truth, the museum ended up being a private showcase for Mr. Morse's adventures, less an anthropological exhibit than a personal one. He dammed Cold Brook, which separates our two properties, and let it flood to form the fishpond that D Dog now found so tempting. He stocked the pond with enormous trout from the local fish hatchery, put a feeding station on a small platform beside the pond, and charged schoolchildren a nickel for a handful of food pellets for the experience of feeding the fish. As the museum declined, poachers sneaked in at night and fished out the pond. Nevertheless, the museum remained the object of countless elementary school field trips. Even today it is easier to give directions to our barn by saying, "Did you ever visit the Morse Museum as a child?" If Warren Township draws a blank from our potential visitor, the Morse Museum often does not.

The museum still stands, though empty now. Morse died; his family had no interest in maintaining it. Before the property went to auction, the Morse family hired a man to clean it out. For weeks local townspeople traveled to the town dump and found stuffed tigers in the burn pile, giraffe carcasses in the metal refuse. People dragged home things that interested them. Walking into a modest Warren home, you may still encounter a Bantu bow and arrow; a Dogon door; a leopard, poised to spring, with a leg cut off and one eye blinking perpetually in half-blindness. A store owner from Maine acquired the prize of the exhibit, a documented Egyptian mummy, and took it back to his shop as a means to increase walk-through traffic. When the Egyptian government got wind that the mummy had resurfaced, they justifiably sued for ownership. The gentleman from Maine, according to local legend, drove the mummy to a bridge and told reporters—who had naturally picked up the story—that the Egyptians could have the mummy. He said it would be at the bottom of the Saco River if they tried to take it from him. He returned it to his store and there—at least for local interest—the story died.

What wonderful folly, I thought, when I first inspected the museum. How did anyone get the absurd notion of building a museum in such a rural, out-of-the-way location? Gradually, however, I learned that Warren had once boasted two large hotels, massive wood structures that provided lake views for downstate sports, downstate being the area connected by railroad to Boston. It was easy to picture the wonderful hubbub of the town a third of the way through the last century: train whistles, muddy roads, and the halting carriage rides through the flats of Warren, then up, higher past the Appalachian Trail, past the Ore Hill Mine Trail, and finally onto the broad, sweet bowl of water at the top of the mountain. Lake Katherine, Lake Tarleton, Lake Armington. Then the thickness of evening, the loons, the moose wading for wild celery. Mount Moosilauke had been the site of the first alpine downhill race in North America; Dartmouth College still ran its first-year orientation program out of Ravine

Lodge, only five miles outside of Warren proper. Records show that the hotels attracted stars from New York. Frank Sinatra—who may well be the George Washington of our most recent generation because he apparently slept everywhere—is said to have vacationed at the hotel overlooking Lake Tarleton. Sammy Davis Jr., too. A museum, given that context, is not so strange an idea.

The Morses often traveled with the Eastmans of Kodak camera fame. Morse's wife, Lilly, needing a place to host the Eastmans and their friends, purchased the barn next door, our barn eventually, to renovate. She envisioned it as a dance hall, a rural haven for her city friends. Money presented no object to Lilly, and some of the features in the barn claim a distinct 1940s elegance. Throughout the barn Lilly's touches remain, nowhere quite as apparent as in the large farmer's porch overlooking Moosilauke. Set under a large portico with five supporting pillars, the porch was constructed of slate-colored fieldstone. By rough calculation, it must have taken several men most of one summer to find the stones, shape them, lay them, mortar the joints, erect the roof, the pillars—all of it, of course, likely done by horsepower. The result is a commodious sitting porch, a place to eat breakfasts of berries and black coffee. Twenty by fifty feet, it runs the length of the building. The sun finds it first thing in the morning. So do the robins and the white-bellied wrens that hop about for crumbs. The porch turned a simple New Hampshire barn into Tara, the prized home of Scarlett O'Hara. One could step out on the porch in riding gear and jump onto the back of a mare. Spring through autumn, we lived on the porch. In winter it would lend a cover to cord wood. We could park our Flexible Flyers beneath the roof and step out on a white winter night to look at the stars.

Over the years, the porch sagged and the mortar cracked. The Rogerses told us that one winter, when they came up to ski, they discovered that local snowmobilers had broken up the

Adirondack chairs and held a bonfire on the porch. They pointed out the black burn marks. The porch needed work, they said. It was sinking.

For an old house, it's best to have an old handyman. I called Clarence Maines. Clarence had been recommended to me by a neighbor when I had needed some work done on the Bridgewater cottage. The recommendation had come with a caveat: "He's a character," the neighbor had said. When I asked if that meant a good character or a bad one, the neighbor simply shook his head and said Clarence was unique. He said Clarence charged nine dollars an hour and would never, ever bid or estimate a job. You either wanted him or you didn't. According to the neighbor, Clarence could do anything a house required—plumbing, carpentry, masonry, roofing, siding, and on and on. Clarence was, my neighbor assured me, the most honest, kindly man one might encounter in this lifetime.

My neighbor failed to tell me that Clarence also resembled, in name and countenance, the angel in *It's A Wonderful Life*. Clarence was a dead ringer for the movie angel, a gray-haired block of a man who had a mirthful glint in his eye and a disposition more cheerful than a bedspring. He was the last man on earth you would want to meet if you had a hangover. He talked until paint chipped from the walls, until the dogs ran for cover, until the squirrels in the trees sat up and looked around. He talked while he worked, while he ate, while he leaned his back against a tree and scratched, talked until his voice drew air out of the building, out of your lungs and ears, talked until you thought you could no longer stand it. He claimed expertise at everything and was, in fact, superbly skilled at a hundred crafts. He had served in the army, had been a logger, a cop, an animal control officer, a custodian, a vegetable farmer, a stone worker, a truck driver, a trapper, a farmer, a mechanic, and a mortician. He had worked in a madhouse and his experiences there afforded him one of his richest veins of conversational coal. I had seen him, at age seventy, lift one end of a 650-pound stove and dance it into place. He snowshoed with his sons and grandchildren on winter weekends, quoted the Bible everywhere he went, yelled at Cub Scouts, always sat in restaurants with his eyes to the door just in case.

"The porch, huh?" Clarence said when I called him. "Stone work, you say. Well, it's an honest day's work."

He talked for an hour, and then told me he would show up two days thence. Wendy made plans to be gone. At first light on the agreed-upon day, long before Wendy could make a break for it, Clarence pulled into the driveway, radio blasting Brahms, a pale blue "Gilligan's Island" cap on his head. He sprang out of the car, began talking to any creature who would listen, and immediately began throwing tools on the porch, the louder the better. It was not quite six-thirty.

I made coffee, dressed in old clothes, and joined him on the porch. I was fond of Clarence and liked working with him. He didn't mind an assistant and I was the best kind: I had a healthy back and I took orders. We drank coffee and walked around the porch, inspecting the sags and cracked places. Immediately Clarence saw things that I had not seen—the sagging, he said, came from the soil beneath the porch. Over the years the soil had dried and shifted. Now hollow gaps sat just beneath the stones, miniature landslides, and with the mortar turning dry, the stones had caved in. What we needed to do, he said, was fill in the hollows, prop up the old stones with small replacement stones, and point the spaces between the fieldstone. Three days, he said, of steady work. Maybe more.

I went to collect sand for the mortar while he dragged more equipment from his vehicle. By the time I had returned, he had tossed every stick of furniture off the porch and was busy spraying it with a garden hose. No matter how many times I worked beside a carpenter or mason, I inevitably forgot the initial step of stripping things clean so you could see them. Some sort of life lesson lurked in the cleaning, but before I had time to dwell on it Clarence started me mixing cement.

Years before, as a Peace Corps volunteer in Africa, I had mixed cement for well-digging projects, and the old formula came back: three to two to one: three sand, two gravel, one cement. I mixed the ingredients with a hoe, scraping back and forth while Clarence worked his pry bar under the first series of rocks and propped stones beneath leverage points, his movements rapid and sure. As he worked, of course, he talked. But he talked this time about an interesting feature of the barn: namely, that the barn had been set, in terms of its alignment, after Biblical instruction. According to Clarence, the Bible admonished builders to set their buildings so that the sun found them from the south. Picture the sun as a hand coming to wipe clean the building, Clarence said. At times the sun might rub low around the base of the building; at another season it would climb on its axis and traverse the roof. But at all times the sun should greet the building from its southern arc.

"My son, Richard, didn't listen," Clarence said, as he continued to work around the porch, lifting and poking huge, flat fieldstones with his thick pry bar. "He set his house on an east-west axis so that he gets blasted by the sun all day long. He has to pull the shades in the morning on one side of his house, then on the other side of the house in the afternoon. His furniture is fading from all the sun. He didn't want to listen to the Bible."

"So this barn is set correctly?"

"As pretty as a peach," he said. "The old builders, they understood these things. If you build your house east-west, the sun's like a can opener all day long. It's always trying to pry the top off the building. The other thing is, now this building takes the worst of the storms on its shoulder. It's like a boat in that way. You like to take a wave on the shoulder of the boat, if you can. The north winds can be sliced by the corner of this building. You see how it goes."

I liked this vision of the building. It was a ship riding into the waves of the north winds. Strange, too, that the ship imagery, the *nave* idea, had returned. Clarence, however, did not spend much time worrying about the poetics of such an alignment. He wanted cement and so I began the ox process of bringing him buckets of muck, pouring at his instruction, watching him pry more here, daub with his mason's trowel there. He clicked his tongue when the porch ate great gobs of cement. To do it right, he said, we should strip the porch of any loose rock, fill behind with soil, then mortar the top stones. But our approach was good enough for government work, he said, a phrase he used to describe work done with only a modicum of style or grace.

By late morning I had begun to enjoy the work. My muscles loosened. The day climbed on top of the barn and hung there like a bright bat. The thermometer read seventy-six degrees. Clarence kept me busy and soon we had a small section of the porch—maybe an eight-by-eight portion—squared away. D Dog, who hung around in the shade, threatened to leave her paw prints everywhere. We eventually banished her to the house. She watched us from inside the screen door, her blackness matching the cool darkness of the barn interior. I thought about getting Wendy and Pie to put their handprints in the cement, maybe D Dog's paw beside them. I asked Clarence if he signed his work—I knew builders often did—but he said no, he had never signed anything. I pressed him and asked if he wasn't tempted to sign his work in unexposed areas, and he said no, God was the builder, he the tool.

We broke at lunch and Clarence ate a meatloaf sandwich. I ate with him on the porch, hungry as work can make you. I felt hazy and warm. A robin hopped by on the grass, the quick short run like a roadrunner's, then the abrupt stop, the gaze around, then another run. When we finished eating, we walked to the fishpond and let D Dog take a swim. Her tail flopped back and forth, a rudder, and she retrieved five or six sticks before giving it up. Cement crackled on my fingers when I threw the sticks. My knuckles flexed with hard, quiet brittleness.

We worked until the late afternoon, when Wendy brought us beers and cheese and crackers. We had done a good day's work. The sun now pushed back at us from the northwest, casting the shadow of the building onto the meadow. When breezes touched the weather vane, I watched it turn like the silhouette of a great heron perched on the eave of the house.

❀

We went square dancing on our second Friday in the barn. I hadn't been square dancing since my embarrassing attempts in junior high, but Wendy spotted a small ad in the *Record Enter-prise,* our local paper, saying that on Friday night at the Went-worth Town Hall, the next town over, Jim the Fiddle Man was ready to call figures. It happened that Pie had a sleepover with his old buddies, Chris and Ryan, so at seven-thirty we drove to Plymouth along Route 25. He was elated to be reunited with his friends, and after a moment of awkwardness all three fell back into their established routines. Comfortable and pleased that he was happily engaged, we turned around and headed to the square dance. I had tried to talk Wendy into wearing a fluffy skirt with starchy crinolines, but she had a conservative bent and opted for overalls instead. I wore jeans and a flannel shirt. She sat next to me in our old Dodge pickup, assuming Pie's usual spot between us. As we drove, the last sunlight clicked off the mountains while the smell of skunks waddling through picket fences clouded our passage, and on either side of the road we saw white rocks peeping up from the streams, and wolf maples resting for another season in the center of a hay field. Halfway to our destination Wendy bent forward to pull on a sweater, elbows swimming into the woolen sleeves. When her head popped out it was nightfall, fireflies puckering the gloominess, and the breeze suddenly chilly. We kept the windows open to smell the hay and cattle. Darkness came across the Baker River in brush strokes, painting the woods beside it paler and paler until the river became a black pearl rolling toward us. I spotted a shallow pool where Pie had winged a flat rock across the surface, the rock first plane, then boat, then plane. Already the river had yanked heat from the trees and earth and now a cold, wet mist rode down the streambed.

We heard the fiddle music from the parking lot. Wendy took my arm as we climbed the steps, the brightness of the room pulling us inside. It took a moment for our eyes to adjust, then we saw Jim the Fiddle Man standing before a small stage, a microphone propped in front of him. The ubiquitous gray metal chairs that appear at every town meeting, Cub Scout troop nights, and penny socials had been set up against the wall. In the center of the floor four squares of dancers clumped through their steps, the women dressed in cowboy clothes, the men in jeans and flannel shirts. Wendy and I hung on the outside, wondering what we had gotten into. Then a gray-haired woman wearing a scarf around her throat stepped over to us and introduced herself. "Mary," she said, welcoming us. Another set would be forming at the end of the next song and we were just in time. I watched the groups wheeling about, their steps more intricate than I had anticipated. The entire scene felt livelier than I had expected, more Friday-night-go-to-hell than I had imagined. I found myself bobbing a little to the music, happy to hear fiddling, happy to have the doors flung open on a spring night.

As soon as the song ended, Mary grabbed us and escorted us to a newly formed set. She introduced us and then backed away, joining another square beside an extremely tall man. Jim the Fiddle Man cleared his throat, struck a chord, then told us the name of the dance. I couldn't quite catch it, but that hardly mattered because he began fiddling immediately. The three other couples in our square seemed to recognize the music without difficulty, and as soon as Jim began calling they performed the steps fluidly.

I employed a sort of one-eyed strategy, making sure I watched the veteran dancers as I honored my partner, my neighbor, bowing and accepting curtseys. It had been a long time since I had seen a curtsey—or had bowed, for that matter. Then before I knew it, we were launched. At Jim's command, we do-si-do'd. We promenaded. We swung our neighbors, swung our partners, we took that girl for a ride around the world, brought her back, then stole our neighbor. I watched Wendy glide away from me, her smile broad, her arm tucked behind her. A broad, beefy man escorted her around the world, while I escorted his wife, a spry, happy woman who whispered to me when I didn't quite catch Jim's meaning. In the end we came back and found our partner, performed an allemande left, and bowed again to our neighbor. Jim's fiddling cut off the instant my body straightened. Wendy reached behind me and pinched my bottom. She had a good smile going and her cheeks shone red. Before we could say anything or catch a full breath, Jim called for a Virginia Reel.

Apparently it was one of the highlights of the evening, because people let out a whoop and hurried to take their places. This, I realized, was the one square dance I remembered from junior high. As I watched Jim wipe his brow with a red handkerchief, I remembered Mr. Gutek, my gym teacher, cueing the old record player, the first strains of the Virginia Reel beginning in static. Jim took our understanding as a matter of course and before he carried us two bars into it Wendy and I were left-handing around, then right-handing, then do-si-doing, and finally clapping as the couple sashayed up, then sashayed back. They peeled off, unwrapping us like a banana, and we passed through the arch supplied by their hands. Jim the Fiddle Man said something about ducking beneath the garden trellis while we snaked through and set up our lines again, clapping and stomping like giddy horses.

Wendy and I went fifth. By that time the group had lost a little enthusiasm, but Wendy and I remained in high spirits. Holding hands, we sashayed down and back in a gallop, peeled off, then made an arch and held it high, just as Jim commanded. The dancers passed underneath us and formed their lines again. Wendy and I collapsed the arch at the appropriate time. Wendy, I noticed, looked as warm as laundry.

After the reel, Jim the Fiddle Man took a break and Wendy and I went out on the porch. The air felt good. We watched three kids stretched out in sleeping bags in the back of a pickup. Their parents, a young couple, stood beside the truck, elbows on the side rails, talking quietly to the children. One of the boys, about Pie's age, wore a headlamp. He read *Harry Potter*, his attention alternately focused between the conversation and the novel. In a little while the parents returned inside. They could easily keep an eye on their children and still enjoy the dance. And the kids—all three—could lie in the back of the truck and look up at the stars. They would fall asleep to the sound of fiddle music and see their parents occasionally swing by, lighted for a moment by the brightness of the building.

jacks

An Ersky Hardware truck out of Littleton, New Hampshire, pulled up with two Bennington Home Heaters on June second. A rainy day. The top of the truck hit the pine branches next to the driveway, creating enough noise to set D Dog woofing around the house. I walked to the open haymow door and peered down. Two fellows wearing Ersky Hardware shirts jumped out of the truck. They looked at the barn, nodded to one another that the building appeared to match the description I had given over the phone, then came around to introduce themselves. Ed was the older of the two and the putative boss, a red-headed man who had rusted. Jim had a bright black NASCAR tattoo on his right forearm and was missing the ring finger on his left hand. Jim had driven and seemed eager to get the stoves off his hands; he made a reference to having had a hard night the evening before. As I invited Ed inside, Jim hustled back to the delivery truck to get the dolly and to free the stoves from their support strapping.

I took Ed down to the basement and showed him the thimble we intended to use for the coal-burning Home Heater. The old Franklin stove that the Rogerses had in the basement hadn't been worth the heat we generated carrying wood to it. Now we proposed putting a steel-bodied heater capable of pouring out 80,000 BTUs an hour in the same chimney thimble, three times the output of the Franklin stove. Ed liked the arrangement. The best place for a heater, he said, was in the basement. Heat rose and sifted where it was needed. Ed and I looked around the house to make sure we had an adequate return vent, a place where air might sip back downstairs and pull toward the stove. We decided the trapdoor outside the kitchen—a trapdoor once used to lower farm gear down to the basement—would work perfectly. It opened beneath the large southern bank of windows, a place likely to be a cold air seep. *Circulation*, Ed said repeatedly, was the key to the whole thing.

The spot we had selected for the upstairs stove, a thimble to the left of the fireplace as one faced it, concerned Ed more. Each stove weighed 800 pounds. That was a lot of weight, double what most woodstoves weighed. Flashlight in hand, we spent forty-five minutes under the basement floor inspecting joists. Ed wanted an upright post. He didn't want to set the stove between the span of beams for fear it would gradually sag the floor.

"It's not one day or even one week," he said. "It's the weight of the stove multiplied day after day after day. That adds up. You want it to sit on a beam, preferably right where a vertical post stands. Like a birdhouse on a pole, that's what we're looking for."

"We don't want it to extend too far out on the floor," I said. "It will block traffic."

"You've got to have it supported," he said. "These stoves have some heft."

We found a post near the southeast corner of the hearth. Using a tape measure, Ed checked clearances. Fire code demanded that we allow specific, comfortable distances around combustibles. We spent a half hour measuring the likely path of an eight-inch stovepipe. When we finally had the stove measurements in hand, we went out to the truck. Jim, who had apparently conquered his impatience, had pushed back in the truck, his legs dangling in the rain.

"Giddyap," Ed said, and Jim sprang to his feet. The toes of his shoes glimmered with rainwater. Jim rubbed his eyes clear of sleep. The rain came harder and had turned the day cold.

The stoves stood belly-button high, and ran four feet deep and as wide as a briefcase is long. They cost $1,000 each and could hold 100 pounds of coal. The coal could burn for twelve hours without reloading. The stoves could also hold fifteen hours of cord wood or roughly a dozen eighteen-inch logs. I liked their appearance immediately. They did not pretend to be anything but stoves. Some of the newer woodstoves we had considered wanted to be anything except a heating element. The Bennington Home Heaters combined beauty in function. They were as handsome as their purpose.

In no time Jim walked the first stove over to the edge of the truck, cranked up the hydraulic platform so that it was even with the truck bed, then slid the stove on top. With a whir the platform sank. Then Jim and Ed wrestled the stove up onto the most substantial hand truck I had ever seen. Ed tipped it back onto Jim and together we steadied Jim as he wheeled it into the basement, carrying the stove as ants might carry a raisin. After forty minutes of backing and shuffling, the stove stood in place, heavy and black, the sides turned to give us its flank.

As we got ready to put in the upstairs stove, Wendy and Pie returned from the grocery store. D Dog went out to wag them inside. I made introductions all around. Pie, seeing the size of the stove, wondered if he could climb inside. We told him no and banished him to his room, where he looked down at us like a juvenile gargoyle. While Wendy took care of the groceries, we hoisted the stove inside and backed it onto the asbestos pad that would protect the floor from heat. In the basement the stove had appeared like any other furnace, but up here, in the large keeping room, it drew my eye immediately. A fine stove. I imagined the winter nights we would spend beside it. I'd read that the decline of the American family was due not to television, as is commonly asserted, but to the proliferation of central heating. With individual thermostats in every room, it's easy to hide in a remote part of the house, luxurious in seventy degrees of baseboard heat. A stove is a different proposition. Set up a stove and we cannot avoid coming together. Reading in a rocker or listening to the wind outside, this is where we would keep company in winter. In a sense we had just delivered the heart of the house. The stove and the fireplace. I enjoyed knowing that our heat could not be interrupted; electric outages, blizzards, even exorbitant heating oil prices could not turn us cold. With a permit to pick up dead wood in the White Mountain National Forest, we could write our own heating bill. We could cut trees and chuck them in our stoves. We could burn anything, order coal and wood. Burn it. Burn more.

After accepting a tip, Jim and Ed wheeled the hand truck out and loaded it back on the flatbed. "They'll throw good heat for you," Ed said as he left. They backed out with the pine branches scraping the top of the truck. D Dog barked them on their way. Jim waved out the driver's window and worked the gears hard going south on Route 25.

Back in the barn, Wendy and I walked around the stoves. I liked them more and more. Pie came down and joined us. He had made another Lego spaceship, this time complete with landing pods. The stove made a perfect runway and he took to swooshing around and coming to a halt at the edge of the steel, his brakes making squealing sounds as he skidded perilously close to disaster. The stoves stood nearly as tall as he. By the time we had inspected both stoves, he had set up a rebel camp on the flat plain of one. Archer and Slam Fist stood like giants in the midst of a Lego village.

"They'll work," I said. "How do you like them?"

"I like them. They're like old Chevys or something. They just look like they will work."

"'Heating with solid fuel,' the brochures say. They say it takes a special sort of person. Do you think you are that person?"

"Absolutely," Wendy said.

Clarence had promised to come over in the next few days to install the stovepipe. Wendy and I discussed doing it ourselves, but we wanted to feel confident whenever we used the stoves, and we felt that Clarence, who had grown up around woodstoves, was the man for the job. I called his wife and left a message that the stoves had arrived.

Afterward we took D Dog for a walk. At the sheep fence I lifted her over and dropped her carefully on the other side. She was pleased to have a new assortment of smells to explore. She kept her head down, her nose a scooter wheel to the ground. Pie ran ahead with her. Wendy and I climbed over the fence, then began down the old railroad bed, a flat tongue of dirt that ran for miles and miles through the White Mountain National Forest. Cornish miners had blasted the rock ledge on either side of the bed, cutting their way from Boston and Manchester, extending the reach of the railroad to Canada. Once upon a time we might have strolled into town and grabbed a train for Boston or New York. Now the railroads had disappeared and the work of the Cornish miners, the great veins of rock, served no purpose.

We cut off the trail and followed an old game path upward, skirting a mica mine abandoned in the 1960s. Mica and schist had once been mined throughout Grafton County, the mica pressed to form isinglass, but that industry had disappeared in the rush toward plastics. The mine still held interest for Pie; he scrambled over the old battlements, the loading docks, happy to shout back to us at each discovery. An old foundation, square and clean, made a perfect fort.

We kept climbing. Wendy grabbed a stick and used it to fence the pucker brush aside. The mine disappeared and we climbed among paper birch and smooth beech, the trees gladed. Someone had logged the land, cutting wide tracks that formed corduroy bridges for the splitter. Deer tracks dotted the bare ground. The deer foraged for the beech nuts, evidently, then pooled in winter into deer yards. Occasionally their tracks remained like small moons in the orbits of larger, rounder moose tracks. Squirrel tracks provided a filigree border. We searched for deer or moose fur in the thorns, but the wind had taken everything.

A few minutes later we spotted the peak. Pie ran ahead, pleased to be the first to claim the summit. A square stone foundation stood anchored at the very top of the mountain, which years ago must have been a fire tower. Standing in the center, mountains ringed us. Carr, Moosilaukee, Sentinel. Rain clouds sawed across the mountaintops, occasionally carrying the tops into the mist and then cupping them. Pie yelled out, hoping for an echo. The echo came back faintly. Wendy whistled through her fingers, a high sharp sound that returned quickly and in the same rhythm of the original whistle. D Dog looked up, a fleck of dandelion frizz nettled into her back. She looked at us, then down the hill, wondering how Wendy had called her from so far down the sloping mountain.

Among the standard collection of ice saws, horse harnesses, and slaughtering hooks left behind by the Rogerses and scattered in the basement and in the dark corners under stairs, I found a hex sign. The sight of the hex sign took me aback, and I recoiled physically for an instant, nervous at what I had discovered. Wendy and Pie had gone to a friend's, so I stood for a second deciding whether I should disturb the sign or not. Then I felt silly. I carried it out to the porch, hosed it off, and set it to dry. I examined it in the morning sunlight, turning it first one way then the next.

The hex sign—a slightly swirling swastika pattern—did not appear original to the barn. It had been painted on a circular wooden sign two feet in diameter. The background was mustard yellow, the swastika a burnished red. I had read about hexafoos or witchfoots, but I was a little spooked to find one in our basement.

While I waited for the hexafoo to dry, I went to find the barn book that contained the information I needed. I found it after wandering amid the boxes—though the boxes had been reduced by a steady flow of unpacking—and carried it back onto the porch. The sun had the porch lined up and I sat on the edge of the fieldstone, my feet flat on the ground, letting the heat bake me.

The swastika, I read, is Germanic. It predates the alphabet and is commonly associated with the sun worship that ruled pre-Christian Europe for more than 1,500 years. Apparently the Germans preserved this ancient emblem and imported it to Pennsylvania. They also carried it on their marriage frakturs (documents written in Pennsylvanian German calligraphy) and dower chests—a decidedly different meaning than it would gain in the swell of World War Two. In using it to represent welcome, joy, and fruitfulness, the immigrant Germans actually embraced an even more ancient and more widely dispersed sense of the emblem. Six-pointed stars and swastikas have been on the temple steps of Ephesus, on the walls of the Byzantine Metropole church of Athens, and on the bronze doors of the shrine of Eyoub Ensaai at Istanbul. The swastika is always shown as whirling or rolling and its root is the Sanskrit word *svasti* or well-being. This sign I discovered in my basement had a heritage older than the crucifix.

In Colonial America, where witches were said to put spells on cattle to dry them up, the whirling swastikas were incorporated in hex signs, or hexafoos, which were meant to ward off evil. It turns out that Warren, New Hampshire, had its share of witches, which might have been reason enough to lay in a hexa-foo or two. *The History of Warren*, compiled over two decades by William Little and published in 1870, supplies an entire chapter on the hamlet's witches and wizards. Local boy Jonathan Merrill, stopping by a brook on a summer evening, was confronted by an "airy figure which to him looked anything but earthly" standing on the other side. Jonathan hopped from the log he had been standing on only to have the airy figure step from the stream bank and stand on water. The boy's hair, Little tells us, turned white in one night.

Stillman Barker's wife, angry at an insult from a local tavern keeper, bewitched the tavern keeper's calf, which fell to the ground afflicted by visions of "a hundred old witches on broomsticks." After the tavern keeper cut off the calf's ear and threw it into his home fire, the calf began to mend, "but only got up smart" when the haying was done. According to Mr. Little, experienced witch killers said scalding the calf would have worked as well.

An enterprising cobbler in the next town over, Wentworth, made Mrs. Zachariah Clifford, a known witch, a pair of shoes with an awl broken off in the sole, which in witch lore would pin her to her place. When she tried them on, she could not move, but stood helplessly imploring people around her to assist her. The cobbler took pity on her and withdrew the awl bit, "whereupon Mrs. Clifford was able to walk as she willed and declared the shoes a grand fit."

But perhaps the strangest story revolved around Caleb Merrill, a deaf boy, who went hoeing one day and was struck by a terrible noise like the sound made from the wings of a mighty bird. Caleb could hear nothing, but when he returned home in a terrified state he reported that Mr. Simeon Smith, the most feared wizard in the region, had come after him. Thereafter Caleb began to act in a strange manner. He would "run up the sides of the house or barn like a squirrel, and would traverse the ridge pole." At other times he would writhe in agony for hours. To cure him the town people procured a bottle of his urine and buried it under the hearth of Simeon Smith's fireplace. Immediately after Simeon Smith was taken with violent nose-bleeds and for a long time they could not be stopped. Eventually the urine seeped out of the bottle—no plastic soda bottles then, I suppose—and the boy began to cut his antics again. Finally they replaced the urine with blood drawn from young Caleb, stopped the bottle with a small sword dashed through the heart of the cork, and buried it again beneath the hearth. This time the sword worked through the cork and into the blood, causing Simeon Smith's death. The hamlet buried Smith beneath an apple tree, where, to this day, the apples are "the bitterest, crabbedest things that ever grew."

By the time I finished reading these accounts, the hexafoo had dried.

Clarence came to connect the stoves early the next week. Arriving in a cloud of noise, he informed us that it had been a while since he had last hooked up a woodstove. His blue shirt, with *Clarence* scripted over the pocket lest anyone forget, had large black swipes of roofing tar across the back. He had spent the past week on a fifty-foot roof replacing shingles. When I asked if he ever worried about falling, especially at his age, he replied that he wasn't concerned about the fall at all. He only worried about the stop. At this he laughed in a big boom, asked for a second cup of coffee, then headed downstairs to tie in the stovepipe.

I followed him down a little later and found him intent on the stove. He had the angle for the pipe, but he was having diffi-culty drilling the holes for the damper. It involves more hope than science, because one has to drill two properly aligned holes on either side of an eight-inch pipe. If the holes did not line up precisely, then the damper—the device in the pipe that slows the outgoing air—would fail to seal off the pipe and our heat would escape merrily up the chimney. As often as I had seen Clarence puzzled, I had never seen him resort to a sort of shoulder-shrugging hope. He asked me to hold the pipe when he drilled the first hole; then he stuck the metal spike through the interior span and tried to gauge, by sound and tapping, where the second hole should go.

"Well, let's try it," he said, when he felt he had it located.

As soon as the drill bit sank through the metal he turned it off and extracted it. Then he had to sink his arms in the stovepipe from either end and fit the damper rod through the two holes. It fit just right. He spun the damper inside the pipe to show off its fit.

"More luck than planning," he said.

"Perfect," I said.

"While you're here, let me show you something. You probably want to call Wendy."

I didn't like the sound of his voice. I called up to Wendy and she came down. After Clarence had demonstrated the damper's working to her, he told us to follow him. We walked outside to the overhang and watched while Clarence shone a flashlight at the joist arch that supported the stove upstairs. It had not sagged, but it was obvious, with Clarence explaining what to observe, that the floor sloped.

"The whole building is slouching a little to north," Clarence said. "Put a marble down and it would roll to the North Pole."

"Is it bad?" Wendy asked.

"It's an old building," Clarence said. "Hasn't settled as much as it might have, but it's on its way. Come here and take a look."

He had dug away the dirt from the central post supporting the barn overhang to reveal a rotted footing. It took a moment to understand the significance of what he wanted us to see. The post had soft rot up to its knee. Little solid wood supported the weight of the carrying beams, the long running traverses that held the weight of the building.

"Here's what you have," Clarence said. "The building has settled. That's natural. But it's going to keep settling if you don't get it back to square. Post-and-beam is all about square."

"How could we do it?" Wendy asked.

"Jack it," he said.

Clarence said the word with relish. I knew from talking to him that he had a pair of fifty-ton jacks, both of them used to lift railroad stock cars onto tracks when they jumped. It was impossible to know if the building actually needed jacking. If it did need jacking, I wondered at Clarence's qualifications. Although he had a hundred building skills, he also possessed a certain recklessness that often made me nervous. He did not lay down a tool when he could toss one; his finish work, while competent, did not exhibit careful, serious concentration. Slap and go, carpenters sometimes say. Clarence had a good deal of slap and go about him. I wasn't sure he was the man to jack up a building more than a century old.

"What I would do," Clarence said, "is leave the stones under the beam just the way they are. They've earned their places over the years. You don't move something like that if you don't have to. I'd cement over them and around them, jack the building, then put in a support beam. Then I'd cut the original beam with a saws-all, do a rabbet joint with pressure treated, and let the building set back down. It won't bring it completely to square, but it won't lose any more ground."

"Is it dangerous?" I asked.

"To me or the building?" Clarence asked.

Then he laughed very hard. I had no idea how to answer. I had no idea if insurance covered such a thing. What if he dropped the building? What recourse would we have? Suing him would be the equivalent of suing a robin for its nest, but I would never sue him anyway. He was a friend, and a good one.

"When would you do it?" I asked, to gain some time.

"Tomorrow," he said, "first thing."

I looked at Wendy, trying to read her expression. She appeared at war with conflicting possibilities. On the one hand, she liked her corners true and square. Clarence might be able to pull that off. On the other hand, this was our house jacked up in the air and this was Clarence. We both imagined him yanking down on the jack and the building teetering up, up, up, then crashing with a woody buckle. Clarence pointed out several other joints where the beam or joist had ridden out of the supporting bracket. Eventually, he said, they might all need repair.

Clarence said he could do it; we knew no one else who would attempt such a thing. It seemed clear, furthermore, that the building would eventually require it. Holding our breath, we told him to go ahead, pleading with him to be careful. He winked and said, "No worries," then headed off to complete the stovepipe installation.

We felt somewhat better that night when we gathered in the basement to try the stove for the first time. Wendy had a bunch of old paint sticks. We broke them into V's and folded them over newspaper. One match forced the blaze. We turned all the flues open and let the air bleed through the stove. In no time the metal began heating. We examined the stovepipe with a flashlight to make sure nothing leaked. Clarence had done his work well. By the time we added a second piece of birch cord wood, the thermometer on the flank of the huge stove read 350 degrees.

"Can we cook on it?" Pie asked.

"If we get an oven and put it over the top," I said. "Mostly baked goods."

"We can make tea," Wendy said.

And we did. The stove continued to heat and we put the kettle on top. The room grew white and warm and the furniture became soft. The temperature climbed in steady increments, rising up above 500 degrees in less than fifteen minutes. Now it was hot. D Dog came and stretched out beside it. In a minute or two she got up and moved away. Her fur, when I touched it, felt like warmed milk.

The fire leveled off at 750 degrees. To go higher we would have had to close down the dampers and press the stove for more heat. Instead we let it fade, satisfied that the test run had worked. It renewed our faith in Clarence, too, and we went to bed that night less nervous. A building could go out of line, we said, but we could set it straight.

Clarence arrived with more gear than usual the next morning. The back of his station wagon sagged with weight. Although he made as much noise as always, he also had a sterner demeanor. This was serious business. I met him and asked him again to be cautious. I would be working beside him; he could use the extra hands. He said that if we took it slow and steady, we shouldn't encounter any problems.

Wendy is handier than I, but she decided she couldn't remain in the house while the entire structure was suspended on one of Clarence's old railroad jacks. She grabbed Pie and headed out to a beach located on Lake Tarleton. She wished us good luck as we set up by the overhang next to the driveway. It was a beach day and the clouds passed overhead like white bear paws.

He set me to mixing cement in the driveway while he studied the job. I had worked with Clarence on several projects and had never seen him so serious. For a moment I considered asking him if he had bit off more than he could chew. Maybe, I thought, he simply needed permission to admit he had overestimated his ability to handle such a large job. From the base of the post, three solid stories stretched straight up to the sky, all of the weight balanced on the end of a pole that had rotted at its base. The roof rode as far away as the top of the pines. A cool blue breeze bent through the needles and wagged the tails of Clarence's navy work shirt as he looked up, estimating weight and thrust and torque. Everything relied on his gut feeling for the work. Gauges or meters would have no meaning on a job like this one. He was stealing from gravity.

While I finished with the cement, Clarence placed the jack close to the weakened post. Then he picked out an eight-by-eight hemlock post and toenailed it into the horizontal beam, forming a 7, if a 7 can be written with a straight downstroke. The jack fit between the earth and the bottom end of the hemlock post. The principle was simple: Lift the sagging beam or the top of the 7 back to square, prop the hemlock post in as temporary support, repair the original post, then lower the barn back into place.

Clarence fiddled with it for several long minutes. His mechanics had to support the full force of the building. The pressure on the upright post, if it inclined a degree in any direction, would be explosive. As Clarence began to turn the jack, he winked at me.

"If this lets go, you better jump," he said.

"I'm not going anywhere near it," I answered.

"It could kill us," he said. "But only once. So you don't have to worry too much."

Clarence brought the jack taut. Then he turned a quarter circle more. An ancient cracking sound shook out of the building; it was the sound of someone prying a nail free from an old board. It seemed impossible that this was a good sound in any sense. Like a physician listening through a stethoscope, he kept an ear cocked while he gave the jack another quarter turn. Then he did a little nervous chattering.

"They build these barns so well that you could roll them across the ground like a big box. I knew a farmer hooked a tractor up to one and tried to pull it down. Then he got another fellow to use his tractor when one wouldn't do it. He ended up with three tractors before they could pull it over. And the thing never did bust up. It just rolled after the tractors like a kid pulling a kite."

"How's it doing?" I asked.

"Oh, she'll give a little," he said. "We want to take the weight off that post."

"How much farther?"

"Wiggle it. See if it's off the ground."

It wasn't. I stood under the horizontal beam, trying to move the upright post that supported it. Beside me, Clarence ratcheted up the wooden bomb he had created. The barn creaked and groaned. A hundred thousand dollars, more or less, rode up on the makeshift jack and cob post. He knelt beside the jack, clearly risking his life. If it kicked—and it could, very easily—he was a dead duck.

With the next quarter turn, the vertical post lifted free of the ground. We had gained perhaps an inch and a half. The post that had supported the barn's weight through parts of three centuries now had become a simple hunk of wood. But we weren't finished if we wanted the corners true, the joints completely square once more. "She'll give another inch," Clarence said. Heat had built under the barn overhang and we were both sweating. I wanted to tell him it was good enough, we could replace the beam, but I bit my tongue.

He gave the jack another quarter turn and the barn shivered. Clarence listened, looked up at the various joists running under the floor, and shook his head.

"That's about all she'll give," he said, although the barn hadn't trued. A few inches remained between the floor beams and the joists.

"How do you know that's all she'll give?" I asked.

"You just do," he said.

He left the jack and came over to inspect the vertical post. Rot had taken three quarters of the grounded bottom. The barn had stood on tiptoe far too long. Give a year or two more, and the post may have buckled. Above the rotted footing, though, the wood remained as solid as ever. Clarence looked pleased that his original idea for repairs would work. Cut the rot away, replace the post with a stump of solid concrete, then set the barn back down.

Wendy and Pie returned in the late quiet of the afternoon. By that time we had cut the old post free, removed the punky section, and cemented a new footing in place. The post dangled like a dog with a bad paw. We braced it with pressure-treated lumber, then called it a day. It was four o'clock. We had worked ten hours. The barn rested on the edge of the jack beam, a rabbit trap ready to spring down. The house itself, now resting on the temporary hemlock, posed no danger. It was not going to collapse in a heap. The danger was that it would slip and sprain, never to be set true again.

Over a beer, I showed Clarence the hexafoo. He looked at it quickly, then shook his head. He knew the meaning. He said he painted the doorframe of any house he lived in with milk. Witches and bad spirits did not like milk and could not pass through the door of a house properly outlined. Milk is stolen, he said, and a witch cannot abide an evil that transpires without her.

Together with Wendy, we explained to Pie that he could not touch the jack. He could not go near it. He could not breathe on it. He eventually understood how serious the matter might be. He squatted like a bushman and examined the technique. He comprehended it immediately. The rest of the night he asked what if the jack gave way, what if the jack slipped, what if the jack twisted out. He asked the questions without regard for anyone's safety. It was dinosaur talk, the talk that let him explore danger without participating in it. Dinosaurs died long ago. Similarly, the jack could kick out like a mule and brain one of us, but he saw it as an abstraction, the sulfur match unstruck.

Clarence returned five days later. He did not bother to come into the house as he usually did, but let the house settle down on the post without telling us. He claimed it was not a big deal. He knew the post would hold and it made no sense to trouble us further. As right as Dixie, he said, an expression I hadn't heard before. But for the rest of a week, and into a month, the barn sometimes groaned and creaked. Wendy thought it was just the barn settling into new alignment, but I could not help worrying that the barn searched for something it had lost and could no longer find. The beams checked and lines appeared in the wood. Nothing, our carpenter friends told us. All beams check.

garden

On an exquisite June morning a brown delivery truck pulled up and delivered three cones of buff parchment paper, each one containing fifty bare root seedlings of winterberry, crab apples, and hawthorn. We had ordered from the New Hampshire Division of Forests and Lands seedling catalog on a whim and, honestly, had forgotten about the order. Our thinking, or at least what we could remember of it, was to plant a hedge line of sorts beside our sheep fence. We wanted color and we wanted fruit for wildlife, nothing predictable like arborvitae or rhododendron. It was a dollar a tree or plant, give or take, crab apples even less. Twenty-five plants for twenty dollars. The trees and shrubs, according to the booklet that accompanied the seedlings, promised to attain a height of twenty feet, maximum, which would give us added privacy without obscuring our views of the mountains.

The parchment cones came with a stern warning to plant the seedlings promptly. Suddenly a hundred other projects became secondary. Our ongoing battle to clean the basement and caulk the windows gave way to the bare roots. We loaded the back of the Dodge pickup with everything needed to plant a tree, then began working around the property line.

A summer morning. Sixty-five degrees, bright, the air moving the grass just a little. Birds flicked around us and lighted on the fence to watch. D Dog came with us. She had firmly established herself in the meadow, going where she liked. We routinely fed her on the porch, so for her each trip outside carried with it the hope that it might start or end with a feeding. But today she followed us outside and wandered as we did. Pie had crept away early and headed out to the sand pit, a place where the local kids went to hold wars and jump BMX bikes over mounds of sand. Now and then we heard the kids hooting, a good summer sound that was far preferable to silence.

Spade and soil. Every four or five feet, I set the spade to the ground and curled a shrug of earth up its blade. I liked the feeling of the blade sinking like a soft brake pedal. This soil had been worked for a century, and the memory of its agricultural past lingered in the loamy yield of each shovel peel. I cut the holes a foot deep and a foot square. The topsoil slipped off like snow on a car hood. I piled the soil in a mound beside the hole, then moved on while Wendy mixed in manure, stirred, and stabbed a seedling into the soft belly of earth. She deliberately planted haphazardly, trying not to fall into a regular pattern. We wanted the planting to surprise us. We imagined the plants carrying dull orange or red berries into late December, the guts turning to an icy liquor, a final fling for cedar waxwings before they clustered and migrated south.

Sun devoured the grass and glinted on the metal sheep fence. By ten we had a good sweat going. Pie returned and wanted to help until he realized helping meant working. He stood in front of us, his T-shirt filthy, his sideburns slimy with sweat. What he really wanted was to plant two or three trees, ensure that they were the best and healthiest seedlings out of the bunch, then head into the kitchen for lemonade or ice water. But Wendy kept him working and soon we had a proper chain gang going, with me digging holes, Pie mixing manure and soil together with a hoe, and Wendy planting behind us both.

As we worked the borders, we tried our hand at a plant census, an idea we had had long before we moved into the barn. A plant census is a common practice among gardeners and landscapers. Our idea was to map the borders and gardens around the property so that in winter we might have the pleasure of contemplating the next year's growth. June had brought on a lushness and vibrancy that we had never suspected on our first visit back in February. The plants on our list already included hydrangeas, irises, peonies, day lilies, phlox, honeysuckle, fire bush, Shasta daisies, rose hips, baptisia, bee balm, cornflowers, hostas, and chives. Our two established gardens—one a half-wild, luxuriant quarter acre of grass and plants, the other a more formal garden set off by the picket fence we had seen on our first visit—contained plants we recognized only as pictures in a field guide. A forest of asparagus had pushed up in the wild garden, had gone to seed, and had now turned into enormous dandelion-type plants, with halos and shaggy sprouts not dissimilar to corn tassels. In the formal garden fescue grass mixed with chives, sage, and lemon thyme. Marjoram. Rose hips gnarled through the spokes of the picket fence and rested, blush-red, beetle-shaped pods waiting for sun.

In the meadow, Wendy used a field guide to identify more plants while we took a break. She first sent Pie inside for a magnifying glass, and he returned with Kool-Aid ice pops he had frozen the night before. The Kool-Aid tasted like oranges and tea. We licked them long enough to satisfy his attention span, then we tossed them. Moving carefully, we counted daisies, chicory, cattails, plantain, bladder campion, fleabane, butter-and-eggs, bird's-foot trefoil, lamb's quarters, chickweed, purslane, goldenrod, sheep sorrel, burdock, Canadian thistle, Saint-John's-wort, quack grass, pokeweed, smartweed, curly dock, mallow, and stinging nettle. We also had bindweed, an invading species like the warriors fighting against Jason and the Argonauts that can split and cast about and finally create ten plants out of the original one. Once, maybe, the meadow had held straight rows of corn and maize, but the years had let it grow as it liked, the soil carrying the plants like conquering armies around and around the acreage.

Purple lupine proved to be the most spectacular of the plants, and the most numerous. We had an entire meadow bulging with lupine, the purple ladder of the flowering head striking everywhere. Whether it was native to the meadow or whether someone had cultivated it hardly mattered. Wolf flower, Wendy said. It grew in patches, a bright legume that helped fix nitrates in the soil. Standing dead in the middle of the meadow, one could look back across a purple field to see the white barn rising off its granite porch, the pillars welcoming, the broad pines flanking it to the north.

In the afternoon we set up a sprinkler for Pie. We trained it so the water splashed the newly planted crab apples and still smashed off his bony legs. He ran like a water bug back and forth, jumping through the scrim of water and shouting in the age-old manner. When he tired of running back and forth, we hooked extensions on the hose and stretched it around the border of the yard as far as it would go, then watered the remaining plants with buckets. By the time evening set in we had properly doused the new seedlings. We shoveled bark mulch around the stems to help them retain water. Then we had nothing to do but stand back and inspect them. The plants—particularly the crab apples—stood no taller than a Japanese bonsai, but they already suggested the shape of what they would become. In winter the black boughs would cut shapes from the whiteness surrounding us. They gave us something to watch in the landscape.

Planting the seedlings inspired us. For the next few days it became our routine to work in the house during the day, then spend the evening in the garden. Often we carried a glass of wine into the formal garden—the one outlined by a picket fence—and spent the twilight picking at weeds. Neither one of us had ever enjoyed the leisure to garden, but the quaintness of the picket fence, the relative limitation imposed by such a clear boundary, invited us to experiment. Besides, we wanted to be outdoors on a summer evening. I bought Wendy a set of garden tools—loppers, snips, a forked weeding trowel. At an auction one town over, Wendy purchased a cast concrete sink that we propped on birch logs and used as a plant bench. The hose ran next to the sink so that we could water the plants or clean tools when we needed. From a nearby nursery, we purchased two lilac plants and two forsythia shrubs to begin a border around the picket fence. We planted them on a blue evening in late June, the stars in a hurry to scatter. When they were solidly in the ground, Wendy clipped the chives that sought to spread everywhere, while I weeded around the fescue grass and pulled dandelions from the pea stone. Later, when we left, we put the sprinkler on and let it speak where it liked, the good garden smells flowing in through the French doors and pulling us out to the porch again.

The balance of the two gardens—one wild and essentially untended, the other striving for wildness within the confined borders of the picket fence—worked for us. Some evenings we wandered to the wilder garden and picked and poked. Purple iris and lupine and the black maw of berry clumps pushed through to the sheep fence. Two adolescent elms centered the garden, but they could not dominate the tangle of wild plants that surged in the early evening any more than we could—the tumble of wild daisies and asparagus brushes and runners of tansy, asters, black-eyed Susan, and Queen Anne's lace. If we had bush hogged the entire garden it would have rebounded with gratefulness, happy to fling itself into the air again. On the nights when we worked in the wild garden, we talked freely and wandered off sooner rather than later, humbled by the fecundity and richness of the growth. Often we found burrs or nettles clinging to our clothing hours afterward, the garden seeking new land on the cotton we wore to protect us.

We hunted for—and eventually found—a few wrought-iron chairs and a small café table to put in the fenced garden. I had a long-standing mistrust of café tables, wrought-iron ones in particular, because they always struck me as fussy. But this was a good table, broad enough to hold a lunch but compact enough to be unobtrusive. Some mornings we had coffee and cereal there; when the berries came in season, we carried our bowls to the wild garden and filled them with blackberries, covered them in cream, then ate while following the sun in our chairs, happy for the warmth. We placed a garden bench just outside the picket fence, locating it so one of us could read while the other worked at the concrete sink. We cut bundles of thyme and sage and hung them from twine lassos on the beams of the house. We planted a honeysuckle vine at one end of the trellis and waited while it climbed not a bit.

The garden also gave us clippings and weeds and these, combined with coffee grounds, onion skins, and vegetable ends, we carried to the compost piles at the far border of the property. In no time we had the beginnings of a nice circle, one I had never pursued before. What we produced and cut away came back to help us as mulch. Soil to plant to soil. Crows and chickadees picked over the compost; worms, whenever we turned the humus, boiled like roots through the castings.

In a final bit of gardening, I bought a dozen hostas and planted them along the stone porch. Rainwater from the roof irrigated them. They grew like bright green ears, curling out of the soil violently and listening for more rain. The plants softened the line of the porch and connected it to the meadow. Now in the evenings we could walk the fence line or wander to the gardens, our hands busy over green things. We made piles of weeds that Pie wheeled away in his red wagon. The compost pile grew and simmered. Birds watched and dove through an old apple tree to arrive for handouts. We watched for nuthatches carrying potato skins, robins with a beak of broccoli.

In July we decided we had better find the septic tank. It didn't do any good to play ostrich at this point, Clarence said. The seller's disclosure had listed no location for the septic whatsoever, an omission Clarence found unpardonable. They knew, Clarence contended, but decided to *box clever*, as the saying went. I didn't agree with that assessment, but I did concur that we needed to figure out the status of the septic. Both Wendy and I had suspicions that the septic report was not going to be welcome news. The town had no system design plans on record, which meant the septic tank was probably ancient and severely under capacity. Depending on local codes and the results of perc tests, a new septic could cost as much as $30,000. That was not, we reminded each other, fun money to spend. Adding an extension or renovating the porch brought satisfaction; a septic system buried itself snug to the house and one only heard from it again when it needed pumping or caused more mischief.

In all my worries about the septic system, it had never occurred to me that the tank could actually be lost. It seemed absurd. When Clarence arrived on the designated morning, he sprang out of the car and went immediately to the fishpond, where he cut some hazel saplings and fashioned a dousing rod shaped like a crow's foot. He explained, as he did so, that it was fairly common to lose a septic system. Some cesspools simply sank into the earth; old tanks, rusted beyond reclamation, fell apart in oxidized leafs, returning to the soil the elements they had borrowed. He didn't know what he would find, he said. No promises.

"Bet you've never seen one of these," he said, accepting a cup of coffee and showing me the hazel dousing rod. "Learned how to make one from an old water witcher. You could use coat hangers just as easily. Whatever comes to hand."

I started to say that I had seen a dousing rod, actually, but Clarence was on a roll, in mid-conversational bombardment. We walked to the corner of the barn next to the fenced garden, where he put his coffee cup on a post and began dousing for the septic. For once he turned silent, his ear cocked first one way then the other. The stick bobbed in front of him like a mime's leash for an imaginary dog.

"Why are you looking on this corner?" I asked him quietly, the way one asks when the other person is involved in a delicate operation.

"The pipe runs this way. I already know the angle from looking down in the basement. Whoever put it in wasn't likely to run a bend in it. No reason to do that. It's going to come straight out at the angle they set down in the basement. No mysteries about this kind of thing."

"Do you feel anything?" I asked.

"Nope. Not a thing."

"Will it bend?"

He nodded and said, "Should be right here."

He pawed at the ground between the garden and the bathroom wall.

"I don't understand it," he said. "It's not the lost city of Atlantis."

"What's next?"

"You'll see," he said.

I could tell it disappointed him to fail at dousing the septic tank. He liked old remedies and loved to pull a rabbit out of the hat. After a little while he disappeared to his car and returned with a gravedigger's pole that he had used, he said, when a county agency had asked him to locate a series of unmarked graves. Like Ahab jabbing his damned rod into the flank of Moby Dick, Clarence paced around the yard with an eight-foot harpoon of metal, stabbing the earth viciously. He jammed the rod in so hard that I winced to watch him. Each time he thrust into the ground, he cocked his head to listen. He clicked his tongue when he received no metal sound from the tank.

"Won't you rupture it if you hit it?" I asked him at one point.

"That's the chance you have to take," he grunted.

From time to time he stopped and waved a compass over the ground, hoping that the tank, if it were fabricated of iron, would produce enough pull to budge the compass needle. But that failed also. I started to feel a nervous pulse rise in my throat. It had been foolhardy, really, to buy a house without fully checking out the septic. Clarence was correct about that. I had images of the septic system resting dead in the ground, the burden of establishing a system on my shoulders.

At ten in the morning, after more than three hours of probing the ground and more dousing with the hazel rod, Clarence finally struck pay dirt. He grinned as I had seldom seen him grin. I must have grinned right back, incredibly relieved that at least something existed under the ground. I understood the pleasure of gold mining.

"Sneaky bastards," he said, clanking the grave-digger's pole around in a small circle not more than two feet away from the wall of the house. "It goes down at a pitch like nothing I've seen."

"A metal tank?"

"Sounds like it. Never had one dive like that. They wanted to sink it right next to the wall, that's why."

"What does it mean?"

"Hard saying not knowing," he said, employing an old New England phrase. He shrugged. It was impossible to tell. After carefully marking the area by making a series of clunks on the tank top, we began digging. The soil above the tank gave way easily. I put a tarp down on the grass beside the hole and scooped the soil away as Clarence cleared it. The tank's rounded body dove down like the dorsal of a whale, a black round object without clear shape or dimension.

"Small," Clarence said after twenty minutes of digging and probing. "Five hundred gallons, tops."

"How big should it be?"

"Bigger."

"How much bigger?"

"A thousand gallons. That's pretty standard. And a leach field. I can't imagine you have much of a leach field. You probably don't have one at all."

"What's next?"

"Guess that depends on how lucky you feel. What we should do is uncover everything and take a look. The tank appears to be in reasonable shape. It's old. It's like an old cannonball down there. But we can't know what to do until we know what we've got. I'll bring my son over tomorrow with a backhoe."

The next day Clarence returned with his son, Richard, and a bright yellow backhoe. Richard, who resembled a younger and thinner Henry Kissinger, stared glumly at the marks Clarence had made over the septic. He wasn't happy at the thought of using a backhoe on a septic tank. If he misjudged the dimensions of the tank, or simply gouged too deeply with the teeth of the bucket, he would puncture the top and render the tank useless. It called for a subtle hand. He backed the truck and trailer around the house, then slowly ran the backhoe onto the lawn. The treads dug into the topsoil.

With Clarence as the ground man, Richard uncovered the tank. It was a 350-gallon tank, not a 500-gallon reservoir, 650 gallons short of the standard tanks used today. The outflow pipe turned out to be a simple, half-inch line, deliberately punched with nail holes on the bottom. By any standard, a crude system. A young man might have been defeated, but at lunch Clarence said he had seen worse.

"I saw a system once where a man had buried a Volkswagen Beetle with one pipe going in the trunk and the outflow going out through the windshield. Fellow had the thing on a slant to get the water levels right. Worked dandy, too. He buried the whole car at night and reported the car stolen the next morning."

"Is that true?" I asked, but Richard got to the central point.

"Did he collect on his insurance?" Richard asked.

"Indeed he did," Clarence said.

After lunch they told me to go away so that, down the road, if asked by a county official about my septic system, I could plead ignorance and mean it. It was a neat moral nicety. I sat inside and watched Richard go back and forth to an old rock pile at the far end of the meadow. He returned with the rocks held in the bucket of the backhoe, an old man cupping an egg in his hand. He dug a long drainage trench and nudged the rocks inside it. This, I understood, constituted the leach field.

I returned to help them cover up the trench and pack away the septic tank. Remarkably, Clarence said, the old tank's tar lining still seemed impervious. It worked, in other words. He hadn't managed to find the hatch, so instead he had cemented a square opening in the topmost portion of the tank. We ran to the hardware store and bought patio stones to place over it. Then, carefully, we covered the stones with dirt. I placed a brick in the topsoil so that I would be able to locate the opening again. We had a septic system, for better or worse, one that would need pumping every fall. Clarence told me to add enzymes each month and to be mindful of detergents. As long as the tank remained solid, he said, the system might well last another twenty years.

That night, in the garden, Wendy and I toasted over a glass of wine. We'd escaped a major expense. Doubtless we needed a new roof someday, but the foundation beams had passed Clarence's examination and the septic now functioned properly. The shell of the barn was solid and we both felt greater faith in the security of our home. Bottom to top, we told each other. That was the way to renovate. We turned on the sprinkler and spent a while watching it hit the garden. The sprinkler threw a fan of water into the air, then gradually pushed it back and forth, waving.

grass
maze

Once upon a time I lived in New York City. That's what I thought about as I constructed a compost bin in the back corner of our land, the place where someone had once kept a few beehives. We had created enough compost by this time to require a system. I had the instructions for the bin from the handyman in *Yankee* magazine. A true Yankee himself, the fellow instructed his readers to take five produce pallets—given away free at most lumber yards—and to place one on the ground as a base. Then, using wire hangers like the rings of a loose-leaf binder, he told his weekend warriors to build a cage out of the remaining four pallets, making one side particularly easy to open outward so that you could actually get to the compost. He also recommended having two or three bins, all of them at different levels of decomposition, so that you could keep an active pile going at all times. Because of the sheep fence, I only had to box three sides of the composters, an adaptation the Yankee handyman would doubtless approve. Birds could take what they liked, I figured, raccoons too. D Dog might stare as long as she liked through the flat slats of the pallets, but she had no way to get to the clippings and decayed veggies she eyed so wantonly. In no time, birds or no, the grass and heat would turn these leavings into humus and soil. The soil would feed the gardens.

It was mid-July now, warm, a Monday, and as I worked I thought about my former life in New York. An apartment on West Ninetieth Street. A dozen three-buttoned suits, all of them purchased at Barneys, shoes to match, crisp shirts starched at the Chinese laundry. A monogrammed briefcase, socks made of thin rayon or silk pulled high to the calf. Stylish ties, fifty, sixty, a hundred dollars on a tie, a cord of wood a tie. Calling people, visiting, a charity ball at MOMA, dancing with women who wore backless dresses, shopping on Madison Avenue, buying deli. Opera, plays, first-run movies, all those books, the reviews, the quick assessment of other people's efforts.

Those worries seemed a long way from composting. As I danced the pallet floor into place, lifted the sides like a mini barn raising, held each pallet steady while I hog-tied it with an old wire hanger, I marveled at how my ambition had redirected itself. Water around a rock, I supposed. What I wanted now, I knew, was clarity. I wanted days outside, stones to work with, sunsets, early mornings. For the first time in my life, my days focused on addition rather than subtraction: the barn, the house, my family now, each year adding to something that went before it. Maybe New York life had been too linear. I had never been able to buy that we were all headed someplace worth going, certainly not in a suit and tie. The seasons, the compost pile, the decomposition of grass and vegetable matter, seemed useful to me in ways that walking a New York street did not. Cut wood, carry water, the Buddhists say. That seemed to be my motto.

Pie arrived in time to help me rig up the last compost bin. We had three in a row. I told him it was now officially his job to carry out our bucket of scraps and dump it. Gross, he said, but he said it without much conviction. I began a short lecture on the usefulness of composting, how it was earth-friendly and a smart way to live, but his eyes glazed over and he asked if he really had to carry out the scraps every night. I said yes, no joke, and then he told me to look at the phoebe perched on the sheep fence a few posts away. We had learned to recognize the phoebes from their tail bobs, the way they fanned themselves and seemed always about to lose their balance, and naturally from their call that repeated *pheee-beee, pheee-beee.* Pie had pointed out the bird to divert me from my lecture.

Then Pie caught the composting passion and decided that if we were going to compost, he wanted to be the first to use the bins. He grabbed a rake and scraped together a pile of dead leaves and brush, then hugged it all to his chest and carried it to the compost bins. We started at the farthest bin, the one we named Old Charlie just for the hell of it, and he gave the bin a light body slam as he dumped in the debris. That gave him the fever, a temporary zeal for work, and he took off around the yard, returning to me like a retriever asking if this accordion of oak leaves would decompose, this broom of twigs, this whisk of dried grasses. I commented on each addition, told him we would never put meat or bones in the pile, told him that animals would start coming around to pick at the leavings. Skunks, I said, which initiated a long discussion about skunk juice, odors in general, about the possibility of skunks getting into chicken coops and killing the hens, and about Nellie, our old golden retriever who died some time back, who had been smart about many things but not about skunks.

"So what did you do when she got sprayed?" Pie asked.

"Took her swimming," I said. "People will tell you that tomato juice and other things work, but they don't. Even a year afterward you could smell the skunk on her if she got wet."

D Dog, to Pie's delight, had never been sprayed. He took this as a sign of her superior intelligence. Afterward we grabbed the tools and carried them on our shoulders back to the barn. We'd done good work. The first bats wicked the air above us. We watched them as they skimmed the porch light, their bodies glinting for a moment before they returned to the pale darkness.

Mid-week Wendy disappeared to Tilton, New Hampshire, and returned by early evening with two table saws borrowed from her father. It was time to begin construction; the walls needed covering. The first order of business, now that the stoves had been installed, was to tighten the house as much as possible. The old barn boards, many of them more than a century old, held the deep, rich color of loam, but they had shrunk over the years and the gaps that so concerned us could wait no longer. Using a razor knife and duct tape, Wendy wrapped the house in Reflectix. Day by day the house grew more silent and comfortable. Henry David Thoreau at Walden Pond talked of a house that communicated with nature directly. He had reveled in the elements blending with the house, the loveliness of walls open to the seasons. Of course he loved nature's intrusion only through summer and early autumn. By winter he had developed a different aesthetic, and so would we. As Wendy wrapped the interior in Reflectix, we grew increasingly aware of how noisy our life had been. Squirrels, birds, and insects had called through the walls. Light, too, had pulled at us during the long wash of sun. Although it would not be fair to say we had been camping, it is true to say we had lived not far removed from Thoreau's ideal. Nature lived beside us and invited us to join. Now, with Wendy's hard work, the world of necessity became divided between inside and outside.

We did, however, regret covering up the old barn boards. Little by little the ancient wood disappeared under bright, shiny silver. An unsettling transformation, to say the least. As it went up, I had a case of the heebie-jeebies. Had we made a mistake with all this tin foil? Should the place remain a seasonal structure? Were we working too hard against the true nature of the barn? Someone once told me that what you lose in the whirligig, you get back in the ding-dong. The phrase referred to two carnival rides, one winging the riders around vertically, the other horizontally. What you lost, theoretically, in one ride, you gained back in the other. I worried that we had taken on too much whirligig and could not recover, regardless of how much ding-dong we found.

"Everything that was in the barn is still here," Wendy reminded me one night when we walked around to inspect her work. "We're just covering it up for a while."

"For a long while. We're going to live here for a long time."

"For as long as we want. Besides, these pine boards didn't represent any architectural marvel. They aren't even matched in places. Old man Gale threw this place together from whatever he had around. All the farmers did. A barn was an outbuilding, plain and simple."

"The Shakers rebuilt the round barns if they didn't think they fit together properly. They took them apart stone by stone."

"And are you a Shaker?"

Wendy's comments, and the disappearance of the tobacco-colored barn boards, forced me to confront aspects of restoration that I had never fully considered. I called a friend, a gifted architect named Jennifer, and asked her to talk about restoration in general. I had worked with her at a summer academic seminar at Amherst College where she had taught an introductory architecture course. I trusted her wisdom about buildings and her wonderful levelheadedness. She once told me that three brick courses on buildings, from mortar stripe to mortar stripe, measured exactly eight inches. To prove it she pulled out a tape measure and stretched it across the brick courses of a dormitory. Now I can no longer look at a brick wall without thinking of her. Eight inches, every three courses. It's something like a universal law, one that I never knew existed until I met Jennifer.

"Unless you're going to restore a barn to its original purpose and house animals, you're lost from the start," she said. "That's not your plan, is it?"

"No," I said, "not at all."

"So whatever you do is going to interfere with the builder's intention for the structure, right?"

"Right," I said.

"It's always a tricky business to renovate. Creating a living building is the key. No one wants a dead building. Some stuffy old building that complies with something or other in the past? That's the alternative. What good would it be to turn your barn into a museum?"

"Keep talking," I said, "I'm feeling better."

She talked about the restoration of a series of mosaics in a Florida museum. A hurricane passed through the area and water flooded the building to the second floor. Several magnificent frescoes disappeared under water. When the flood water receded, the museum curators went crazy debating what to do. They had the precise details of the frescoes on computer. In principle at least, they could have restored the frescoes to exact copies of what they had been, blending old and new sections until they had a fair representation of the originals.

"But is that the original fresco?" Jennifer asked. "Or is that a reproduction of some sort?"

"I see the problem," I said. "What did they decide to do?"

"They made a conscious decision to leave the destroyed sections blank. They put a putty compound where the portions had fallen out and decided that solution was the truest approximation of the originals. On the other hand, hundreds of museums restore paintings and change them slightly to bring new life to them. They spruce them up. They would tell you that's the same thing as long as it's true to the original."

"So are there any sins to avoid?"

"Probably counterfeiting. I knew a woman who had a Cape reproduction built for her in Barnstable, Massachusetts, the whole thing right from the ground up, at enormous cost. A guy down there specializes in doing this kind of thing. She had a fieldstone foundation, just like yours. She had wide birch boards bought from an old house and put down over a subfloor of plywood. She had painted cupboards from Indiana or someplace brought in and put up in the kitchen. All that stuff. It was a new antique, in other words. A lot of people are doing it. They're doing it with furniture and everything else. It's frowned upon, to say the least."

"By whom?" I asked.

"By those who feel it's their right to frown on such things, I guess," she said. "The one thing to avoid would be trying to make the building look original when it isn't. Or parts of it. You're going to lose something, but the current thinking is that you should be honest about it. You'll gain something, too. Show the new work. Don't kill yourself trying to hide the details."

"So new boards will be okay?"

"Depends on how tasteful you are," she said. "That's the final judgment, so to speak. Almost everything old is eventually renovated. Very few buildings pass through a century or two entirely unchanged. It just doesn't really work. If you reinforce a building, is that still the same building? Are the structural aspects of a building the same as the finish details? You know what I mean."

"Someone already added a chimney along the way."

"Exactly. You don't find chimneys in a barn. It wouldn't make sense. It's the last thing you would want. Not many windows, either. You might decide that your governing aesthetic is an accuracy of feeling. Is the renovation in keeping with the feeling of the barn in the first place? Does the renovation keep in hand the barn-ness of the place?"

I told her I thought it did. She said not to worry then. Putting a new roof on a building, she said, is a necessary renovation, and no one would argue against doing so if the building began leaking. Leaks beget rot, and rot begets decay, and decay begets ruined timbers, and ruined timbers beget collapsed buildings. Ditto caved-in foundations. Ditto sagging sills. A building is a representation of a concept, she said as we finished. We needn't worry disproportionately as long as the truth of the concept remained. The conversation gave me a renewed feeling for the work. I liked the phrase *an accuracy of feeling*. It seemed as workable a guideline as any.

The next day I helped Wendy begin cutting boards. Wendy had learned carpentry by working with her father. She was a thousand times more competent than I, and quickly I became her assistant. I carried boards to her when she needed them. I held one end of the plank when she sawed. I was clearly the sous-chef, whisking soups and chopping ingredients while she put together the final menu. I liked my role. I liked the brute work of carrying things, and being Wendy's extra pair of hands. Wendy proved herself a Yankee builder. She hated waste. Measure twice, cut once served as her motto. Her caution made the work go faster in the end. We did not have to redo anything once it was done. An added benefit was that she became increasingly parsimonious about the boards. She did not use a board without considering its end product; she wanted each square inch of wood to count for something. It was a thought I had never had about a carpentry job. Not only did you have to cut boards to fit, but you had to use your products wisely or risk shortchanging the job. At that particular aspect of the job, Wendy was a true master.

The beams running through the walls established a natural partitioning. The large X's of the barn wall, the vertical straights, allowed us to mark our progress. By five o'clock we had covered half the southern wall with shiplap. The new pine looked sugary and yellow. It brightened the walls and made the entire house lighter. When the evening sun bent through the skylights in the roof, we called a halt and fixed ourselves two tall Scotches. Then we walked away, counted to three, and spun to look at the work.

It was difficult to *see*. Naturally we could see that here was new work, fresh boards, and that they differed substantially from what went before it. But what did they look like? What did they suggest about the rest of the work that would consume hundreds of board feet? How did one see whether this was a change for the good?

We didn't discuss it at great length. It wasn't something you could discuss sensibly. You either approved or disapproved of the changes, and explanations didn't amount to much. It reminded me of rearranging table lamps around a living room. Why, exactly, did the light in this space improve the composition of the room, while a lamp over there appeared to drain vitality from the furniture? Jennifer's words came back to me. Had we remained true to the concept of the building? Had we continued the accuracy of feeling the barn had possessed for two centuries? I felt we had. The new wood, from what I could see, seemed precisely in keeping with the sense of barn-ness we had loved in the first place.

That night, as we ate dinner, I looked frequently at the wall we had just completed. Reflectix stretched everywhere around it, but the new wood, the portion we had completed, held the color of dry hay. I was reminded of a conversation I had had with a painter who said at some point you have to draw a line. You have to scar the canvas, in other words. If you're painting a landscape, eventually you must decide what is sky and what is earth. We had accomplished the same trick with our day of work. The trick, I recall the painter saying, was to know if you had done it well or not.

That night a full moon greeted us as we tucked Pie into his trundle bed. It blazed in through his windows and searched the house. Pie lay with his head propped on the pillows, his stuffed animals everywhere, his faithful D Dog beside him. He was in good spirits and lively as a cricket. High summer floated through the windows and the barn, all the floors and walls, rested everywhere beyond the light. Because it was on my mind, I asked him how he knew he saw a thing when he saw it. He listened to the question and cocked his head. An adult might dismiss it, but the idea had intrigued him. He said he saw things when he blinked his eyes. In other words, he took a snapshot of them, his snapping eyelid a camera shutter. It struck me an ingenious answer, though I wasn't sure he had seen the question as anything more than a puzzle he had to solve. I finished tucking him in, petted D Dog, then went downstairs. The new wall, the pale boards, glowed in a buttery glaze, but they did not push or pull my eye. I couldn't say that I saw the full impact of the new construction. I was reminded of a story I had heard about a famous actor who had a tile floor designed for his newly renovated apartment. The tiles and laborers came from Italy; the cost for both constituted a small fortune. On the day the workers completed the floor, the actor walked in and shrugged and said he didn't like it. End of story. He had seen, like Pie with his blinking, a snapshot of what the floor represented. He didn't like it and the cost did not prove a determining factor.

How wonderful, I thought, to be clear about your desires. And better still, to be able to afford such decisions. Wendy and I had to be much more careful, which made taste slave to finance. We could not afford many wrong turns. In some sense, that made our efforts more interesting. Like tailors embroidering silk, we could make the garment only once.

Wendy came down behind me and I grabbed her around the waist and we stood together for a while looking at the new work. Crickets had taken over for the peepers. Fireflies blinked across the meadow, the last of the sunlight carried in their phosphorous. I asked her if she ever wondered about filmmakers who make catastrophically bad films. I asked her if she ever wondered why someone in the prescreening didn't stand up and shout that the film was terrible, that the concept was ludicrous, that they had to begin again. Did they all go along, I wondered, because they wanted to keep their jobs? Or did everyone on the project become deluded, entranced by the day-to-day production of the film until they lacked all perspective?

"You're worried about the construction?" Wendy asked, going straight to the point.

"I like it," I said. "I think it looks good."

"But you worry we're making *Heaven's Gate*?" she asked, referring to a cinematic bomb of the early eighties, a film often cited as the model of enormous cost overrun.

"Not really," I said. "Honestly, I like it. I just don't know if I'm liking a monstrously false move."

"It's okay," she said, "we're doing it right. It's just a change."

"I want to be able to see what it's going to be."

"That's the trick of it, isn't it?" she said.

We went to bed shortly afterward and woke to work the next day. Sawdust formed a skirt of work around our coffee cups when we set them down anywhere at all.

At nine on a Saturday in late July, Pie and I went into the meadow to design a grass maze. We had seen a road sign earlier in the spring, Grass maze. The grass maze had matched Pie's interest in mythology. In third grade he read the myth of the Centaur. We could cut a maze in our back meadow, he said, then challenge people to try it. When I asked him to draw the maze he made all manner of nutty designs, conveniently forgetting that we would have to cut the maze with a lawn mower. What occupied us most was devising a trick we might build into the maze, a secret only we knew, a key that would be both obvious and devious.

"We could leave signs with backward writing and you could use a mirror," Pie suggested as we wheeled our old Tecumseh lawn mower out to the meadow that morning. It was a dry, hot summer day. "Or maybe really small writing that you would need a magnifying glass to read."

"Or maybe you could write it on a piece of paper, then eat the paper."

"Maybe," he said.

Pie and I figured the maze should lead to something tangible, preferably something vile and horrible, but the best we could come up with was the weathered picnic table we had brought from the Bridgewater cottage. We dragged it to the center of the meadow, then went back and started the lawn mower. Together, Pie in the brackets of my arms, we mowed a waggy circle, a half-moon, an arrow. We finished at the table and then retraced our steps, arcing off in haphazard directions, trying to make our maze duly complicated. The grass grew as high as our knees; we could not see the next leg of the maze before we were upon it. At times our efforts seemed to take us, literally, in circles.

In an hour we mowed a good quarter-mile trail through the grass. It snaked everywhere, doubling back, then linking up with an early strand of the maze. Pie let go of the mower handle and ran in front, scouting. Grasshoppers and ladybugs chittered up. I followed him with the mower, cutting the timothy grass and smelling the tired ache of lawns in mid-July.

"Let's get Mom," Pie said, as soon as we finished.

We had not even attempted the maze ourselves before he dashed into the house and returned in about five minutes with Wendy. Pie could hardly contain himself. He ran ahead of her like a miner's canary, chirping and flitting whenever she seemed about to make a wrong move. The maze turned out to be harder than we had anticipated. The grass stood high enough to obscure the next turn and in ten minutes, maybe less, it managed to disorient us sufficiently to feel like a maze. A unique experience, I thought, to feel the sense of a maze under your feet instead of under your pencil. As the grass grew higher it would become more difficult. If we kept the pathways trimmed, the meadow rising around them, we stood a chance of making the maze genuinely confusing. It felt oddly Victorian to be strolling around the maze, the grass our stage, the barn lingering in the background.

Pie had brought along a pocketful of Kooshes, rubber spoked balls on an elastic, and he ran ahead and dove to the ground in hidden areas, only to spring up and shoot a Koosh at us. We collected the Kooshes and shot back at him. He poked up at strange intervals along the maze, more turkey or prairie dog than eight-year-old. D Dog wagged after him, intrigued by a human down on her level. Pie hated when D Dog ferreted him out in her dopey, kindly way. He jumped up and pushed her away, then darted off and resumed hiding. D Dog plodded after him. When they wandered far enough away, we saw only D Dog's tail bobbing like a black shepherd's staff over the grass.

wolf
maples

The first maple turned in the third week of August. The maple flared suddenly, so much so that Wendy and I remarked on it the same day. One August night a cold wind frisked it red and orange, and the next day we spotted it. We had seen glimmers of color—rusted leaves, and scissored cuts of brown tucked among the faded green canopy—riding on the swamp maples in the wetland areas we passed on our daily commutes to and from Plymouth, but suddenly in August the wolf maple had exploded.

It is nearly impossible to see a New England autumn creep in without resorting to cliché and sentimentality, but the good, defined aspect of the wolf maple stood quiet and delicate. Loss of sugar, not sweetness, turned it. The tree pulled back inside, reducing the flow of nutrients to its outer branches. Like blood pulled away from an injury, the vast roots drew the sap down and stored it beneath the ground or passed it deeper to the core of the tree. This maple had begun to hide its essence for winter. Already, merely three weeks into August, it stood nearly dormant.

We have always loved wolf maples—the wild, dominant tree that has survived the farmer's ax, its bulk growing and expanding until it stands without equal on a flat plain of tired meadow.

Cows know it; so did the farmer who may have once eaten his lunch under it. Wolf maples most often grow near stone fences, their round boles a plug in the fieldstone. Because it is difficult to lay rock on roots, the trees tear their confining skirts and push the stones to ground. Frost helps. So do the occasional animal visitors, the luggage-skinned black snakes that use the stone walls for a hunting ground, the busy chipmunks that cannot rest in hollows or on flat rocks but must be eternally active, the deer that occasionally come to rub and lick. The wolf maples have a kinship with rocks, but it is hard to pinpoint it. Perhaps it is that each tree is a wall, a circular stair of sap and leaf and shade.

The wolf maple Wendy and I saw that week in August grew in Rumney, New Hampshire, a town not far from our barn. We had noted it separately on our rides to and from Plymouth, the tree impossible to miss because of its size and fierceness. It stood on the edge of a meadow, its rocky outriggers crumbled by years of frost and heave. An old dairy barn, gray as ash, presided over the tree and the meadow. Someone had once farmed the land, but now the barn sagged pitifully, its oak bents exposed to the weather, its siding long ago stripped for use elsewhere. The barn knew the tree, it seemed, and the tree the barn. Both had been part of a farm that had sunk away into the earth, leaving them floating on the skin of soil.

We parked near the barn and we took our picnic from the back of the truck. The picnic consisted of apples and a few sticks of celery, fresh tomatoes from the Longview Farm Stand, a few plums, and black bread. We walked across the meadow and spread a blanket beneath the maple. The leaves smelled of candles and the window shades of schoolrooms. Pie nibbled a little food, but we had brought along a kite and he wanted to fly it. Years ago I had learned that an inverse relationship existed between the money you spent on a kite and the performance you gained. Cheaper kites flew better, bar none, and the shark-shaped kite we had with us cost under three dollars. Pie got it going in no time, his arm raised in classic fashion, his shark trailing behind him. The kite gnawed the wind and fluttered above. He stopped running halfway across the meadow and became bored, gradually, by watching the wind shove the kite around. We knew he would return to us soon.

Autumn. I lay back on the blanket with Wendy, and autumn surrounded us. Summer had gone. Asters pushed their expectant heads up along the stones walls like guests arriving too late for a party. We would still have some warm days, and the sun would pretend to linger in the sky, but soon frost would tongue the ground and turn it white. With Wendy's head on my chest, I looked up through the bright orange leaves. Sun and clouds and soon black cats and cardboard cutouts of turkeys. The leaves that shone so kindly right now would turn brown and pale and drop to the ground. They would hang for a while in the weary meadow grass, then sink farther still, dying like a footprint in the white mist and first snow.

Pie returned with the kite string hopelessly tangled. Wendy sat up and tried to unscramble it, the shark baring its teeth at each twist and turn, threatening to gobble her arm. While they worked I walked over to the old barn. The roof joined in a classic gable style, two playing cards set together to form a peaked structure. The animal loading ramp led up to it from the gable end, a later innovation to avoid snow and ice falling on creatures as had so often occurred with side-entrance barns. It was a good-size building, bigger than our barn by half. Like our barn, though, it had not been built into a hillside as so many barns were built in Pennsylvania and elsewhere. It sat flat on the meadow, the sills fractured, the framing of the walls and roof as bare as a cartoon desert skeleton. The cellar hole, built of fieldstone, had gradually begun to swallow the wood.

I counted six bays through the missing boards and siding. Hay lay around the bents, and the floor was covered with dried manure years and years old. A dairy barn, then. The cupola—a sheet-metal ventilator typically used on agricultural buildings–had rusted brown as a coconut. It gave me pleasure to realize I could read a barn. From the barn, the rest of the farm took shape. It had probably been a self-sufficient operation. Cows and corn. Maybe some potatoes and some local lumbering. Hang a deer or moose from the rafters in autumn to bleed out. A bit of maple syrup in spring. The barn did not seem so dedicated to one proposition–as chicken barns are, for instance–so that one would know at a glance what commercial engine drove the farm. This and that, probably, although cows had certainly been housed in the stables. The barn had served as a multi-use out-building, a place to store and harbor things. When the function of the farm had faded, when agriculture had migrated west, the barn had been consigned a low priority. The barn's state of dilapidation, really, was like that of an old hand tool–say a cobbler's last–that no longer holds a purpose for a modern shoemaker. Farmers who knew what it was to connect a rope between the house and the barn so that they did not get lost in a snow squall would not lament the barn's disappearance any more than a modern cobbler might resent machine-made shoes. Hard work to manage a barn, the farmer might say. Hard to keep it going.

I skirted the barn and looked for an old house foundation. I soon found an abandoned fieldstone foundation on the south-west corner of the barn, the sides caved in, the house small. The main keeping room looked to be about eight by twelve, with two ells wandering halfheartedly off in different directions. The ells did not have full basements beneath them. The fieldstones that had served as footings had been covered by grass, by yellow peeps of black-eyed Susan and a final mat of rye. A ridge of phlox, too, worked its way from the doorstep, doubtless planted by the house's inhabitants. I tried to imagine how many years the phlox had pushed up untended, fighting and spreading until it had achieved a pink eyebrow forever marking the empty socket of the house.

Many New England barns are attached to houses so that the farmer can tend his cattle without going outside, but not in this case. Here the farmer stepped out of his back door, also marked by a granite step up, and walked a forty-five-degree tangent to the front of the barn. Slide the doors open. Hear the contented munch of his line of cattle. Listen to the fading slurp of the cows as they caught their cuds, the muddy cluck of their hooves on the thick plank floor. Bells might sparkle, too, and the chickens, high in the hay, might stir their legs in bicycle motions.

I followed his steps and entered the barn a few paces. The floor did not look solid, but the rest of the barn, the oak bents, the peaked rafters, seemed perfectly joined. The barn still smelled of hay and animals and something older. Standing in the doorway, I saw cobwebs winking at each corner of the purlins and queen beams. I remembered Joseph Campbell's thoughts about why it is that when we step into Saint Patrick's Cathedral in New York City the street sounds, the noise of the taxis, suddenly fade away. Even if no sign is posted asking visitors to be quiet, we lower our voices. One could argue, Campbell said, that it is the sacred nature of the church that causes us to speak softly, but it is also architecture that persuades us to quiet.

Maybe that's making too much of it. Nevertheless, the barn is an echo of the cathedral, and as I stood in the doorway I could not help feeling a sense of human aspiration. This had been a serious undertaking. This construction had required great and lasting effort. Now that it lay empty and abandoned, its sense of purpose was even clearer. What must it have taken, I thought, to bring rock for foundations, cut trees for timbers, broad-ax the beams, use a draw knife to shape the mortise and tenon joints, quarter cut the planks for flooring. All of this work had been performed before electricity. Coming to the work site as the farmer raised the barn, I might have encountered the bouncy drone of a pit saw, or heard the jingle of draught oxen, but the whine of gasoline-powered saws and drills would have been absent.

Lately farmers have become cagey about these abandoned structures. A dozen firms specializing in post-and-beam construction have gone into business dismantling old barns. At considerable cost, an antique barn, or a portion of the barn, is dismantled piece by piece, marked for reassembly like a Lincoln Log set, then transported to a wealthier environment. In many cases the barn boards are removed and sold at exorbitant prices—prices that, frankly, the original farmers would have found astounding. The slab pine weathered by years of pushing away the freezing rain has taken on the value of fine cherry wood or tiger oak. The post and beam spans, cut of necessity from hemlock and maple, bring a prime dollar. To reconstruct a building on a new site using materials from a vintage barn costs upward of $500,000. Remarkably the barn beams remain wonderfully cured; many were originally soaked in water, quickly aged, then used within weeks of their green cutting. The first New England farmers lived by the adage, "When the moon is new to full, timber fiber warps and pulls." February was the preferred month for all woods, the thought being that wood cut in the month of the Hunger Moon could not regain its moisture. A saying brought over from England with the first settlers advised, "If you'd have your flatboards lay, hewe them out in March or Maye." The farmer who constructed this barn probably would have known these bits of folk wisdom. Early New England woodsmen believed the moon had the potential to influence the various woods so subtly that cutting the same type of wood three hours before the new moon and six hours afterward would create a difference in the soundness of the timber.

Pie came and found me. I tried to interest him in the details of the building, but that was hoping for too much. He informed me the kite was ready to fly again. I took another look at the interior of the barn. It would collapse eventually, I knew. It had already listed ten or twelve degrees and finally gravity would not be ignored. Maybe someone would make an offer and put together a crew to take the old wood joinery apart. They would need mallets to hammer the joints apart. After so many years, habit lay in the wood.

The turning of the maple marked a third of a year now spent in the barn. Wendy noted it. *Four months*, she reminded me, and I had to go to the calendar to see it for myself. It was true. We had gone through most of the summer. A staggering amount of work remained to be done. We had to bring in and stack five cords of wood; order ten tons of coal in fifty-pound sacks and stack that, too; finish insulating the walls; insulate the pipes; coop up the windows; cover the perennials with pine boughs; fabricate wooden doors to cover the haymow opening, and another door to insulate the bathroom's outside entrance; and get to work on the kitchen. That was merely the work that couldn't be delayed; the entire barn still needed cleaning. The dark, ugly room beneath the stairs needed to be completely rearranged. Old tools and hunks of horse harness hung from hooks everywhere. In addition to inheriting close to a century's worth of ancient farm gear—hexafoos and witchfeet included—we had contributed our own messes. We had shoved things one way, then another, simply to have them out from underfoot. Our construction made piles of scrap lumber and mounds of sawdust that waited for any breeze to blow through the barn so that it might scatter, like pods of miniature yellow mice, to each corner of the building. At any given time we might say to ourselves that we were winning, but truthfully moments arrived that seemed to defeat us. How do you get a handle on construction? How do you live around it? Tools wandered everywhere, appearing next to our cereal bowls in the morning, finding their way into books as markers. Night and day we talked about construction, about what needed to be moved. Every spare moment was given over to the barn.

On a rainy day in late August we called a time-out. The temperature dropped to fifty degrees by noon and showed no sign of rising. Wendy fixed a corn chowder recipe her mother had sent her and we cooked it slowly, dark rye bread warming in the oven. Even Pie seemed to slow. He took out a *Harry Potter* book and settled in for a comfortable afternoon. For the first time since it arrived, we started the enormous woodstove in earnest. We ignited rolled newspaper and added cedar chunks from the Rochester Shoe Tree factory—heels and toes of wood used for shoe trees. The factory sold the discarded hunks for kindling at a dollar per potato sack. In minutes we had a bright, honey-colored glow burning in the cavernous core of the stove. I added a few short sticks of birch, then maple. The fire climbed through them and shoved them around. The stove gave off the dark, winter smell of woodstoves and stovepipe. The magnetized thermometer on the flank of the stove began to register heat.

Home, really, had to be something like this. The warmth of the stove began to push through the room. Pie's pages turned softly and the fragrance of corn chowder reached us from the kitchen. I felt my body relax. Renovation is hard physical labor, I realized, and we had been doing a great deal of it. Together we had trimmed the hedgerow on the north of the building, cut down a beech that grew too close to the house, torn out a patch of nettles that invaded from the south, trimmed under the hydrangea bushes, hayed a section of the meadow by hand, and carried all the lumber upstairs for Wendy's building project. We had moved a hundred boxes, rearranged furniture, scrubbed floors, erected a fence around three acres of land, dug a gate post into granite-filled loam, and cemented sections of the porch. We certainly couldn't match an early New England farmer's schedule, but it was true that we carried on the renovation work while continuing the usual daily chores—cooking, cleaning, laundry, and childcare. Our schedules, in other words, did not allow us to concentrate solely on renovation. We worked around our work.

The woodstove began to push serious heat. I appreciated its huge black flanks, its rectangular slab of warmth. A pretty good stove. Wendy filled a pan of water and set it on top; to our satisfaction, drops of water from the pan frizzled and steamed on the stove. The partially insulated walls blocked sound from the outdoors. We were left with the clunk of wood falling in the stove, the white bleed of steam out of the water pan.

We ate the chowder next to the fire. Pie told us the adventures of Harry Potter between spoonfuls of soup and bites of rye bread. He told the story haphazardly, pretty much as it came to him, so we had to take on faith that a narrative existed in the books. He especially liked the magic elements in the stories. We talked for a while about magic in general, about witches and Halloween, then he asked to be excused and went back to his reading. Wendy and I sat beside the stove and baked.

"How much have we spent so far?" Wendy asked from her rocker, her feet pushed out to the stove.

"Enough," I said, "but not more than a little."

"Tell me," she said.

"I haven't calculated it."

We rarely discussed the finances of renovation. I knew, roughly, what we had spent, but we had decided long ago not to dwell on it. I saw, though, that Wendy wouldn't be satisfied with such an answer.

"Six thousand dollars, give or take," I said, "and we're committed to at least ten more."

"I want to redo the kitchen."

"Call it fifteen thousand then."

"Is that too much?"

"No," I said, "not too much. Do you think it is?"

"No, it's nothing. Not for this old barn."

And it wasn't. We had set money aside for the purpose, but writing checks for large sums made us nervous. Except for Clarence's work on the porch and septic, we had done the work ourselves. We had always intended to do the majority of the work. If we spent $20,000, the total expenditure for the house would still only be $95,000. Undoubtedly we would go on to spend a good deal more than that, but any house would demand ongoing expense. Still, even $100,000 for a 6,000-square-foot house worked out to something under $200 a square foot. Cheap by any measure.

We napped and the afternoon grew long and dark. The wood-stove turned the room into a warm red stone. Pie woke us excitedly to tell us a bird had flown through the house. A black bird, he said. A downy woodpecker flew across the open expanse of the barn and landed on the westernmost skylight. It clung to the latch on the window and pressed its body against the glass.

I thought of my mother, of the bird that had flown into the house a few days before her death years and years before, but then I put superstition aside. Just a bird, I told myself. Wendy, for all her indifference to pain and her ruggedness when it came to the work in front of her, did not like being around small animals. Spiders turned her into a wimp; dead mice might have been radioactive for how uncomfortable she felt near them. When she saw the bird, she covered her head with an afghan and told me to get it out of the house.

This was a good adventure on a rainy day for Pie. The wood-pecker did not appear upset at having to cling upside down on the skylight. When we crept below it, Pie using a voice right out of a Discovery Channel wildlife show, the bird looped down and shot toward the second skylight. It landed there, then fluttered its wings against the glass. Off again. Back to the first window. Wendy yelped when it swung down toward the couch.

It shot off the skylight and disappeared up, probably following the dim daylight to the cupola. Pie and I ran off with a whoop. He stopped halfway up the stairs to the second floor and suggested ten different devices to trap the bird. A butterfly net, a cardboard box, a fruit basket. I sent him to the bathroom for a towel, then climbed up the stairs, oddly nervous myself. I imagined the woodpecker arrowing toward my eyes, its horny beak rapping me on the forehead. But when I reached the second floor, the bird had disappeared. Pie arrived a moment later, a towel cradled against his chest. He had the high, bright color of kids after a hide-and-seek game. He ran around and inspected the corners of the building while I closed off access to the skylights. The woodpecker had to be in the cupola.

With Pie right under my feet, I climbed the hand ladder up to the cupola. The bird had reached the windows before me; it remained pinned behind a window screen, its body desperate against the pane. I told Pie to be careful. I let him climb up beside me so we could watch the bird for a moment before figuring a way to release it. We peered up like two soldiers over a foxhole. Only our heads remained in the actual space of the cupola. Our bodies dangled on the ladder, waiting to go up or down.

"He's beautiful," Pie said.

"Yes, he is. He's a downy. A hairy woodpecker is bigger."

"What's the really big kind?" Pie asked.

"Pileated," I said. "Remember, we saw one once?"

"In Bridgewater," Pie said, "I sure miss that place."

"Really?" I said, surprised.

"Yes," he said.

"Why do you miss it?"

"Because it was small and I never felt scared."

"Because we were nearby?"

He nodded.

"Well," I said, "I can understand that."

"But I like the barn, Joe," he said. "It's nice."

"You don't sound so enthusiastic."

"Sometimes I'm scared. The way my bed is up, I think something is underneath it."

"Got you," I said.

"Did you ever worry about that as a kid?"

"Yes," I said, "I did."

We watched the bird for a while longer. Somehow the bird's anxiousness, its panic at being trapped, had triggered something in Pie. I felt him beside me, his tiny, gentle body quivering. I put my arm over his shoulder. Then I reached up and tilted the cupola window out. The bird pushed back against the screen, not believing it could be free again. But I held the screen and forced the bird out, over the roof. It flew in dips to a fat pine at the southern tip of the yard. We saw it through the cupola windows, a white fleck, a red crest, shaken in all that green.

The woodpecker's flight upstairs had reminded me that the cupola, too, required attention before winter settled on the building. Wendy was not wild about heights, so while she worked on the boards downstairs, the sound of her table saw rising and falling in quick, hungry bursts, I carried a tool chest up the narrow ladder to the cupola. I liked the cupola a great deal; its presence, in part, had sold me on the barn. It was unique. Who else had a square box on top of a four-story building that might serve as a tower? From up in the six-by-six structure, we could see most of Warren. We could see Carr Mountain and Moosilauke and twenty other peaks. It was a boy's dream tree house, a place that Pie and I promised to camp in if we could just figure out how to lie comfortably in the cramped quarters.

But the wooden structure, I had noted on the day Pie and I had chased the bird upstairs, was painfully dry. It had baked in the sun for more than a century, the topmost portion of the building to catch the sun. The windows, eight over eights, showed the wear and tear of so much exposure to the elements. The window caulking felt flaky and insubstantial. The glass panes had settled in the frames, glazing and bunching in the corners. Inching up the stairs, I wasn't entirely certain what I hoped to do in the cupola. *Coop it up*, I thought. Get it ready for winter. I brought plenty of weather stripping.

The cupola, derived from the word *cupa* or tub, was, in our case, a squared turret set exactly in the center of the barn. Farmers along the Connecticut River Valley initially built their barns without roof ventilators. The cupola, when it appeared as a regular feature of barns, represented a chance for the farmer to express himself architecturally by designing an individual style of roof. Godly farmers believed that lightning was God's will, and they often refused lightning rods because they didn't want to interfere with God's plan. On the other hand, early scientists argued successfully that the heat of fresh hay attracted electricity. A good ventilator, they said, would repel lightning. Farmers who refused lightning rods accepted the cupolas as ventilators—a small step forward for science. As anyone who has worked to store hay understood, green hay, stored in a virtually airless mow, provides an enormously dangerous threat of spontaneous combustion. Farmers could salt the hay, or turn it repeatedly, but ventilation proved to be key. Cupolas took up residence on barns throughout New England.

Someone had nailed triangular seats in each of the corners of the cupola; maybe Farmer Gale, in a bit of whimsy, had provided himself a place to sit and enjoy a quiet moment. I sat on the southeast wedge, letting my senses become accustomed to the dropoff below me. The roof slanted away at something like a thirty-degree grade. Steep. When the wind blew, as it did almost continuously at that height, the trees bobbed back and forth but the cupola remained stationary. It instilled in me an odd feeling of dislocation—like looking out the window of a submarine, or through aquarium glass. Gradually my vertigo calmed and I began to look seriously at the state of the windows.

They were a mess. We knew that various features of the barn required work, but we seldom knew exactly how much work was involved. It was one thing to look at a project, another actually to see what it entailed. But working on a project also makes us understand it. I opened my toolbox and began by scraping dried paint from the windows. The paint came off with little effort, volunteering to complete its disintegration. I chipped dried putty from the frames, then opened each window carefully and inspected the hinges. Most had lost a screw or two along the way. I drew out the screws, added wood fill, then reset them. Slowly the pleasure of the cupola began to soak through me. I worked four stories off the ground in a small, wooden box, the meadow and mountains spread out below me. Sun heated the interior, but wind cooled it instantly when I swung a window open. The windows seemed glad to have attention. The work followed straightforward demands. Do this, clean that, replace them. One window at a time, I worked clockwise around the cupola. When I had caulked the windows again, checked the hinges to make sure they held the frames securely, I painted the dried wood. The paint disappeared as soon as it touched the frame, drawn into the wood so rapidly the application became an exercise in Pointillism more than house painting. It took an hour to do one window. When I finished, the window gleamed white and fresh.

Wendy came up with ice water as I finished the second window. Sawdust flecked her hair and arms. She sat for a minute or two without really studying the view. I understood she needed a few minutes to steady herself. With the windows open, the pull of the mountains ledges, the cool breezes passing through the tidy window frames, she gradually allowed herself to look around. Her body relaxed. She drank the ice water and passed it to me.

"I could get used to this," she said. "I hate heights, but this is okay."

"It's a tiny bit too short for a bed. Pie wants to sleep out up here. You could watch the stars all night."

"The trapdoor is in the way, but maybe we can figure something out. It's worth figuring out."

"I would have loved something like this as a kid," I said. "My father and I used to sleep out on our screened porch some summer nights in New Jersey. I still remember what that was like."

"You can see the Baker River from here. It looks like a black eyelash."

She climbed back to her work. It did look like an eyelash. I continued around the cupola, working slowly. As my hands moved over the wood, dabbing paint and cleaning the windows, I felt myself not entirely here, not entirely in the moment, but back in New Jersey with my father. How many years ago? I remembered how he let me spread the porch furniture cushions on the floor, covering them with a sheet and a light blanket, while he stretched out on the wrought-iron glider, his late cigarettes calming and reassuring. He slept in his boxers and undershirts; I slept in briefs and the jersey of a Baltimore Orioles baseball uniform. He didn't mind if I listened to the baseball games late at night, so together we tuned in the Yankees or Orioles on a transistor radio, or the Cleveland Indians coming to us from a station a universe away, or the Phillies reaching us from the south, a pale, limp edition of our own broadcasts. The shouts from the beer vendors, the ash crack of a bat on the ball, even the puff of the announcer's cigarette, matched by Dad's inhalations, all drifted into the warm atmosphere of the porch. Daylight, when it finally arrived, came as another inning. Then my father would leave for work and the porch gathered sun from the forsythia around it, the green leaves suckered to the screen, the summer heat trapped in the cicada's call.

Back to school. I woke Pie at seven on a day in late August and whispered to him that it was the first day of school, time to become a genius. He groaned in the ancient honored fashion and pulled the covers over his head. D Dog, who slept beside him, yawned and circled deeper into the bed, a black Lab puck on a chilly morning. This day, of course, had rattled like a train toward Pie since the start of summer. We had attended a back-to-school session at the Warren Elementary School, met his teacher, and introduced ourselves to the principal and the custodian, who also happened to be the local constable. We had performed the annual pilgrimage to outfit Pie with enough office supplies to run a small company. A new Pokémon lunch box; a Pokémon pencil case; a thermos with a picture of Homer Simpson on it; a thumb-size eraser, pink as a prom dress; a pair of blunt-tipped scissors; a miniature stapler; a ruler; a pencil sharpener with a tiny brown plastic beaver attached, so that sharpening a pencil fed the toothy grin of the enormous rodent. Wendy had also visited Old Navy, where she picked up khakis, polo shirts, one or two button-downs, new boxers, socks, a brown leather belt, and three pairs of jeans. Together with Pie, she had scoured the shoe store for the correct pair of sneakers—Pie had his notions about sneakers—and eventually had sunk close to a hundred dollars into a pair with vertical, luminescent stripes, gray shoelaces, and a black tongue. To my delight, Pie lifted his foot like a horse being shoed to show me the tread. Excellent traction, he informed me, which translated, at least in his mind, to greater speed, superior leaping ability, and general athletic excellence. It was wonderful to discover that new sneakers, whatever the outlandish price, still initiated the same monkey-headed reasoning from eight-year-old boys.

"Time to wake up," I said. "This is the first day of the rest of your life."

"Oh, God," he groaned.

"This is your chance to begin your future. Your future starts here. Here we go. Today is the beginning of your career as a great scholar. Up and at 'em. Your pencils await."

He started laughing. I loved it when he laughed. I tickled him a little and got him squirming under the covers. "Oatmeal," I told him, which was his meal of choice. Then I headed downstairs, feeling good and lively. I poured Wendy a cup of coffee and took it to her. I made her sit up to hold the cup, because otherwise she would crumple back on the pillow and snooze like an old hound. I told her it was time to shake a leg. She groaned too and sipped the coffee. I told her this was Pie's first day at the Warren Elementary School, hardly a day to be pokey, that we had to be sunshine and happiness. She groaned again. I went to fix oatmeal.

Pie had showered the night before, even though he had pointed out that he had taken a swim a few days before. A shower, to his way of thinking, hardly seemed necessary. When Wendy had informed him that he was showering for the first day of school even if it was the last thing on earth she did, he relented. He appeared downstairs in a fresh pair of khakis complete with leather belt, a white polo shirt, presumably somewhat clean boxers, and his new sneaks. He looked like a million bucks. He perched at the breakfast counter and told me he thought school would be easy, but that he had heard his teacher, Mrs. Mathews, was wicked strict. She sent kids to the principal's office like that, he said, and tried to snap his fingers. That reminded him that he couldn't snap his fingers, so we spent a while practicing snapping our fingers until the teakettle finally whistled and the oatmeal was ready.

I drank coffee while he ate. Wendy staggered out of the bedroom and disappeared into the bathroom, raising her own coffee cup in a salute as she closed the door. A few minutes later she returned and sat on a stool beside Pie. We had put out a few feelers in his direction about walking him to school. Did he want us to accompany him to the school, or did he prefer to hop the fence and take on the educational establishment by himself? Wendy and I had agreed to let Pie direct us. But Pie, true to his nature, didn't catch the hint.

"Pie," Wendy started, "we want to talk to you about something."

"Yes?" he asked, cheerful as a robin.

"Today when you go to school, do you want us to walk over with you?"

"No," he said, looking at his mother as if she had sprouted a third eye directly in her forehead, "it's right over the fence."

"I know, sweetie," Wendy said, "but we thought you might be a little nervous starting a new school. All that kind of thing."

"No, but could I bring D Dog to school?"

"No, I don't think that would work," I said. "No dogs allowed in school."

He had already hopped down off the stool and hugged D Dog. He was being theatrical. Sometimes he did that to obscure his feelings. I couldn't read him. Wendy looked at me and lifted her eyebrows. *What do you think?* was the clear question. I shrugged and told him to hop up and finish his oatmeal. D Dog watched for crumbs. Pie understood he now had center stage. He liked that. He wagged each spoon of oatmeal around to show off. Wendy told him to stop it. He finished the oatmeal in three overly large bites, purposely pushing his mom. I still couldn't figure him out on this one.

I decided to go outside and check the weather. I took D Dog with me. We did a slow circle around the perimeter of the meadow. The grass felt wet on my legs, but the day was warm enough to make the moisture welcome. I watched the teachers arriving. They drove the traditional teacher cars. The playground was newly mown. Here was the start of a new school year. I tried to remember the first day of any of my school years and failed to come up with one. Other than a general sense of new clothes, maybe a few stationery supplies, the days mopped together in a wash of confused emotions. I admitted, frankly, that I was relieved to be seeing Pie off to school, not going myself.

Halfway around the walk, the screen door slammed open and Pie galloped out, yelping and gleeful. He wore his backpack, complete with rubber Pokémon figures dangling from the back, and as he ran the pack thudded against his shoulder blades. He didn't care. He yelled to D Dog and yelled to me, then he picked up a tennis ball and chucked it. D Dog shot off as if to grab it, then forgot the whole enterprise and busied herself sniffing at a patch of vetch. I looked past Pie to spot Wendy on the porch. She had stepped out with a coffee cup, but when I caught her eye she raised her hands to indicate no decision. I saw that Wendy had slipped on a pair of blue jeans and a sweater in case he wanted us to hop the fence with him. We waited on him. Like dousing for water, we had to watch to see which way he might bob.

He caught up with me next to the compost pile. D Dog rousted around the edge of the pallets, sniffing at the possibilities. The day built warm and bright, more summer than autumn, more a time for swimming than for school. A bumblebee droned over the pile, lighting on smashed tomatoes and empty husks of corn.

"You ready?" I asked Pie.

"All set."

"What time do you have to get going?"

"Pretty much right now."

"Okay," I said, "you want us to walk you to the fence at least?"

"Sure," he said.

His inflection indicated that the whole issue meant more to us than to him. I waved at Wendy and pointed toward the fence. She nodded. With Pie I finished the loop around the yard. It felt a small treachery to have summer paying a late visit on the first day of school. An eight-year-old boy should be out playing, not cramped up in a classroom on such a day. But the season had changed; we felt it at night and even this morning autumn rusted the leaves of the sumacs and the bright maples behind the barn. Grasshoppers chittered up and flew in their Frisbee flight to different sections of meadow as we passed.

Wendy joined us as we came to perihelion, our closest approach to the barn. We put Pie between us and walked slowly toward our fence. The overriding metaphor was inescapable: Here was our boy and we were sending him off to the world. He would literally hop a fence to join with the rest of his age mates, leaving us behind and joining in the current of milling children. He knew one or two of the kids and he kept a sharp lookout for them. He recognized his teacher, too, and he raised his hand as if she would see him beyond all other students. When she didn't wave back, he continued undaunted. He expected no hurt, therefore he perceived none.

"Okay," he said when we reached the fence.

He bent and hugged D Dog. Then, to my surprise and delight, he kissed me on the lips. Then he kissed Wendy. He did not make anything of it. Then up and over the fence. We had placed two stumps as fence stiles on either side of the sheep grid so that he could stand on one, swing his leg to the school grounds, then follow it with the other. It was the equivalent of mounting a horse, and Pie did it without any clumsiness. The Pokémon figures jangled on his backpack.

He ran when he cleared the fence, which broke my heart a little. Where was he running to? He knew no one, really, and his bravery, his joy at meeting new people, dug into my stomach. What a fine, good boy, I thought, what an open heart. Wendy grabbed my hand and that was a cliché, too, but what else could we do? We watched him disappear in the swirl of children, then reemerge to wave to us. We waved back.

black
roof

S hortly after we moved into the barn a friend clipped out an article from the *New York Times* and sent it to me. Titled "Symbol of Rural America Fades With a Way of Life," the article detailed the demise of barns across America. Half of America's barns were already lost. Nearly 1,000 barns disappear each year in Iowa alone. To a large degree the decline of barns reflects the decline of farming. In 1900, 50 percent of all Americans lived or worked on a farm. A century later, that number has shrunk to less than 1 percent. Furthermore, farmers today rely on machines that can be sixteen feet tall and twenty feet wide, much too large to be stored in old wooden barns. As a result of mechanization, farmers have not been building barns in significant numbers since the 1940s. Although some old wooden barns have been preserved as offices, theaters, and churches, the price of renovating a barn for human use can be expensive. Just installing a new roof can run $20,000, a great deal of money when weighed against the cost of building new or building with steel. Preservation committees are active around the United States, but they're short on cash and long on hope. Barns may one day become a strange relic of an agrarian past, not unlike sickles and scythes, or the ash yokes found hanging in old carriage sheds.

Later I read an article in the local paper, the *Record Enterprise,* detailing the rise and fall of the Smith Bridge. Built around 1900, the Smith Bridge was a covered wooden bridge that spanned the nearby Baker River for most of a century. When I first moved to the area in the mid-1980s, the bridge was in disrepair. Someone formed a committee and raised money for the bridge's restoration. I contributed a few bucks myself, happy to throw in a dollar at the supermarket when someone did a cake sale. Clearly this was a project of love. A metal bridge, built in a few short months, would have spanned the river more efficiently. It would have also provided two lanes, whereas the covered bridge relied on a stop-and-nod system, in which one driver let the other go first, then the next let the first, and so on. But covered bridges, like barns, are part of New England's history, and I was happy to watch the bridge project go forward.

But just as the crew prepared to start their restoration, an arsonist sneaked in at night and burned the bridge. It was such an odd thing to do, such a bizarre attempt to halt the building project, that local police attributed it to simple arson. Someone wanted to watch flames consume a large wooden structure, the reasoning went, so he lit the bridge on fire.

Other locals, who perhaps had suffered for years the tight squeeze of the covered bridge, argued that someone on the Rumney side of the bridge—the less populated side, in other words—had grown tired of waiting and nodding to get across the Baker River, so he had torched the bridge to have a two-lane span. That, too, would have been a Yankee sort of thing to do, especially because rebuilding the wooden bridge seemed a fussy enterprise. Efficiency is an aesthetic concern, too, and maybe someone got tired of quaintness at the expense of his or her daily commute. The true cause of the arson remained a mystery.

To everyone's surprise, the burning steeled the community's resolve to replace the covered wooden bridge. The committee that had been in place to raise money for the refurbishment now took on new vigor. Someone found substantial federal transportation monies; a local builder, known internationally for post-and-beam structures, became interested in the project. Someone offered to use a team of oxen to erect the bridge in the old manner, thereby giving the project an old-timey flavor. Suddenly, the Smith Bridge—or Quincy Bridge, as it is sometimes known—became a cause célèbre. Here was America honoring its past by rebuilding a structure from a simpler day, an opportunity to practice outmoded crafts, to put on display what we, as thorny old citizens of New Hampshire, could do better than nearly anyone else. Editorial writers preached about American virtue and the resiliency of our early settlers. Although people spouted enough hooey to float the bridge on hot air alone, the structure represented American know-how to thousands of people who read about it or chipped in a dollar at a local can shake. It didn't matter that early settlers would have known nothing about covered bridges. The fact that covered bridges were squarely nineteenth century in their origins halted no one from linking them to our Pilgrim past, to Jamestown and Plymouth Rock. The myth of the bridges was more compelling than the truth. In such a situation, it is always better to go with the myth.

My own interest in the bridge derived directly from our barn. Covered bridges, for the most part, relied on the precise building techniques employed in our dwelling. To watch the bridge go up was to witness the original building techniques used on our barn. True, the purpose and shape of the bridge would be different from that of the barn, but the wooden joinery, the choice of beams and purlins, would replicate the skeleton. When a diagram appeared in the paper detailing the proposed bridge, I saw features of the barn ready to be carried into reality.

Covered bridges arrived on the American scene much later than barns. The first American covered-bridge patent was issued January 21, 1797, to Charles Willson Peale, a famed portrait painter who painted George Washington. As a member of the Town Board of Philadelphia, he became interested in building a bridge to span the Schuylkill River. Eight years later, an exposed bridge built by Timothy Palmer on the site suggested by Peale opened, but Peale's bridge never got beyond the draft stage. An article in the *Railroad Gazette* for October 8, 1886, provided some history:

When the Market Street Bridge was finished in 1804 it was the intention that it should remain open, free to the action of the sun and air, exposed as well to rain and storm. Judge Richard Peters, a prominent stockholder of the company which erected the bridge, was the author of the plan of covering it at the sides and surmounting it with a roof. It was his opinion that if the timbers were left open and the roadway exposed to the alternate action of storms that would soon lead to decay and destruction. So the sides were boarded up, with the exception of spaces for windows. A long roof was placed over it, and the bridge was nothing more than a wooden tunnel, leading from one side of the river to the other.

The American covered bridge had been born at that moment, several years after the first patent was issued. In 1842, Charles Dickens wrote about his experience on bridges during a visit to America.

We crossed the river by a wooden bridge, roofed and covered on all sides, and nearly a mile in length. It was profoundly dark; perplexed with great beams, crossing and recrossing it at every possible angle; and through the broad chinks and crevices in the floor, the rapid river gleamed, far down below, like a legion of eyes. We had no lamps; and as the horses stumbled and floundered through this place,

*toward the distant speck of dying light, it seemed inter-
minable. I really could not at first persuade myself as we
rumbled heavily on, filling the bridge with hollow noises,
and I held down my head to save it from the rafters above,
but that I was in a painful dream; for I had often dreamed
of toiling through such places, and as often argued, even at
the time, "This cannot be reality."*

A budget for a bridge built in Gaylordsville, Connecticut, in
1832 takes into account the bills submitted by a man working
with a pair of horses for a full day: $2.50. A team of oxen could
only demand $2.00, probably because they worked slower. The
work with horses involved grading the approach of the bridge
from either direction, hauling wood and stone from wherever it
was procured, and participating in the ongoing carpentry.
Here's the budget.

4,000 feet of two inch oak floor planks	$ 100.00
1,800 feet of long string pieces	$ 324.00
Mud sills of heavy chestnut timber	$ 25.00
Boards to cover the bridge	$ 60.00
Carpenter work complete	$ 400.00

The budget added up to $909, and the final cost of the
bridge came to $1,500.15.

I drove south to the Smith Bridge one Saturday to take a
look. I walked down to the construction site and studied the
bridge. It spanned approximately fifty yards from riverbank to
riverbank, a modest arch that tied West Plymouth to Rumney. A
football field had been drawn out of a corn meadow just beyond
the bridge, a pretty rectangle of grass ringed by hazy mountains. A temporary Bailey bridge, swung into place shortly after
the old covered bridge burned, stood next to the foundation of
the new wooden bridge. The metal bridge lay as flat and as

uninteresting as a train trestle. Years ago as a kid, running an HO Scale car set around an old ping-pong table, I had snapped pieces of plastic together to create similar bridges. A Lego trestle, in other words. The wooden bridge, by contrast, seemed green and growing. The beams glowed nearly yellow, having just come from the forest. The architect or builder had established a camber, or arch, to the run of the bridge. This was to take care of any sag when its own weight set it to place. The proper camber was one of the builder's secrets, because only he could add together his inaccuracies compiled through the building process.

I stood at an angle to the bridge and for a few minutes let my vision run up and down the beams and cross braces. The builders had erected steel staging next to the wooden frame so that they could move about it safely, and the staging pushed my eyes too rapidly over the true bridge. The staging halved and quartered the arches and trusses, leaving them cut into grid shapes. It lent the bridge a busyness it did not take on itself.

The single greatest problem of all bridge building is to make one long arch that will still be strong. Introductory architecture classes often construct pasta bridges to drive that point home to students. When students hang a bucket on a pasta bridge, gradually filling it with sand until the bridge collapses, they gain a sense of what is involved in creating a span to traverse an open gap. Their experiments replicate the design struggles that took place in the mid-nineteenth century. The simplest and first truss used in America was the king-post truss. It consisted of a center upright, or king-post, in the middle of the span, with two compression pieces slanting downward and outward toward either shore. Only small bridges could be built this way because the compression pieces were not long enough to absorb the weight. To adapt this principle to a longer span, two uprights, or queen-posts, were spaced across the span. This became known, rightly enough, as a queen-post truss. By using a cross instead of an inverted V in the middle of a queen-post truss, a stronger design known as a Warren truss was born. Each truss held a supporting patent, but most barn builders were familiar with these structures. A typical farmer of the day might easily apply his carpentry skills to laying out a bridge. Barn or bridge, the construction job amounted to the same thing.

Certainly beneath the grid work of the Smith Bridge, underneath the modern cranes that lifted beams and materials from one bank to the other, I saw the trusses used in our barn. They had been fortified against the vibration of modern conveyances with iron bolts, but the joinery in the bridge might have been pulled directly from the beams and purlins in barns around the area. The bridge builder had opted for something resembling a Burr truss, a graceful curved arch strengthened by king-posts throughout. Everything about the bridge appeared gratifyingly substantial. As in covered bridges before it, militia groups could practice drilling in it and church congregations could hold their suppers in its interior. I imagined such bridges before electricity reached the rural parts of the nation. The slow creep across a covered bridge lit by oil lamps on an autumn night must have been a little spooky.

What struck me most, however, was the communal nature of the post-and-beam structure. A bridge could not be raised alone anymore than a barn could. Balloon framing—the stick framing used in modern housing—seemed a solitary enterprise by comparison. Although it would be difficult work, a builder could, and often does, construct an entire house by toenailing and pinning two-by-fours together. Stick construction, as it is known, allowed houses to be built by individuals in diverse locations around the country. Receive a shipment of two-by-fours one day and an amateur builder was off to the races the next. Barn building—and bridge building, of course—relied on many men to come together. Huge beams could not be lifted alone. They required teamwork and careful planning. The building of the structure might be said to build structure within a community. Everyone involved with it held the trust of a bridge or barn. A single-family home, built of two-by-four sticks, literally splintered people away from the communal enterprise of post-and-beam construction. Stick construction made settlement of the West possible, but it robbed us of something as well.

For a little while longer I let my eye travel as it liked over the structure. I made a few mental notes, vowed to bring Pie back to study the construction with me, then called it a day. I drove over the metal trestle bridge to Plymouth. We needed groceries. The trestle carried me over the Baker River, but it was indistinguishable from the road before or behind me.

❀

The first frost came like a white sheet pulled over furniture to keep things clean for the winter. Feeding D Dog out on the porch in early light, at five-thirty, I watched mist rise off the meadow. The sun skidded on the icy glint and for a few minutes I thought maybe it wasn't frost at all. Maybe, I thought, this was just a chilly morning and the white scatter was nothing more than the cold air brought low. But when D Dog finished her food and we walked into the meadow, the nettles and flower heads carried the heavy weight of winter. They hung suspended in a white glaze, stiffly nodding, frozen as though they had forgotten what it was to grow. A few of the poppies had turned black in a single night, their red vibrancy rinsed off and twisted silent for another year. We left dark dents in the meadow where our feet touched the ground. The Baker River was a white trail of smoke, a train stack of winter riding south through the mountain crevices.

Cleanup day. By coincidence, we had declared this first Saturday in September a day of cleaning and arranging, and the frost seemed an encouraging note. We had circled it on the calendar and talked it up with Pie to make sure he made no other plans. He was excellent at play, good at learning, but he had a lazy attitude about work sometimes and Wendy, particularly, had decided to do something about it. We had already composed a list of chores for him and posted it on the kitchen door. From this point forward, he was in charge of D Dog cleanup, D Dog water, carrying the compost bucket out every evening, shoveling out the fireplace, keeping his room straight, and keeping the wood boxes filled. He didn't have to do everything perfectly, but he had to take responsibility. To let him do less was to turn him into a spoiled egg.

First thing, Cheerios on the porch. Pie ate with me. He liked Cheerios, though he had purchased a variety pack a few days before and had gone through the more sugary, more disastrous brands in short order. Cheerios with bananas, I tried to tell him, was the way to go. But he had some wacky cereal that resembled dark raisins sprinkled with sugar. At any rate, he would have enough energy. He ate and talked about work. He needed gloves, he told me, and maybe some work boots. I assured him sneakers would be okay. As for gloves, we had a pair for him somewhere around the barn. I told him he could wear a bigger pair when we moved wood. At that, the proposal to move wood, he gave out a lovely groan.

Wendy joined us on the porch. She had coffee. We sat for a while and watched the sun plow up the meadow. It wasn't going to be a warm day; the frost had made a sweater necessary, but that seemed exactly right for working. Pie repeated what I had told him. Frost, he said, in a voice reminiscent of an old farmer informing a city fellow of the day's predicament. Listening to him, I wondered if he had stolen the phrasing from me.

"When do you think we will be finished?" Pie asked.

"Absolutely when we are," Wendy said.

"And when we are, we will be," I added.

"I'm serious," Pie said, "when do you think we'll be finished?"

"Around eight tonight," Wendy said.

"I'm serious," Pie said.

"More like nine-thirty," I said. "I'll pull the truck around so we can work by the headlights."

Sweet torture. But I saw Pie's face collapse a little, so I told him to put away his cereal and come with me to start the wood-stove. If we planned it right, we could work until noon, then have a nice lunch beside the fire. I hoped not to work much beyond one o'clock. I wanted to take D Dog for a walk and get out among the red and yellow trees.

Before we went inside, Pie tried to walk backward in his tracks across the frost. It was funny to watch. He walked backward for thirty feet, looked around him, then fit his feet carefully in the tracks as he returned. I'm not sure where he got the idea in the first place, but it was surprisingly convincing. If you let your mind go with him, the tracks appeared to rise out of the meadow, sourceless, the birth of a grass creature approaching the house. Pie was pleased with his trick. His only disappointment was not having someone besides Wendy and me to show off for. I told him a riddle about a man being found frozen in the middle of Central Park, dead, no track around him. It was a game that involved asking yes-or-no questions until you discovered the silly core of the matter. In this case it was not a man at all, but was the jack of diamonds instead. But Pie couldn't be bothered. He gave up in about thirty seconds, announcing that he had invented the tracks as if they belonged to a spaceman. His creature, he wanted us to know, had been beamed down from a spaceship. My riddle stayed lost the rest of the day.

A nice moment occurred when I stepped back inside the barn. Maybe it was the coolness of the air outside, or maybe it was the change of light from exterior to interior, but I actually *saw* the barn again. I saw it new. I saw it as it had appeared when it slammed into our hearts long before. Here again were the great span of the keeping room, the gray granite chimney, the sweeping beams. I had become so accustomed to the dimensions of the barn that I now took its spaciousness for granted. This house, though, was built on a wonderful scale. It was built, really, so that someone could step through the doors and breathe deeply, satisfied to be inside. We would never feel cramped here. I watched Pie flutter into the kitchen and saw the thin shelf of ice on the skylights, and I felt an overwhelming sense of satisfaction. I would always want to live here.

We had sufficient scrap wood around to make fire-starting an easy job. Pie asked to start the fire and I let him roll some newspaper into the body of the stove, line up some smaller scrap pieces, then light the match. The flames took over the stove almost immediately. Moisture had been frozen out of the air; now the wood and paper burned without coaxing, happy to have a job. Pie squatted before the hatch opening like the witch out of Hansel and Gretel tending her stove. He was eager for reports of the fire. When we lay on three birch logs and a piece of oak, he swung the door shut and made an elaborate show of clapping his hands together. One job finished.

"Ready?" I asked.

"Ready," he answered.

Then in one of the moments that I could never predict but always found so remarkable, he told me he loved me. He said it so sweetly and with such peace in his voice that it passed through me and made me happy to have him in my life, made me grateful that I got to watch him grow, made me amazed that this gentle, kind soul loved me. And I thought that I would never want anything, anything in the world to hurt him, or to turn him callous, and that no one had ever informed me of the great whoosh of love you could feel for a child. Why hadn't anyone explained? I went over and lifted him up and hugged him. Then he said he wanted me to be a horse, an old game between us, so I made a clicking sound like hoofbeats and let him down. He climbed halfway up the stairs to his room and, as the game demanded, I passed by, galloping, making my hoofy sound louder as I approached. He flung himself around my shoulders, light as a scarf, and spurred his heels into my sides.

I let Pie down, then went over to the garden where Wendy was busy digging out weeds. She had already accumulated a large pile of clippings, so we told her we would be back to clean up in a while. She said okay and continued working, intent as she usually is when she sets her mind to something.

I pulled out my ten-year-old wheelbarrow from the barn overhang. It makes a rasping sound when I push it and the tire goes flat more often than I'd like, but it has saved me endless hours in moving wood around my property. Immediately Pie asked for a ride. He plunked his hindquarters in the wheelbarrow and swung his legs as I pushed him around the driveway. When we reached the loose woodpile against the northern fence, I tilted the handles up and toppled him out. He deliberately fell, then got to his feet when I reminded him it was time to work. Together we loaded the wheelbarrow with about ten green pieces, then creaked over to the barn overhang and the wooden pallets left empty by the wood we had already burned.

The first order of business, I told Pie, was to cob an end for the new stack. Cobbing, as the old Yankees call it, is a process of setting logs in a square, generally three on three, creating a brace to hold the regularly stacked wood in between. The derivation of the word is difficult to determine. Cob, of course, is the central core of an ear of corn. It is also a male swan. Less commonly, the word may be applied to a stocky, short-legged horse, or to a self-important man. It can also convey hitting someone with a paddle, particularly on the buttocks—a definition, when I told it to Pie, that he liked the best. In carpentry a cob job means a botched project or one thrown hastily together. But to cob, as it applies to a woodpile, probably derives from Middle English *cobbe,* or cob work, which is building by thatching or laying wood crosswise. A log cabin could fairly be said to be cobbed.

Whatever its derivation, the practical benefits of cobbing are obvious, although Pie found such fastidiousness tedious. I told him he was lucky, that some New England wood stackers arrange their entire woodpile in a cobbed form, building each section of the woodpile in the thatched method. That seemed, frankly, like more work than necessary, but it certainly creates a stable pile. As a rule I cob one end, build out from that point, then cob the other end when and if I get there. Pie, once he got the hang of it, ran back and forth from the woodpile to get more likely logs.

"It's like Legos," he said.

"You've got it," I said. "See, work isn't always terrible."

"Hah," he said.

We worked for an hour without stopping. Pie, once he got into it, proved to be a good laborer. He didn't complain and didn't ask for inordinate breaks. We kept stacking wood in the wheelbarrow together until he got the hang of stacking wood beneath the barn overhang. Then he became the wood stacker, while I brought him wheelbarrows full of cordwood.

As we worked, I grew curious about the weight we had handled throughout the morning. My back and arms felt the workout. At eleven we hauled Wendy's clippings to the compost pile, then voted unanimously for a break. Because we always need wood by the upstairs fireplace, we each carried three representative logs inside. On a whim I decided to weigh them. Our bathroom scale was by no means a precise instrument, but each log registered close enough to five pounds to make me comfortable using that as an estimated weight-per-lift. Sitting at the breakfast bar, we played with the calculator. Pie got to punch in the numbers while I gave him the equations. The figures quickly became impressive. One wheelbarrow load containing ten pieces equaled fifty pounds.

In twenty trips, we would move a thousand pounds of wood. Over the course of the summer and into fall, I estimated we would move—at a minimum—two hundred wheelbarrow loads of wood across our door yard. In short, coming and going we stood to move approximately 10,000 pounds of wood each year. That works out to five tons a year. As often as not, I had to handle the wood more than once, so the numbers doubled without much pinching.

Pie whistled. Then he grabbed his heart and staggered around the kitchen for a few minutes. We told him he could go play if his heart wasn't hurting him too much. He let out a whoop and headed for the mica mines, a place where he and his friend, Christopher, a little blond-haired boy who lived up the road, had established a fort.

I was so impressed with the scope of our calculations that later that same afternoon I called Northam Parr, Grafton County Forester. I had talked to him once before about another matter—about what I could grow in a Zone 4, northern New England climate—so I had his home number and was lucky to catch him there.

"Sounds about right," he said, when I finished outlining my question. "Depending on the type of wood, a green cord weighs about 5,400 pounds. About half of that weight is water, so if your wood is dried out you might reduce it a little. But yes, we move a lot of wood in New Hampshire. It adds up."

"Any idea how much?"

"Well," he said, "the Governor's Office on Energy would have a better idea, but I seem to recall it topped out after the Middle East oil embargo in the seventies. New Hampshire burned about 600,000 cords that year. Now with greater affluence pouring into the region people tend to use wood mostly as a backup. Of course that changed in the past winter or two when oil prices went up again. You have to remember, in the old days a farm might burn thirty or forty cords."

"That much?"

"Sure. We've cut and burned the forest twice across New England. You figure the White Mountain National Forest has something like 750,000 acres. You can calculate a well-wooded acre holds about thirty cords. That roughs out to about a billion trees in the National Forest."

I asked him if it was true that a tree twenty inches in diameter at chest height will yield a cord of wood. He said that was about right, then told me that while softwoods form the backbone of the timber industry, red maple is the most abundant tree in New Hampshire's forests. He also recommended it as the best all-around wood for burning. It grows fast, he said, burns well, thrives on wet soils or dry ones, and can be split easily. In all, he said, about 55 percent of New Hampshire is given over to hardwood.

"But you can't go wrong with red maple. Other woods might have more commercial value, so people should keep that in mind. No sense burning a tree with a good, straight grain when you might burn one that's bent or twisted. You can always have a county forester come out and do a wood-lot evaluation. Lately we've been advising people to cut beeches. Unfortunately, beech trees are doomed because of a malignant spore."

He finished by saying something that went against everything I had ever heard about burning wood.

"Pine doesn't necessarily produce more creosote than oak. That's an old wives' tale. It all comes down to dryness," he said.

After lunch I went to clean up my work and finish what I had started. As I stacked the last of the day's wood, I kept in mind an adage told to me by Clarence. He said that when a squirrel approaches a pile of wood from the side, some of the holes between the logs should be big enough to scamper through. But a cat chasing the squirrel to the same pile should have to go around or over.

A few days later Nory Parr sent me information on the heat values of various woods. I pinned it up next to the woodstove.

BEST HEAT VALUE

(One cord of air-dried wood of these species is equal to 165–200 gallons of No. 2 fuel oil. Each species forms an excellent bed of coals with few or no sparks.)

Apple
Red oak
Sugar maple
Beech
Ironwood (hop hornbeam)

MIDDLE HEAT VALUE

(One cord of air-dried wood of these species is equal to 130–165 gallons of No. 2 fuel oil. Each forms a good bed of coals with generally few sparks.)

Red maple
White birch
American elm
White ash
Larch (tamarack)

LOWEST HEAT VALUE

(One cord of air-dried wood of these species is equal to 100–130 gallons of No. 2 fuel oil. These woods produce an inferior bed of coals with an overabundance of sparks.)

Hemlock
White cedar
White pine
Spruce
Aspen
Poplar (popple)

Remarkably, no one who showed an interest in my woodstove ever concurred about the heat values of various woods. Months after their visits, friends would send me a clipping reporting a new tabulation. Several men seemed to take the matter personally. One friend sent a rhyme about kings warming their feet by ash logs and pointed out, correctly, that ash can be burned green.

At an auction across the state line in Vermont, Wendy purchased a two-person, swag-bellied saw. We waited for fierce, windy nights, then loaded the saw into the truck the next morning to look for downed trees. *Going downing*, we called it. We looked for oak, mostly, though, true to Nory Parr's prediction, we found more maple than anything else. Standing over a makeshift sawhorse, one end of the log propped like a knee on a footrest, we sawed the wood down to stove-length hunks, throwing the handle back and forth like men tossing hot coals. A truckload took an hour to gather, twenty to burn. We could have cut the wood faster with a chain saw, but then we wouldn't have heard the birds or the leftover rain falling through green branches. We liked rolling the honest, yellow butter ends to the truck, rolling them up the loading ramp, rolling them down to the wood lot at the barn. A year later, handing an oak log to the fire, we often stopped and remembered where the wood had come from, what forest had produced it. Time, shape, grain mixed in with the wood so that we recognized individual pieces. At times, burning the wood felt a little like betrayal.

A nor'easter. The storm that appeared first on our television as a curled fist of clouds rising out of Georgia and moving up the coast promised to be the first major storm we had faced in the barn. *More rain than snow,* the forecasters said. Or freezing rain. Or sleet. New England weather forecasters like to build drama, and they often have ample opportunity given the changeable nature of the weather patterns, but in this case it appeared we were headed for trouble. The cloudy knot on the radar screens rose to Maryland and then up into New Jersey and Connecticut. New Hampshire state officials posted a weather advisory. High winds; gusts to fifty miles an hour or more; danger of small streams flooding; avoid electric lines; potential power outages.

By the time Pie returned from school, we were under assault. Wind smacked us from the south, slicing the corner of the building. The barn began to moan, not in pain as much as in appreciation of the wind. I reminded myself, and Wendy, that the barn had withstood more than a century of such winds, but nevertheless the storm made me feel like a cat in a room full of rocking chairs.

The sun set at six and by that time the storm had fully arrived. It battered the side of the house with horizontal spray. Pie, who loved movies, kept saying he saw a cow flying past à la *Twister*. To calm us, Wendy made a chicken dinner. She suggested a good, quiet meal would be just the thing. When she served it at the upstairs table, however, we watched the wind push against the two-story bank of glass on the southern wall. The glass, at one point, actually bowed inward, and for a hungry second I believed we faced catastrophe.

"Go downstairs and finish your dinner," Wendy told Pie. "This wind is too strong."

"Did you see that glass?" Pie asked. "It's awesome."

"Go downstairs," Wendy repeated, and this time Pie understood.

But he returned a moment later.

"Something is dripping," he said. "It sounds like water is running somewhere."

My heart ached as I went downstairs, the chicken dinner abandoned. He was right. Water gushed through the fieldstone foundation and ran in a brisk current over the basement floor. The charm of the foundation suddenly paled; without mortar between the stones, and with the ground beginning to be frozen outside, the water had no place else to go but inside. It did not appear to threaten the integrity of the wall. It simply ran through the dirt fissures and produced a fine puddle on the floor. I set out six plastic buckets to catch what I could of the incoming freshets. Then I went back upstairs.

Wendy had left the dinner table and for a second I couldn't find her. Eventually I heard pots clinking and I followed the sound until I found her. Like a character in a bad TV sitcom, she stood on the catwalk, head cocked back, trying to gauge where the holes in the roof let water enter. Ten leaks, twenty leaks. I counted a dozen pans already arranged for the tiny bombs of water drops coming through the rafters.

"Damn it," I said.

"It's just water," Wendy said, her eyes still up on the roof.

But we both knew it meant more than that.

Given most weather patterns, we possess an internal clock that tells us when a storm is about to abate. The brunt of the storm, usually, does not last very long. But on this night the storm did not relent. Wind continued to hit the house hard, and twice more we watched the transom windows bulge in, pregnant with gusts of cold, freezing wind. We kept Pie downstairs and we started the woodstove. After a while the electricity snapped off. The stove gave off excellent heat, but in the candlelight we listened to the wind yanking at the high profile of the barn. Often we heard the weather vane turn in a rusty screech, announcing a change in wind direction. Even in the instants of calm between blasts of wind, we heard the pans plinking as they received drops of rainwater. The steady gush of water through the foundation did not slacken.

"There's a truck outside," Pie said. "It's got a flashing light."

I looked and saw a town truck parked near Cold Brook, the stream that ran across the northern edge of our property. The flashing orange light spun around and around. I pulled on boots and a slicker and went outside. Two workmen with long, metal rods dug at a drainage grid. The road had flooded. Cold Brook had leapt its banks and now gushed out onto the street, covering a cement bridge that forded the stream. The men chopped at the grate, trying to clear it of debris. Some of the water had frozen in the eddies. Walking across the shallow areas caused the ice to shatter like window glass, white shark's teeth of frozen water.

I had a shouting conversation with the men. Yes, the road had flooded. Yes, drainage grids up and down Route 25 had clogged. The Baker River had run its banks. Yes, town trucks were out doing what they could. Some people had been flooded out of a house overlooking Lake Armington. A tree had come down across a set of power lines near the Appalachian Trail. A mess. A freaking mess. No easy fixups. Electricity would probably be out for at least a day or two. Did I have a woodstove? Yes, well they had to move on, good luck.

They pulled off, water now swirling down the storm drain like a miniature whirlpool. The drain undoubtedly helped, but too much water still swirled out of the stream to know for certain. Walking back to the barn, I saw that the top of one of the pines had snapped free and had fallen inches from my old Dodge Dakota, a huge hunk of pine that now rested on its supple arms, gazing at the barn. I tried to pull it out of the driveway, but it was too heavy.

By the time I made it back inside, Wendy had beds made up in the dry section of the basement. Pie, naturally, saw this as a holiday. We had no TV or lights, but he had a sleepover in the middle of the week. He wanted to tell ghost stories; he wanted to make animal shadows with the flashlights we kept beside us. We humored him for a few minutes, but he slowly understood we were in no mood for clowning around. Wendy and I held hands, squeezing a little each time a new wind ran at the house. We kept Pie between us and soon heard the heavy breathing that meant sleep.

I woke late, just before sunrise, and listened for the wind. It had gone. The drip of the foundation had lessened, too, and I felt the wonderful relief of having endured a terrible storm. We were safe. I stood and threw two more logs on the fire, then climbed back into our makeshift bed and fell asleep. We did not wake until the sun reached us through the vent windows looking out at the storage area beneath the barn overhang.

Rain, unlike snow, required no community cleanup. It would go where it liked. To Pie's great sorrow, the superintendent did not cancel school. Electricity had been restored. Roads had drained sufficiently to permit buses to pass. Some schools delayed opening, but the Warren Elementary School rang its bell at eight-thirty, ready for business.

I was out of the house early, too, inspecting damage. On his way to school, I showed Pie the treetop that had snapped off one of the large pines. "Cool," he said. I sawed off enough of the branches to permit me to drag it out of the way. The butt end weighed a hundred pounds. I sawed it in sections and threw them next to the sawhorse. Pie helped for a while, then headed off when the warning bell rang. As he crossed the meadow his feet made plunger sounds.

Over coffee, Wendy and I decided to call a roofing company. Just for estimates. It did not fit into our budget, but both of us had found the leaks incredibly discouraging. Renovations relied on foundations and roofs, and both of those elements had proved faulty the night before. We consoled ourselves that it had been a horrible storm, but the fact remained that water had gushed in well above acceptable levels. We didn't have a choice.

Tom, a fellow from Black Ox Roofers, a company out of Vermont, showed up three days later. He wore a hooded sweatshirt, a pair of faded jeans, and boots the color of pumpkin seeds. He presented himself as clean and orderly; his clipboard, when he held it in front of him, served as a small desk space. Everything on the board had been arranged with clamps or paper clips. I had the sense that he could produce a tax return from the clipboard if required to do so by a client. His goatee, trim as piecrust, had a ruby-red dye patch dead center below his bottom lip.

I liked him immediately. He had come on a recommendation from a former student. A friend of a friend of a friend. Black Ox did most of the metal roofs in the area, and Wendy and I had already decided on a metal roof. We liked the look of metal, and we liked the fact that snow did not remain on the eaves to create ice dams and water problems. We worried how it would look on the building, but metal roofs, after all, had long been used on barns. The asphalt shingles we currently had on the barn did not fit the character of an agricultural building. Metal would be more definite and clean, we figured, and a thousand times more worry-free.

Walking around the barn, Tom did not flinch at the size of the building. No problem at all, he said. Mostly straight cuts, some work around the skylights, and that was it. With the new metal extruding machines, he explained, they would run a single piece of roofing from the peak to the eave. Then another. Then another. Fairly simple, really, he said. The expense came from the extruder and the crew of roofers required to do the job right. The extruder alone cost several hundred thousand dollars.

"How expensive?" I asked.

"Looks to be around seven thousand," he said. "It's as big as a church. Luckily, we don't have to remove the old roof. We'll lay it right over the asphalt. But I'll figure up an estimate, then you can decide. We have an opening next week. A company over in Fairlee, Vermont, canceled on us, so we can book you right in. They were going to do a service station."

We thanked Tom, told him we would call him, then went into executive session. Seven thousand dollars was more than we had planned on spending. We danced around the figures in various ways, but the simple fact returned to us: All the renovation in the world wasn't going to do much good if water came through the roof and rotted everything. A solid roof was the key to the long-term welfare of a building. Keep a building dry and it will essentially last forever. Once the roof goes, though, a building is on the way to the gallows.

I called Clarence and asked him what he thought.

"Can't beat a metal roof," he said. "Except slate, maybe, and no one can afford slate. A slate roof will last a century. Metal will probably go fifty years if they do it right. If you can afford it, it's the best money you'll spend on your barn."

"I was hoping we could get another ten years out of the roof," I said. "I figured we'd need to replace it down the line."

"Well, a building isn't a thinking thing," he said. "You know the old saying: We only regret our economies. You think about it. You go to the store and you buy yourself a pair of socks, you never say, gee, I wish I hadn't bought those socks. But if you don't buy them, well, then you regret it. Sometimes, anyway. We regret our economies."

I checked our bank accounts, talked again with Wendy, then called Tom and told him to put a roof on the barn. Black, I said when he asked the color. Matte black. He said he thought that would look good. The shutters on the building were black already, he pointed out. Should work, he said.

On the appointed day, he pulled into our driveway with two trucks. He parked them in back, right on the bib of the meadow. A moment later two more vehicles arrived, both of them extra-cab Ford pickups, and five young guys hopped out. I had been upstairs when I heard the trucks, and by the time I made it downstairs to shake hands with Tom, one young fellow had already scaled the building. He stood on the ridge, a hollow triangular cap piece in his hands, already nailing brads into the existing roof.

For two days the guys climbed all over the house. By noon on the second day, the crew foreman, a young fellow named Hank, stood on the top of the cupola. He appeared absolutely fearless. In minutes he began laying metal sheets across the cupola. The roof looked so small under him, the height so severe, that I had difficulty watching him. He did not falter, though. The job was a tricky one, however, and when he finished around four, the others did not suggest he continue working on the remaining portion of the roof. Hank struck me as a roofing gunslinger, a specialist whose skill demanded the most difficult assignment, the most frightening circumstances. He lounged in the grass the last hour of the job, drinking a sapphire PowerAde and shouting out insults to the rest of the crew.

Then they left. Two full days and the job ended. I shook their hands as they piled into their pickups. Tom had returned to inspect the job, to drive the extruder back to base, and to give me the final bill. The black roof looked terrific, I told him. He promised if I had any problems with the workmanship, any concerns about leaking, to call him immediately. A fifteen-year warranty, he said. No questions asked.

When Wendy came home that evening, we walked out by the property line and then turned to look at the house. For a moment the roof scowled; it was too sharp, too clean. Gradually, though, the utility of the roof became its beauty. I liked the corduroy ridges, the wide bands of black metal that led inevitably to the porch roof. The cupola, bright white, stood out from the field of black. The whole barn appeared brighter and newer.

Only in northern New Hampshire would one receive calls from neighbors congratulating him or her on a new roof, but for the next few days local folks called and commended the addition. One fellow allowed that he hadn't been certain, at first, whether the metal roof would blend in or not, but now that he had had a few days to study it, he was pleased with its appearance. I thanked all the various callers, told them what company had done the job, and recommended them to anyone interested. I avoided naming the price, although several neighbors hinted around that such a roof could not come cheap. I let the comment linger long enough to make sure they understood I had no intention of answering them.

Three days after the crews had left, we had a nice sleety rainstorm. The sleet ran on the roof with the sound of mice rustling in a paper bag. I liked the sound. That night, with the sun going down, we inspected every inch for leaks. Not here, we said, making a game of it. Not over there, either. Dry and solid. Not even snow would stay, we said.

old
man's
month

I n Wales long ago the last stand of corn harvested each year was the cause of much excitement. Workers bombarded the final stalk with their scythes and whoever managed to strike down the last stalk won a cask of beer or whiskey. The final ear of corn, along with the stalk, was called the Hag. In other cultures it was called the Old Woman or Baba, but the meaning of each was the same. She was ceremoniously thrown out of the field, thereby ritualizing the desire of corn to run from the thresher's blade. Sometimes she was carried to other fields, where workers still labored, and then thrown at the slower teams in mockery. If the person throwing the Hag were caught, however, he could be stripped of his clothes and made to dance. If the workers managed to sneak the Hag into the manor house, dry and properly prepared for threshing, then the owner must provide a round of good beer from the "cask by the wall," meaning the better brand of beer. Sometimes the Baba, or Old Woman, was dressed in women's clothing, then burnt at the top of the annual bonfire. The corn's spirit, bruised by cutting, was cauterized by the burning, her ashes spread to bring fertility back to the fields. Sometimes the Hag was thrown into a nearby river, by that means ensuring future rain.

In some cultures the last stand of corn is called the Old Man and is awarded as an invidious trophy to the woman who falls farthest behind in binding the stalks in the field. She must carry the sheaf to the landowner's house, and say solemnly, "I have brought you the Old Man." Then a feast is held and the Old Man is given lavish portions to eat. As he cannot eat it, of course, the portion is given to the woman who brought in the Old Man. Then the Old Man is taken outside where the woman who brought him to table is called upon to dance him around a ring. She carries the name Old Man until the following harvest, when the next Old Man will be killed.

I thought of these rituals on a night in mid-October when Wendy and I ran through a cornfield on a full-moon night. Pie had gone to Christopher's house for a sleepover. Our original thought was to take a swim in the Baker River, but the crispness of the night, the bright, gloomy radiance of the moon, made us reconsider. Instead we found ourselves in a harvested cornfield, the white stalks like canes. The sawed-off canes could cut, but we ran anyway, not exactly sure why, but letting the air hit us and push us. Smells came from every direction: wind and pine and water and dirt. Inside those fragrances, the corn swayed white and brittle. We could not get enough of the air and the feeling of pushing through the stalks and we kept running, not playing tag, just running.

After a little time we came to the Baker River. It ran like black steps at the foot of the cornfield. The air beside the river was damp and demanding, and without really discussing it we knew we wanted to be back in the pasture. We found a spot and lay down, our eyes trained on the sky. Wendy lay perpendicular to me so that her head rested on my belly. We both found ourselves out of breath; trying to catch our wind, the heaving of our chests made the stars dance sideways.

Everything about the night had come bright and orange: The moon had cleared the clouds, the pines had nailed themselves to the white ground. A black-cat night, I told Wendy. Later we walked around the cornfield, grabbing stalks and bending them. A few tasseled heads remained, disappointed to be left. A coyote yelped somewhere across the river. Then another joined it, but they didn't manage to paint their voices together. Maybe they had been disturbed by us and merely wanted to alert their pack. I liked thinking of them running in their waggy ways, their tongues out and licking at the corn and mice they found.

At the barn we lay for a long time in bed and watched out the windows. For a time we talked about whether this was good, about whether this was what we had both wanted. We hadn't married, deliberately so. Theoretically, either one of us could leave. But it was working. So far so good, we both said. I got up and opened two more windows, leaving the breezes blowing in and covering the comforter. Later, D Dog hopped in bed with us, and we fell asleep eventually. D Dog slept on my side, down by my feet, and she twirled late that night to chase something in her dreams. I reached down a hand and left it on her side. The wind blew across the meadow and winter couldn't wait.

The next morning, without discussing it, we worked like field hands. The gardens had died; we covered them with mulch and compost, cut pine boughs for the sensitive rose hips and lilacs. For the most part we had planted native perennials, which meant our work in fall was kept to a minimum. I took a sharp spade and chopped irises and day lilies through the heart, carrying the departing half to a new ridge of curled soil near the barn overhang. The hydrangea had turned pink and rosy and Wendy cut bunches to hang from the trunnels scattered around the barn. They dangled like farmers' lanterns, still belonging more to the outside than the inside. The late morning had bloomed into a spectacular October day, red leaves, white birches, crunch underfoot. The feeling from the night before—the feeling of wanting to run through the cornfields—had returned, only this time channeled into work. We moved quickly, completing jobs now that we had put off again and again. We ate lunch on the porch. I had made some quick penne pasta with butter and basil, the last of the summer tomatoes cut up and served beside the plate in a white bowl. We ate bread and drank a beer each. Then we went back to work.

No insects. No bug bites. I cut down twenty saplings that had encroached on the northern hedgerow. Light surged into the open spaces, squatting under the remaining branches like someone slipping through a tent flap. I lopped down a thousand fingerling trees; Wendy followed behind and raked my clippings and cut anything remaining with a pair of hand shears. The stacks of chopped saplings became waist high. Oak, maple, beech, tamarack. The cherry striplings smelled of soda fountains. Now and then we uncovered frogs and snakes, once a turtle, lazy and somnolent already. Soon the turtle would head to the bottom of the lake, burrowing into the mud while it waited for the stars to turn, the spring to release lactic acid in its blood. Then it might rise, like gas, to join with the sunlight again. That slowness was already in its blood; it carried autumn in its bloodstream.

We deliberately left piles of cuttings for snakes and amphibians. Birds like the brush piles, too, and we liked birds. We could burn the piles off in the spring, we figured, and until then they would be mounds of sticks and warmth for animals. A barn for crawling creatures. Snow would soon cover them and then they would be white parts of the landscape, swells of hummocks forgotten until spring. The rest, the larger hunks of trees, we lay across the tailgate of the Dodge and cut into stove-length pieces. Then we threw them into the flatbed and carried them off to be stored under the overhang for a year, maybe three years from now.

Leather gloves handshaking wood, splashing the limbs and twigs out, the green bark fragrant. Wendy stood in the back of the pickup and kicked wood to me. I stacked. Over and over, log by log, until the wood flowed to the rafters of the storage space. I asked her if she remembered the boat that had been here the day we had first looked at the barn. A million years ago, she said. But it was only a little over a half year before and we both shook our heads, happy in the dazed way couples have when their time together seems longer than the outside world could know. Then while I finished stacking, Wendy sat in the back of the pickup, her legs dangling over the edge.

Once, she said, she and her father and mother had taken down a barn. They had been living in Maryland and her father had been working hard. An electrical union job. He rose at five, got a quick breakfast, out of the house by six. In exchange for doing an electrical job for an acquaintance, he was paid a barn. No kidding, Wendy said, when she saw me stop stacking. It was a barter thing, she said. I knew, glancing at her, that she had been waiting to tell me this story for a time but hadn't found the opportunity.

He ate dinner at five or so, then took the whole family out to help take down the barn. He must have been exhausted, but the work had to be done just so. Boards couldn't be ripped free. The nails must be extracted with pry bars, the wood lifted softly away. They made a large stack beneath the remaining portion of the barn. It had been a tobacco barn, so the wood had been particularly lovely. Like old baseball mitts, she said. Her mother had worked beside her father.

Wendy's job, as the oldest of three girls then (Dee was born later), was to watch her sisters. Spread on a quilt in the back of a pickup, she played with her sisters and listened to the wooden twang of boards coming loose. Because it was a tobacco barn, no trees had grown beside it to comfort it with shade. The Maryland nights had been warm and thick and her sisters had grown cranky in the back. It wasn't easy, Wendy said, to keep them happy. All through the summer they stayed in the back of the truck, watching the sunsets. When the sun turned amber in the west, bats flew around and around the barn. Maybe they came out of the barn at sunset, a braided tongue shooting out of the eaves, but in any event the bats flew above the truck. Her sisters, even then, understood the bats. They lay together, all three of them, watching the bats skim past the flat bed of the truck. She worried that the bats would collide and drop like burnt stars into the pickup. Then eventually she would fall asleep, the creak crack of her mother and father going on into her dreams.

"You never told me," I said when she finished. "How come?"

"I don't know why," she said. "I didn't have the right segue. Sitting in this truck made me remember it. And you working over there."

"Okay," I said.

"And the barn," she said. "It seemed funny to talk about taking down a barn when we're trying to keep one up. Sorry."

Pie came back at five and we again ate out on the porch. Then we went out to the fire pit and burnt sticks and hunks of logs until we had a good flame going. Wendy brought out marshmallows, stale ones, and we roasted them. Pie ate with wide, greedy bites. Sparks went up into the sky and became eyes winking back at us. Darkness came and it grew colder around the campfire. Pie asked me to tell him a story—he often asked for stories—and I told him a sillier than usual version of Pie and the Flying Carpet. He liked being the central figure. Cinnamon made the carpet fly, I told him, and I whispered in his ear the magic word, *mashed potatoes*, that made the carpet return to you.

Then it was bedtime. Wendy and I put water on the fire and watched the white smoke genie into the sky. Pie went off to hide from us, hoping to jump out and scare us on our return to the barn. The meadow had grown and frost clung to the tops of the seed heads. Clouds, when we looked up, jigsawed the mountaintops. Deep in the barn, D Dog woofed our approach. Smoke from the woodstove made a gray flag of combustion extending from the chimney.

I drove my Dodge pickup deep into the woods, up toward Sunset Mountain and the abandoned mica mine, in search of suitable stone. For reasons that had no logic behind them, stone had started to interest me. Maybe it is the occupation of old men, or older men, who like to use the leverage of their years to move weights they shouldn't be moving. Or maybe it is a sense of putting something permanent in place before one's life gets too rickety. Whatever the motivation, I had begun to take an active interest in stone walls. I read several accounts, all of them thin and serious, and I experimented enough to understand the two-on-one-on-two dictum. It is the basis of most stone masonry, even brick laying, and I saw it everywhere. Put two rocks down, one on top, two on top of that, and so on until infinity.

Now I had a project worth doing: a facing for a well. I needed stone and I had spotted a mound of schist during a hike with D Dog. The rock had been black with white flecks, fancy for stone walls, but it was abundant and free, and it would look handsome when it was laid up. The trick was to bring it home.

The woods stood quiet and bare enough to accept my entrance. I drove carefully, easing the old Dodge over the ruts and snags in the dirt trail leading up to the mine. D Dog rode in the passenger side, her head bobbing like a dashboard dog at my starts and stops. Two large planks clunked around in the flatbed; I had leather gloves, a stout pry bar, and a snake coil of old rope. As I drove, I checked clearances. It was one thing to get in with a relatively empty bed. When I loaded, though, and then trickled back down the hillside, the truck bottom could scrape. It was a standing code of northern driving that you did not get your truck into places you could not get out of. I particularly didn't want to get hung up, only to have a local pull me out while muttering I was a Jersey boy or a pilgrim, or, worst of all, a flatlander.

A mile uphill, I passed the first cement foundations of the abandoned mine. Birch saplings slapped the top of the truck cab as I banked a slow right, keeping the accelerator steady. First gear, up and up, more gas. D Dog watched, no expression whatsoever touching her. At last I saw the beginning of the mound of rock. I cranked the steering wheel and managed to K-turn slowly, getting out twice to make sure I didn't drop my back tires off the ancient roadbed. No one had been up this road in years from what I could tell, and the trees had encroached from every side. When I finally had the tailgate as close to the stone as I could get it, I turned off the engine and sat for a moment until silence supplanted the engine noise. Chickadees began scolding from the branches above me. I pushed open the door, held it while D Dog hopped out, then walked behind the truck to take stock.

Not an easy job. The stone lay ten or fifteen feet away, which didn't sound like much until you tried to lift one. The stone had been purposefully splintered out of huge boulders just north of the pile, because the shape and size of each stone appeared roughly uniform—a breakfast tray of rock, half a foot thick, as pleasing as morning toast. Igneous rock, I remembered from my eighth-grade Earth Science class. The rock had once been magma; it had cooled under the earth's mantle and finally worked its way to the surface, trapping other elements as it chilled and solidified. I immediately liked the color and the heft of the stone. It would not take much to make a great well facing. If I managed to load sufficient stone, it would come together easily.

I stretched a little, knowing that there is no good way to begin such a job except to begin it. I bent and got my hands under a stone the size of a bathroom trashcan. I lifted with my legs and back, cradling the rock to my gut. Then I monkey-walked to the back of the truck, grunting and wading like an ape bringing back primordial weapons.

I ughed it into the truck and skidded it up to the front. Easy enough, I thought, though risky on the old back and knees.

D Dog returned from wherever she had been scouting and walked with me back to the mound of rock. I needed larger stones than the first one, but to get loose I repeated a second lift, this time scraping my legs a good lick as I grumbled the stone to the truck. Two aboard, I thought. This was good, mindless work. Actually, that isn't quite fair. It called on a dim spot of intelligence deep in my forehead, something that knew about shapes and sizes, because already I had begun to organize the stones in a pattern. I lifted again. I waddled with the rock and thumped it into the truck. It skidded up with the other two, knocking together like shuffleboard disks. Then I hurried back to the rock pile. I didn't want to pause or slow down. *Here we go*, I told D Dog. I tipped a large rock up on its end, then flipped it. It clunked on the rocks below it, but traveled its diameter toward the truck. Again and again I flipped it. It did not move more than the force of my lifting; it volunteered nothing, in other words, and it required fourteen flips to get it near my planks.

Planks proved handy for the Egyptians while building the Pyramids and they proved handy for me as well. I flipped the rock onto the lower eighth of the planking. The planks vibrated and made a loud thwacking sound, but then I had the stone where I wanted it. I pushed it from underneath and of course the planks lifted too. The entire enterprise sustained a moment where it might all slip from the truck, slide back and crush my instep, when at last the planks steadied and the rock slid up. When it crossed the fulcrum of the tailgate, the planks sprang up in Three Stooges fashion, trying their best to whack me in the vitals. I steadied the stone and lifted the planks. The large rock made the truck curtsey as it received its weight.

I bent down and grabbed D Dog's front legs and made her do a short cha-cha. This was good work. The forest could not have been more beautiful. October sky slid above the green trees. Everywhere new light reached the forest floor. The tangle of spring and summer, the green, choking growth had come suddenly to a halt. Whatever seeds had found new earth were already gone to ground; whatever sap had climbed with the trees' push to the canopy had now begun its descent to its rooty storehouse. My breath came in white scarves. D Dog's muzzle showed silver when I studied her profile.

More stone. I duck-walked three more mid-size rocks back to the truck. Then another big foundation stone, one the size of a ram's head. This one went up the planks with no worries, almost as if I had the hang of it now. A blue jay swung down to the rock pile where I had unearthed grubs and worms. It yanked a few dark things from the darker mud, then glided back to an aspen, its iridescent blue queenly and dignified. The foundation rock, meanwhile, cracked up with the others. I did a quick survey of the truck to make sure it had not sagged too much. It's an old truck with 160,000 miles on it, and its shocks are no longer supple. But it seemed to be taking the load well, so I went back and brought out another foundation stone, this the biggest of all, a rock as high as my knees. Small rocks look handsome, but one likes a sense of footing in a wall, so I chugged this one end over end onto the planks.

It refused to budge. I heaved at it and tried to horse it upward, but it remained resolute. *You tricky bastard,* I muttered. I shoved some more. Then I had the idea of lifting the planks instead of the rocks, skidding it in the back of the truck like the old parlor game, Shoot the Moon. You could send a metal ball all the way to the moon by simply playing with two wands spaced just far enough apart to the let the ball drop, then catch itself. In any case, the planks would not budge either. The stone felt immovable.

It was as good a time as any for lunch. I ate sitting on the tailgate of my truck. D Dog sat beside me. I ate bread and cheese, a Vermont Cheddar a friend had sent me. Then I ate five or six chocolate chip cookies. D Dog finished off the cheese and bread, her tail wagging to show her appreciation. I had a half-gallon of cider, and I drank that with long pulls. I still felt the rocks in my hands; their abrasions had roughed up the skin on my fingers even under my gloves. I closed and opened my fingers to make sure they performed okay. Lately I had felt a little weakness in my hands. It had not been much. Once or twice, while I thought I had something securely gripped, my hand had given way. Peculiarly, it had not felt to be in my control. Whereas before I could will my hand to maintain its grip, now something else forced it open. Maybe age. Maybe weakness. I didn't like to think about it.

I lay back in the truck and fell asleep. I hadn't meant to, although I like a nap in the afternoon. But my eyes clamped shut and when I woke I understood that I did not have to hurry. It was okay to be in the woods. D Dog had stretched out beside me, her dark fur warm and good to touch. For a time I looked up at the sky, watching the leaves parachute from branches. Then I pushed off the truck and grabbed the recalcitrant rock and made it move up the final few feet to the truck. Same rock. Strangely, I could move it without difficulty; the stone obliged me and went exactly as I directed it. Perhaps it had been fatigue that had slowed its progress. I did not pretend to understand the rock's new willingness.

I rounded off the load with five or six mid-size rocks. When I climbed behind the steering wheel, the truck felt fat and full. I bounced the first few feet over the dirt road, carefully going at an angle to any bump. The truck did okay. I drove the entire distance in first, letting the gears hold me back. The load did not rattle around. Now that the stone understood where it was going, it seemed almost to cooperate.

Pie was waiting when I returned. He wore a red plaid parka shirt and a bright orange hunting hat. He had the school-day mania about him. He had been locked up too long for such a marvelous day. I told him to climb aboard and help me push the rocks off the flatbed. He liked explosions and avalanches, so this was right up his alley. Together we shoved the rocks off the end of the tailgate and listened to their bowling-ball thumps as they found gravity in their new location. When everything had cleared, I hopped down and showed him what I proposed. On a scale of stone masonry, it was a distinctly minor operation. The large cement collar of our well had bothered me since we had moved into the barn. It stood like a pale doughnut, a manufactured product, while the meadow around it remained natural. I wanted to build a rumble wall around the well, stacking the rocks against the cement collar. Grass would weave into the rocks and obscure the harsher line of the well. It would still resemble a well, but after applying the stonework it would be a country well, not a prefab one.

Whether Pie got it or not was hard to say, but he liked the idea of us building something together. I told him the rocks were heavy; he could easily pinch a finger, or even break one, if he wasn't careful. He brushed my cautionary remarks away. He promised to be careful. He stood on the stones and tried to make them move. A circus bear on a large ball. He fell off a dozen times before I sent him off to feed D Dog her evening meal.

"Chow bow wow?" he asked D Dog, which got her prancing and raising her feet.

"Just a little. She had some cheese and crackers."

Ideally, when constructing a stone wall, one would dig down four or five feet to the frost line and begin building from there. But I had no intention of taking on a major excavation. An ornamental facing, I reminded myself. I had flattened the soil around the well, sprinkling in a few yards of crushed stone. Frost might tip the stones eventually, but that would hardly matter. Besides, we could lean the stone against the cement collar. Of course no one can build a stone anything in New England without thinking about Robert Frost. *Something there is that doesn't like a wall,* I remembered, then laughed at the spottiness of my recall. I could recite most of the verses of "She Wore an Itsy Bitsy Teeny

Weeny Yellow Polka Dot Bikini" and the complete inane intricacies of the "Name Game," but I could not conjure up many complete poems. There was a comment about society somewhere in that, or maybe about me, but I shook it off. Stonework does not stew well with social criticism.

I circled the well while Pie fed D Dog, and when he came back I was ready with a plan. The largest of the stones, the one that would not budge until I had eaten my lunch, needed to be the first to go. I wanted it at the front of the well, the side we glimpsed from the house, because its mass was so pleasing to the eye. Together with Pie, I rolled the stone into approximate place. Then I asked him to stand back and I tilted the rock up on end, the earth side grinding the crushed stone, and leaned the hunk against the well tile. It stood beautifully, carving out a dark, stony presence against the ghostly white of the cement. An improvement. I asked Pie what he thought.

"It looks good," he said and shrugged.

"Really good? Or just okay?"

"Good, Joe," he said.

"You ready for the next rock?"

"Sure," he said.

His interest had already begun to wane, but he stayed with me for three more rocks before he left. His friend Christopher appeared on a bike. I watched the short conflict play out behind Pie's eyes. They had been building a fort in the wood that had lately been visited by coyotes. Tracks everywhere, they said. Pie had thought Christopher was grounded for the day. Now his friend's appearance was thrilling and unexpected. Christopher straddled the bar of his bike and kept it steady while he explained that he had an hour in which to play. His family intended to drive over to Lebanon for groceries around five. He also said his dad had seen more coyotes up in the woods beyond the railroad bed, that they had tried to find the den but couldn't.

"Do they den in the fall?" I asked.

"My dad says they do."

His dad, I knew, hunted regularly. Pie had returned from a sleepover to tell me about the frozen bear head they had in the family freezer. I told Pie to go ahead and play for an hour. He let out a whoop and hurried off to get his bike. A minute later I watched them disappear up the old railroad bed, heading toward their fort.

The rest of the work came easily. I set the stones in courses, following the prescription of two on one, one on two. Wendy came out and brought me a Scotch on the rocks, though the pun was inadvertent. She wore a thick black wool sweater, a white turtleneck, a pair of faded jeans, and Birkenstocks. She sat on the tailgate of the truck and said the well looked better, much better, that it already blended more with the meadow around it. I asked her if she could remember Robert Frost's "Mending Wall," but she didn't get much further with it than I had. Then I asked if she could remember "Itsy Bitsy Teeny Weeny Yellow Polka Dot Bikini" and she rattled it off.

I had a few sips of the Scotch, then finished setting the last stones. The final course went level with the lip of the well. For all intents and purposes, the cement had disappeared, eaten by stone and shadow. It was not a bad piece of work. Across the meadow, crows fell on the compost pile, yanking out tomato peels and desiccated corncobs. They squawked and carried on and we turned and watched them for a while. By the time we turned back the afternoon had disappeared and winter had crept a little closer.

We wanted a chair. I'm not sure who first started the campaign, but on a day in mid-October we suddenly felt our furniture was drab. Not drab, maybe, but it needed a slap up. We had worked tirelessly at combining our furniture, and that, perhaps, was part of the problem. We wanted something new, something neither of us had owned before, something we purchased together specifically for the barn. Added to that was the pleasure we took in finishing the insulation in the walls. After five months of worry and work, we were finally done. We cut the last board on a Sunday evening, Wendy setting it with a pneumatic hammer. As soon as the last board shivered solidly in place, she stepped off the work platform and announced she needed a shower. A scalding hot shower. Then a Scotch. Then a long night's sleep.

But instead of rest, we ended up moving furniture around while drinking the Scotch Wendy had requested. Pie had already gone to sleep but we suddenly had the decorating itch. Now, with the walls complete, we saw the barn as it would be for years to come. The honeyed shiplap pine, the enormous granite fireplace, the acres of birch flooring—everything had swirled around in our vision for months. Finally it had begun to slow and we felt capable of making decisions about furniture. This was the fun of it all.

Undeniably, the granite hearth anchored any conceivable arrangement. Wendy called it the decorating sun, the center of the furniture universe. The large, blank log that served as a mantel drew the eye; the stones and mortar, rising to the peak of the barn, dominated everything around it. We placed the old camel loveseat horizontal to the fireplace, then moved it vertical, then moved it back. We put a cordovan-colored Adirondack chair next to a pile of cordwood, the chair arms pointed toward the fireplace, then settled a wooden crate beside it as a side table. Finally we moved a wing chair, ice blue with yellow curls of goldenrod printed across the material, to counterbalance the Adirondack chair. The general shape of the arrangement worked, but in the lamplight the chair appeared tired and shoddy. It drained the other pieces of furniture, the blue material dingy from D Dog's naps, the winged backrest faded from sunlight. It had to go.

When we had the furniture roughly arranged to our temporary satisfaction, we spent the rest of the night hammering
hooks into the walls for pictures. The scope of the barn made it
a daunting job. Smaller pictures, either photographs or paintings, shrunk to postage stamps on the wide walls. We drank
Scotch and moved the pictures around. Only one picture, a portrait we had purchased at an auction of an English lord waking
from a four-poster bed, had the size and density to adequately
hold its position on the wall. The rest, unfortunately, swam like
brown oak leaves on a cement walkway. We surrendered eventually. It was going to take time, we told each other. That was the
pleasure of it.

In bed that night Wendy read from the various quotes she
had collected concerning house decorating. The quotes appealed
to her droll sense of humor. They also served as warnings to us
both not to get carried away by something we called the country
magazine mentality—the devotion to quilts and clever doorstops,
to headboards made from picket fences, tables formed of paint-
chipped shutters. We had once attended a dinner at which the
hostess had served six courses, five wines, all delivered on place
mats made from the dust jackets of 1930s novels. A thin line, in
other words, between kitsch and culture. We played with the
notion constantly, hoping we stayed on the more authentic side
of things. We understood, too, that sometimes our approach to
country things approached self-parody. *Loving hands at home*, we
said to one another when we ventured too near the glossy-
magazine-layout approach to decorating. We remained vigilant
against egg baskets, cast-iron muffin pans, duck decoys.

Wendy read from a description accompanying a layout in
the March 1999 issue of *Country Living* magazine:

> *"I wanted this place to feel airy, like a little tree house,"*
> *says Cornella Sidley Parker of her fifth-floor apartment in*
> *a landmark building in central Denver. So she painted the*

living-room and sunroom walls sky blue, whitewashed the wood floors, and left the historic building's original casement windows bare to take advantage of the views. Buttery damask fabric covers a down-filled sofa that Cornella inherited from her grandmother; her great-grandparents brought the low slung coffee table home with them from after a 1910 trip to Morocco.

From *Bed and Breakfast in New England* by Bernice Chesler:

Peter, the vegetable gardener/song leader/former wholesale lumber businessman, took tap dancing lessons to celebrate his 60th birthday...Kay, a skier too, is the good cook who wrote the Moose Mountain Lodge Cookbook. *Before breakfast she spins her goats' mohair.*

From *How to Open and Operate a Bed and Breakfast Home* by Jan Stankus:

Other ideas: Place a tiny table-and-chairs set from a doll house on the table as a centerpiece. Or display a toy tea-party set. Or create a miniature farm right in the center of the table, and use some of the pieces for a place setting: Put a cow next to the glass of milk. A tractor can haul the spoon. (Maybe a large green placemat would make a good field for the tractor.) Or think about a jungle theme, with toy lions, tigers, bears, elephants, and maybe a Tarzan model. (And how about a napkin made of black and yellow tiger-striped material?)

The next morning we went chair shopping at a furniture store in Meredith, New Hampshire. We dropped Pie at a friend's house along the way, then drove on a leisurely course past a number of antique stores we liked. Antiques, in this instance, weren't the solution. We wanted fabric, upholstery, a traditional easy chair. The barn had a tendency to bleach things with its size; we needed color and texture, not more wood.

Our trip to a furniture store that sold new things went against the grain. We had become steady customers at auctions throughout the area and had decorated a good portion of the barn with odd and ends—cast-off objects and lots from estate settlements. Until recently, my concept of auctions had come from James Bond movies where 007, who apparently had no home whatsoever, decided to outbid the Bad Guy for the privilege of owning a three-million-dollar harpsichord. Why James Bond wanted the harpsichord was never made clear, but I admired the manner in which the bids were lodged, discreetly raised eyebrows correctly interpreted by the auctioneer to signify a bump of $20,000.

Country auctions don't have quite that ring of sophistication. People who go to country auctions are cheapskates, for the most part, and Wendy and I were no exceptions. Two things about auctions quickly became clear. First, it was ridiculous to pay much for anything. Retail prices, especially in antique shops in New Jersey, Connecticut, or Massachusetts, are so far out of whack with what one pays at auction as to be nearly insulting. Drop-leaf maple tables, for example, sell for $150 to $200 in antique stores, depending naturally on their condition and provenance. At auction the same table might sell for $10 or $25, tops. Mark-ups of 3, 4, even 500 percent are not uncommon in chic boutiques around the eastern seaboard. Wendy and I, after we got the hang of auctions, delighted in investigating toney antique shops and marveling at the prices of things. It was everything we could do not to catch the eye of the shop owner and give a big wink over the outlandish pricing.

Second, we learned that America provides such a flood of merchandise, furniture, fans, hats, stoves, and so on, as to be entirely inexhaustible. Miss a good buy on a lamp? Don't worry.

You will find ten lamps at the next auction, a hundred two weeks from now, a thousand the day after. Want a VCR? Ten thousand copies of *National Geographic*? An FDR memorial cigarette holder? Everything in America, in other words, is destined for a yard sale. It is a great, giant river of goods, of junk, of objets d'art. Unless you have visited auctions and flea markets, yard sales and VFW tag sales, you cannot conceive of how much stuff floats through the American household each day, each year, each decade. Soon after visiting our first auction, Wendy and I agreed that it made no sense whatsoever to buy retail—with the possible exception of upholstered goods, which get musty over time—again in our lifetimes. Never. No more new pots, pans, cups, glasses, bowls, saucers, platters, ashtrays, plant pots, or candleholders. No more new towel racks, bathroom scales, rubber stamps, log andirons, milking cans, or tables. With a sense of humor and a good eye, we decided we could decorate our barn for a fraction of the retail cost.

But we still needed an upholstered chair. We found ourselves trying to explain the barn to the brightly dressed woman, Dolores, who escorted us around the furniture showroom. She wore dangling earrings fit to catch trout. A log cabin, she said, misunderstanding. The country look, she said, when we corrected her. She seemed fairly certain she knew our house better than we did. We offered to look around and to call her if we needed anything. She disappeared with her clipboard pressed to her chest, her earrings casting the shoals along her neck.

A million chairs. We looked at Laz-Z-Boy recliners—no way, Wendy said—and at beautiful, silk-upholstered vanity-table chairs. We looked at leather chairs—too many meat associations, we decided—and at Southwestern, ranchero-style armchairs. That seemed a little giddyap to us.

Wendy spotted a sign that said BARGAIN ATTIC, and we followed it upstairs. The Bargain Attic was poorly heated and less carefully arranged. But it had tons of stuff. This was where beanbag chairs went to die. The attic ran the length of the store, which was enormous to begin with, and pushed furniture at us everywhere we looked. All of it was new, I suppose, though much of it, because it seemed relatively out of fashion, had a grandmother's attic quality. A few items had been damaged. Most of it, though, had simply failed at being bought.

Our eyes lit up. Much better pickings. We separated and started working our way down different sides of the building, calling attention to different items if we found them amusing or bad enough to be good. Our search, I realized, had been blunted. We now looked for a chair, sort of, but we had also given in to the experience. Maybe we didn't want a chair, after all. Maybe we wanted a faux Victorian birdcage, or a fifty-gallon aquarium, or a ten-tiered combination plant stand and CD rack.

Halfway down the right aisle, I spotted a sofa. It sat back behind two standing lamps, back next to a Michael Jordan lamp/headboard/hoop wastebasket. Red did not describe it. The sofa glowed the color of certain tomatoes after they had been sautéed in olive oil. Or glowed like the deep crimson of expensive oriental carpets, or like a woman's freshly painted toenails. I knew that I had discovered something, and I approached it carefully, afraid to look at it too directly for fear I would uncover a hideous element.

But it stood up. "Wendy," I said. She knew from my voice that I had found something. She came over and spotted it immediately.

"Brocaded," she said. "It's a sectional."

"Really?" I asked, because I hadn't noticed.

"That's okay. It would fit. It would enclose things a little around the fireplace. I don't mind that at all."

"Aren't sectionals kind of like recliners?"

"Not always. There's something to be said for them."

We moved closer. The longer end of the sectional extended to the right—a letter J that had fallen forward onto its back, the shorter portion now straightened and sectioning off the fireplace. It would work. We could both see that. It had a size and depth that made it instantly appropriate for the barn, and it provided a needed shot of color. It may have been a bit risky—to buy anything so large and red is a risk—but we felt it made sense.

Dolores appeared. She wondered where we had gotten to, she said. We sat on the sectional and tried it out. Comfortable. She stood before us and explained that the piece had actually been commissioned by a woman in Wolfeboro, but it had come the wrong way. The letter J, in other words, needed to be the letter L. Dolores didn't know the price on this piece off the top of her head, but she assured us that her manager would be willing to work with us.

"It's a beautiful piece, but how many people can fit it into their house?" she asked. "And then, some people need it to go the other way. Sectionals can be tricky."

"Good point," I said.

"It would look great in a log cabin," Dolores added.

We bought it for $750. Two days later a pair of delivery men showed up in a van. They had phoned to say they were coming and Wendy and I had prepared the space and pushed away excess furniture. Wendy had also taken measurements to reassure us both that it would fit correctly. Still, we could not be certain the sectional would fit the barn's style. The brocade, in our nervousness, seemed too genteel for the rough motif of our barn. The rest of our furniture, too, suddenly seemed provincial. Waiting for the sectional to arrive felt like waiting for a rich, judgmental aunt to show up, elaborate luggage in hand, her stories of adventure both welcome and intimidating.

But when the two young guys—Rob and Tom—carried the sectional in and plopped it down in front of the fireplace, we knew at a glance that it worked. Suddenly the room had a center, a focal point, a place to be. The hearth, certainly, demanded attention, but the rich quality of the brocade added necessary warmth to the arrangement. Even the faded wing chair, the original reason for our search, took on new vigor.

Of course any new addition of furniture is the beginning of an avalanche. Once one piece changes, others must follow. As soon as Rob and Tom departed, we started shuffling furniture. Wendy remembered an old blanket trunk we had bought at an auction in Fairlee, Vermont. We carried it down from the top walk of the barn, a great coffin of a thing, wheat-colored and buff, and put it in the island created by the sectional wings. *Ahhh,* we both said. Then we went on with the fussy business of arranging coffee-table books, magazines, lamps. Presently the room acquired a grace that had escaped it before. The touch of brocaded elegance enhanced the parochial elements of beam, strut, and board.

That night, long after Pie had gone to bed, we sat on the couch, a good oak fire burning in the hearth. We turned out most of the lights, isolating our red island. We sat so that we could rub each other's feet. We talked for a long time about the building, about what was left to do before winter, about the pleasure of putting the sectional into place. The sectional, on top of everything else, was spectacularly comfortable. We sank into it. Heat from the fire reached us. Wood smoke puffed out sometimes and we smelled the oak, the underlined hint of pine and ash. Moonlight fell through the southwest skylight, a white sword, a dagger, a finger of winter.

séance

Geese began flying at night in mid-September. We heard them up in the stars, honking and calling to one another. All geese repeat *Hurry, Hurry, Hurry*, but sometimes the wind makes their words unintelligible. By the first week of October they had disappeared, though we continued to listen for them. Pie told me he could not stop worrying that a flock had gotten a late start and might leave too close to winter. Someone had told him a story about ducks becoming frozen in the ice, and the story stuck with him. We talked for a while about geese navigating at night, how such a thing was possible, and I told him about starlings navigating by the stars. In an experiment I remembered from high-school biology texts, scientists had turned the interior starscape of an observatory and the starlings had flown to follow south according to the stars. When the scientists rotated the starscape, the starlings rotated with them. Then we discussed the possibility that geese had sensitivity to electromagnetic waves, that they responded to elements in the earth we could not perceive. Pie said he had heard dolphins could do the same thing. I wasn't sure he was correct, but he was so convinced of this fact that I believed him.

The geese did not land in the fishpond next door, but ducks did. They splashed in on their feet and then sank like light wood into the water. The old blue heron that fished for trout in the shallows beat his way slowly over the pond one last time. He could not raise himself abruptly enough to make it over the pines in one pitch, so he canted back and forth, stitching his way out of summer and into the gray autumn clouds.

Crows came to our field every day, squawking and wrestling over bits of compost. I liked the sight of them: black and definite against the softer hues of empty grass. A few red-tailed hawks circled the meadow on their way south. They hung like mottled hens, though twice as graceful, and then followed the thermals down the seaboard toward their winter grounds. I did not see one stoop for mice or smaller birds. They seemed too well suited to flight to bother with eating.

The field lay ravaged now and when I walked it with D Dog one morning I marked the advance of raspberry shoots and black weed brambles. Everywhere the grass seemed trampled and spent; it pressed up red against the sheep fence, and ran like a comb around the three acres of our land. One Saturday morning I took out our old Tecumseh lawn mower and tried to hack it back, but it was useless. The lawn mower choked and clogged every twenty feet. I relented and rolled the mower under the overhang, put Stabil in the gas tank to prevent water from icing until spring, then went back out to inspect the field. It did not look good. True, winter would eventually crush the grass and smother it into the soil, but the bushes would take hold and weave into the fabric of the meadow. One could argue for abdication—let the berries take it—but the barn benefited from the long, sweeping meadow. A meadow was useful for play. Pie and his friends could bike across it or play hide-and-seek. Besides, in a week or two we planned a Halloween séance, and we hoped to have the place looking good. The meadow needed a final mowing.

Shortly after we had moved in, a man had stopped by to say he had mowed for the previous owners some years back, that he knew the field, and that he'd "do us decent" if we engaged him. At the time it had been too early to make such arrangements, but now I felt ready to track him down. I couldn't remember the fellow's name, so when I stopped in the Warren Village Market on Friday morning, I asked the clerk if he knew anyone who might mow the field. A tall, rugged-looking fellow who stood behind me in line heard my question and said if I didn't mind sheep he had a small flock he would love to put to graze on my land.

"John," he said when I turned and introduced myself, "John Lester."

"You keep sheep?" I asked.

"About a dozen. I do a bit of weaving."

"The village lawn mowers," the store clerk said, "can't beat them."

I had heard about a New Hampshire state project through which sheepherders were given free access to the land beneath power lines, so that the sheep could keep brush from building up around the stanchions. In the past, power companies often had sprayed herbicides to control vegetation. Sheep, by any standard, were preferable to sprays. I knew Wendy would like the idea of sheep grazing idly in our meadow. Clouds come to rest on grass, as one poet put it. I told John to bring the sheep by. He could at least graze them there for a while.

"Sheep?" Wendy said when I told her. "Do you know the first thing about sheep?"

"No," I said, "but I assume this guy Lester does. They'll mow the grass."

"And anything else that grows."

"Let's see how it goes," I said. "We can always ask them to leave. It's better than a brush hog."

Not a full hour later, I heard the sheep bleating from the town common. John Lester, apparently, was as good as his word.

We also learned, later, that he was famous for wedging his sheep onto any plot of grass in the county. No one showed surprise—when we told the story to local folk in the ensuing weeks—that he had taken us up on our offer so readily. The sheep, they told us, had eaten everything within the town limits.

Meanwhile, Wendy found me in the kitchen and gave me a look that clearly stated that anything concerning sheep fell squarely on my head. Then Pie started shouting that he saw sheep coming up the driveway. As quick as a trout rise, we had livestock.

I went out to help or to at least stand around with my hands on my hips. John and two of his sons, Andy and Steven, drove the sheep up our driveway. I felt satisfied to see a dozen sheep spill out against the farthest corners of our land. We lived in a barn, after all, and the cheery bleating made sense given the history of the building.

John obviously had done this before and set up like a desert nomad arranging camp. His wife, Sarah, appeared in a pickup, with batteries and electric fencing in the flatbed. Several large buckets of feed jiggled when she rode over bumps. She raised a hand to wave while Steven and Andy, howling and barking like wolves, kept the sheep pinned to the far corners of the meadow.

It took an hour to complete the job. John bisected the meadow with an orange electric fence, a pulse running through it every three seconds, but the sheep knew better than to approach it anyway. Sarah handed over a few buckets of feed, then John took off with the truck and returned with an aluminum hut. Steven and Andy filled the water buckets while I helped John stake out the shelter. By five o'clock the sheep had settled and had begun merrily to chew their cud, stuffed already by our clover and timothy grass.

After the Lesters left, Wendy and I had a glass of wine on the porch and watched darkness cut slowly across the meadow. The sheep moved like white grains of a massive Etch A Sketch.

The bells around their necks tinkled softly and their bleating, not frequent, knitted the sounds of frogs and crickets together. Pie came out later and led D Dog to the fence. She woofed a little, but gave it up quickly.

We told Pie we would time him running from one end of the field to the other and so we spent the minutes until darkness watching him run through the tall grass. The sheep watched him suspiciously, then finally gave up worrying. They clucked and burbled over the grass. We challenged Pie to make a bleating sound and he did, dramatically hamming it up. That night going to sleep we did not listen for geese, but instead to the sheep wandering the fields with their pointy toes. Later, when first light hit the meadow, I went to the French doors and looked out at them. They lay on their bent knees in the tin shelter, chewing. Only an old mother worked the perimeter of the fence, searching for clover. Steam floated off her back, a white cloud, a sheep above a sheep.

We wanted to hold a séance. The weather was right; the barn, potentially, had a ghostly feeling. We thought, too, it might be a good way to entertain for the first time. We had never had people over on a formal basis. A séance gave us a good excuse. It would be fun and a little scary.

Like many people, I had assumed séances served as a sort of Rotary meeting for wandering spirits. As I discovered doing research the week before the séance, it turns out séances had more to do with mesmerism and animal magnetism than with ghostly wanderings. Spirits did not cause mediums to become elongated or hover above oak pedestal tables. The mediums themselves, blessed with particularly fine spiritual tuning forks, as it were, summoned the phenomena through their corporal bodies. Séances did occasionally contact the undead, but that specific purpose attributed to séances occurred more often toward the end of the nineteenth century than at the middle. In our mass consciousness, the two—séances and hauntings—became blended.

The best story I came across in my brief reading period, and one that combined the elements of séances with ghostly presences, concerned a haunting that took place in 1855 in England. In November of that year a nursemaid going along a passage at eight in the evening saw a figure in light gray. The nursemaid put out a hand to touch her, but the figure avoided it. The nursemaid saw the figure the following March. She also saw a ghostly male figure, and heard footsteps, scuffling sounds, and the noise of something heavy being dragged downstairs. The butler confirmed the sounds—like barrels rolling and planks of wood being stacked—and in March he saw the figure, too, all except the head, which appeared like a black mist. The following day the master of the house decided to hold a séance and imported a table-turning medium. They learned during the séance that the ghost was eager to tell them about a box of jewels that had been buried in the cellar.

The next evening, at eleven, the ghost reappeared during a second séance, dressed this time in Japanese silk. Her feet were in a dark cloud and she threw up her hands, clutching at her hair. Her face was long and haggard and she had a thin nose. Her hair was torn and hung almost to her waist. Her eyes were cast upward and resembled balls of fire.

The assembled séance participants took the table to the basement, and by tilting it the sitters determined the ghost wanted them to start digging. They got the flagstones up and found the soil had apparently never been disturbed. Then they found a hole, but there was nothing there. They summoned the ghost again, who appeared agitated and reported she had forgotten where she had buried the jewels. Unknown to the master of the house, the former owner had been a suicide, hanging herself by a skipping-rope from a peg behind a bedroom door. No remnant of her jewels had ever been found.

That story remained stuck in my mind as guests began arriving Saturday afternoon—the day of our séance—in a wonderful flux of confusion and noise. Wendy and I quickly discovered we had not worked out a greeting policy. Where did you take a guest when she or he arrived? We didn't know because we had never actually entertained before, but it worked out anyway because D Dog barked, Pie jumped around wanting to show everyone the sheep, and Wendy and I, undecided about which rooms were to hold which guests, stalled everyone by saying they should simply put their bags down and drink a glass of wine.

Because this weekend possessed the flavor of a British comedy, it might make sense to introduce formally the other players.

Sarah, Wendy's sister, a 28-year-old social worker. She recently returned from the Peace Corps in Eritrea and now worked with AmeriCorps in adult literacy programs. Known as Bozo to her family, she is the traveler.

Steve, a horticulturist, responsible for all plants at the college where I teach. An avid bicyclist, he is tall and thin, a graduate of Temple University's Ambler campus, older, at 44, than anyone else in the group. He lived through the back-to-earth movement and stayed with it to some degree.

Leslie, a Dartmouth senior who wants to do stand-up comedy in Boston. Bright, funny, a native of Cleveland. She brought a Ouija board for the weekend.

Chris, the rock climber. An outdoorsy kind of guy, a friend of Steve the horticulturist. He went with his brother, at seventeen, on a trip to the innermost regions of Labrador. His first hike, ever, turned out to be the Appalachian Trail, 1,800 miles south to north.

Deb, my niece, a fifth-grade math teacher. Tall, an All-state basketball player who set high-school scoring records. A dry wit who washes dishes once a year for my sister and only at Christmas.

Dave, an ex–Navy supply sergeant, the most organized man in the universe. He drinks Diet Pepsi for breakfast.

Catie, another niece, a recent grad of the University of New Hampshire and now an occupational therapist. She had applied to the Peace Corps and was waiting to hear the result of her application, meanwhile killing time with her uncle.

Then the tour. We clumped up and down stairs, walked all over the yard, Wendy and I getting a kick out of explaining what we had done here, what we hoped to do there. We walked down to the old railroad bed at the foot of our land, a ten-foot-wide footpath that ran all the way to Canada, the trees crimson around us.

A happy afternoon. Earlier in the summer Pie and I had discovered a hillside covered with raspberry bushes, so we headed in that direction. Berry Hill, as Pie had named the find, squatted at the knee of White Mountain National Forest. We walked and picked these late berries, mindful of the thousand bees that winked among the leaves. The berries tasted intermittently sweet and sour and you could not guess which juice a berry would hold until it squashed on your tongue.

On our walk back to the barn, it was difficult to feel we were embarked on anything ominous. Steve pointed out the various plants along the railroad bed—American dogwood, tansy, Queen Anne's lace, sumac, yarrow, wild iris—and we walked in shade, then sun, then shade again. In the meadow light clung to the top of the grasses, turning insects to flashing cinders as they drifted between the plants. We walked as children do in gangly groups of loose conversation, chill temperatures pushing us homeward, the bulbs of shade thrown by the oaks indisputably cold.

We had drinks on the fieldstone porch. The pond to our north glinted in the last sun as Wendy served plates of raw vegetables—white bowls of cherry tomatoes with fresh farm scallions beside them—and a dill dip. She garnished the dip with chives from the garden. D Dog, a specialist with tennis balls, made the rounds of the guests, dropping her ball into their laps. Now and then a guest would stand, take an old tennis racket we kept on the porch for the express purpose of knocking the ball into the meadow, and whack the ball as far as possible. Then D Dog, tail up, knitted her way through the field, her nose searching endlessly for the yellow balls. Before long, the sun had dimmed and D Dog had become hazy in twilight.

At seven we served peasant pie. I caught Wendy's eye several times as the guests passed the food around the table. This, our look said, is a wonderful place. With guests around the table, good food, laughter, a bit of wine, we were reminded of why we had fallen in love with the barn in the first place. The fireplace light threw intriguing shadows everywhere and the splendid height of the building, the century-old timbers, browned from years of smoke and animal heat, stretched and carried the ceiling up and away. Through the windows opening onto the porch, we could watch the last light play on Mount Kineo. In a span of ten minutes the mountains lifted and shrugged with the passing clouds, and then night joined sky and ground and the meadow slipped away into darkness.

Over coffee our conversation turned to séances and to spirits in general. Nearly everyone at the table had a story to relate. Steve, our horticulturist, proclaimed himself a staunch skeptic. Chris, his buddy, agreed. My niece Debbie told a long story about a haunted dormitory, which proved to be the kind of story that depends on the teller turning quickly to grab the person beside her at the climax. Debbie grabbed my niece Catie's arm, and Catie, obligingly, screamed in one shrill squeal that made D Dog stand up and look out at the meadow, a bark ruffling her throat.

But Dave, the ex-Navy sergeant, had been doing his own research on matters of the occult. He said he had been fascinated by vampire myths for years, and had recently read a tract about vampires being linked to the nineteenth-century fear of being buried alive. Between 1850 and 1867, burials in the major cities of Europe, particularly among the poor, remained haphazard affairs. Often no physician viewed the corpse. One of the leading medical journals of the day, Dave said, discussed the topic of premature burial. He had brought along a copy of the document. It read:

> *Truly there is something about the very notion of such a fate calculated to make one shudder, and to send a cold stream down one's spine...The last footfall departs from the solitary churchyard, leaving the entranced sleeper behind in his hideous shell soon to awaken to consciousness and to a benumbed half-suffocated existence for a few minutes; or else, more horrible still, there he lies beneath the ground conscious of what has been and still is, until, by some fearful agonized struggle of the inner man at the weird phantasmagoria which has passed across his mental vision, he awakens to a bodily vivication as desperate in its torment for a brief period as has been that of his physical activity. But it is soon past. There is scarcely room to turn over in the wooden chamber; and what can avail a few shrieks and struggles of a half-stifled, cramped-up man!*

Many nineteenth-century notables made provisions against premature burial. Wilkie Collins, the well-known novelist, left a letter on his dressing table adjuring anyone finding him dead to call a doctor and make certain. A prominent society woman, Madame Martineau, left her doctor ten pounds to see that her head was amputated before interment; another woman asked that her heart be pierced with a needle; another man requested that bells be tied to his extremities, probably so that he could ring in distress if he awoke in a pine box.

Dread of vampirism, according to Dave, resulted from the twisted and contorted configurations of exhumed corpses, the manifestation of premature burial. People studied the bent bodies and assumed a titanic battle had occurred beneath the churchyard soil. According to folk legend, the entombed soul sent forth an astral projection, searching for sustenance on which to feed. All of these threads combined in Bram Stoker's *Dracula,* published in 1897, in which, interestingly, the vampire becomes corporeal, a creeping peril with codified powers and limitations. Dracula, as Stoker made clear, is the mirror image of Christ, with blood ensuring everlasting life. Though Christ pushed back the stone of his tomb, thereby bringing light into the darker recesses of the human spirit, Dracula chose to keep the stone tight to the opening, darkness the counter to the intrusive light.

All of this talk put us in a fine, creepy mood. By the time Dave had finished, the barn was completely dark except for the fireplace light and the candles we had kept on the table. Wendy made her way to the kitchen and brought back a bottle of cognac. A few people poured drinks. Then we started the séance.

The little reading I had done on séances put me a few steps ahead of the others at the table and therefore made me the medium. I told the participants to hold hands. It was important to keep our hands joined throughout the séance, because the various writers hinted that to break the circle might place us all in jeopardy. Certainly the trick of holdings hands—while using counterfeit hands, or prostheses, to carry off an eerie effect—was well established in table-knocking circles, but I had no tricks in mind. My only plan was to beseech forthrightly the powers of the universe, to let them enter our circle if they desired, and to see what became of the evening.

When we joined hands, we couldn't help laughing. I saw no point in attempting to make the proceedings serious. Whatever might happen would originate from an outside source; we obviously had no power over such an entity. Debbie asked who had kicked her under the table. Dave said he felt a cold breeze from somewhere. D Dog shifted on her bed, her tags rattling softly from time to time. People continued to laugh and poke fun. Then, surprisingly, they didn't.

The nervous laughter around the table began to give way, incrementally, to anticipation. Most of us at the table, I realized, remained at least open to the possibility that something might contact us.

"Is there a ghost in this house?" I asked when the room finally grew quiet.

My question set off another round of laughter, but then a log popped in the fireplace and immediately the tone became serious again. I said some other mumbo-jumbo about the spirit, if it existed, making itself manifest to us. Nothing happened. We sat in silence. Then something did happen.

We debated later about whether the light appeared outside the building or inside. I felt fairly sure that a light in the kitchen had blinked on and off. Others claimed the light hovered outside the window, suspended above the autumn lawn. The light, a ceiling bulb set on a very old breaker and 1930s-vintage wire, had blinked any number of times before. The twist, though, was that I was nearly certain I had turned the light off myself. In our months in the barn, the light had never flickered when the switch had been closed. The connection may have been poor, but once the juice had been cut the bulb remained inert.

"Oh my god," Catie said.

"Shhhh," someone else said.

"Did you see the light?" people asked on either side of me.

At all the talking, D Dog got off her bed and wagged around the table. No one seemed in a mood to resume. Steve claimed he had seen nothing whatsoever, and Leslie thought it might have been a car headlight passing over the window. Wendy stood and switched on the lamps while Sarah threw another log on the fire. Outside the sheep began bleating in quick, random bursts, and for a second we all listened. Then the wind smoothed out the sound and whatever remained of the séance passed away from the keeping room, the barn jolly again.

The Warren Halloween tradition was to throw a party at the school, one with plenty of candy and a hayride—contributed by a dairy farmer who had a wagon and a smoky old tractor. We went at five-thirty, Pie dressed as a mummy. Wendy had wrapped him up and down with white bandages and she carried a few spares in the pocket of her coat. The bandages inhibited his movement a little, but he didn't care. He remained in role the entire way to the school as we lumbered across the meadow, his arms out, his groans intermittent but persuasive. When we entered the gym, he put new emphasis into the action. He staggered after the little kids and pretended to lose body parts. An excellent mummy. The PTO had done a fine job decorating the place with hay bales and cornstalks. One mother ran an apple-bobbing tub. A little girl in a princess gown chased a few apples around the water, her nose as eager as a crocodile's.

A good, chaotic time. Kids ran everywhere. Someone had square-dance music playing, but the kids paid no attention. The older children—the sixth-graders, mostly—rushed back and forth with an air of seriousness. They had planned tons of tricks to play on the hayriders. Pie had returned from school daily with reports of a boy who had a compelling way of losing his arm, another who had a chain saw ready, without the chain, and another who had such good camouflage he could run invisibly through the forest.

We drank cider and talked to the few parents we knew, then went outside at the sound of the tractor pulling into place. The kids charged out of the gym and clambered onto the hay wagon. Alan, the farmer, waved at everyone; he was a kind-hearted fellow with a broad, happy grin. He wore only a flannel shirt and jeans against the cold.

Wendy and I climbed aboard with Pie between us. He only stayed between us for an instant before he shot to the other side of the wagon to sit with friends. The tractor pulled out at a snail's rate and headed down the old trail. Our house barn looked pretty in the hazy light, the tall front pillars more grand from a distance than they are at close range. Slowly we passed out of all light and the squirming, squealing kids became quiet. Here at last was the old Halloween fright. I looked up and saw a mottled sky. Maples lined the path and touched hands overhead. The forest smelled of pumpkins and wet leaves and one had a sense, looking into the deeper forest, that things were on the move. Animals searched for shelter and the plants had now desperately cast their seed. It was all over, the big show of summer and most of autumn. Now winter waited to come tumbling down the hills. Soon the rivers would slow and the occasional puddle, the weed-edged creeks, would turn into icy windows.

Ahhhhh! Suddenly a bunch of sixth-graders shouted from out of the woods. The children on the wagon pulled their legs up and screamed back. Most of the sixth-graders simply charged the wagon, but one, a boy I had seen around town, hung back and shone a flashlight from his chin up. It turned his hideous mask into something surprisingly terrifying. He appeared a tortured soul living out his soggy life in the woods. Then he lowered the light and charged the wagon, joining all the sixth-graders trying to pull the little children into the woods. The screams clicked around the darkness.

On the way home that night, Pie's bandages had become a straggled affair. He resembled a player who had run through the Thanksgiving Day football game's crepe-paper school colors and had it all stick to him. He had a bag full of candy. He had eaten three cinnamon cupcakes and two apples. He had bobbed and snagged a Macintosh with his front teeth; the water had smeared the scars he had painted on his face at the beginning of the evening. He was tired now, but happy, and I wondered, holding his hand, if he would remember this Halloween long into the future. Probably so. I wondered how scary the sixth-graders appeared to him, how the night and the forest and the hay wagon had registered. I liked that the wagon had pulled us past our house. Whatever else he remembered about Halloween, I liked that he might remember the barn waiting there for him.

turkey

The appreciation of pleasing decay is an important one, because it is so neglected. It is always worthwhile looking at a building twice before pulling it down. A building in a state of pleasing decay should be looked at three times...to be sure, first, that it has no virtues in itself that will be sadly missed; second, that it will not be missed as an enrichment of its present surroundings; third, that it might not form a useful point of focus, whether by agreement or by way of contrast, in future surroundings."

This quote, from *Buildings and Prospects* by John Piper, came to mind when we heard of a barn that had received its death knell. The owner had other plans for the land and he wanted the barn to go. Its time had passed. We learned about it by blind happenstance. A volunteer fireman, a neighbor, told us his squad had been given the barn to burn as a training exercise. Once we got a corn snow, the first granular precipitation of winter, they would burn the barn to the ground.

Fire is the fear of every homeowner, of course, but none so much as a barn owner. Barns are wood, plain and simple, and usually dry wood at that. I've read they make a beautiful fire. The only equal to a barn fire is a blaze at sea. Wooden ships and barns, to no one's surprise, burn about the same way. They go fast and they go bright. Both sit on flat surfaces, their height spectacular in combustion.

I asked my friend if he could direct me to the barn. He said he wasn't sure about the trespassing concerns, but it was a few miles along a dirt road we both knew. It wasn't much of a barn, he said. The farmer owner had called several demolition firms to inquire whether the boards, beams, and purlins might be worth extracting. They were worth something, he was told, but when weighed against the labor cost of getting them out, the profit would be negligible—assuming, naturally, that he could get a firm to do it in the first place.

It turned out not to be much of a barn at all. I was curious and drove over to it one day in late November and parked on the dirt road overlooking it. It was a shed, really, a gable-and-hip barn about twenty feet square. Someone had run a roof off the southern end as a place to store wood, or maybe old plows, but its useful life clearly lay behind it. The owner had apparently picked it clean of anything he wanted. The remaining bents, the bright ribs on the place, had cracked and folded. The entire structure leaned thirty degrees to one side, a stumble that would never permit it to regain its balance. Besides, whatever purpose the building had provided long ago had now become obsolete. No one farmed nearby; no animals grazed the old fields. A lone apple tree marked the only sign of domestication.

As I studied it, though, I saw movement in what must have been the hayloft. I stayed and watched and in the gloomy light two raccoons waddled out of the topmost level. The barn had become a tree to the coons, and I supposed it afforded pretty good shelter. The coons lifted onto their back legs to inspect me, determined I was merely a truck, and continued on their way. They waddled up and over a stone wall that ran at the eastern edge of the old meadow. Their backsides were the last I saw of them.

The barn burned a few weeks later, right before Thanksgiving. A brief corn snow powdered the hills and the fire department got their exercise. My friend called me to go along, but I wasn't around that day. He said the barn burned without any backfires, meaning it had gone straight up. The bents had collapsed one by one. The exercise hadn't been an attempt to save the barn. It had merely vetted their equipment, made certain they could respond appropriately. The farmer plowed in the burn, but he left the fieldstone foundation exposed to help himself to the stones.

It was difficult to romanticize the barn. One couldn't argue that its end hadn't arrived. Time had made it derelict, a gray ghost of something spent. The dignity of the framing, however, still spoke of men coming together to erect a substantial structure. That counted for something. It had endured a hundred years or more and that counted for something, too. In that time the barn had become the focus of that small landscape, and when I drove past months later, I hardly recognized the field. The field now matched a thousand New England plots, a dipped concave in a granite ring, anonymous except for the pines and stone wall. The apple tree remained, but the foundation had grown over, pokeweed and berry bushes taking hold. The green curl of the forest had pushed closer. In ten years it would be new growth.

I thought of the raccoons. Resourceful fellows. They had probably found a knotty pine, no doubt, and taken up headquarters there. It occurred to me, though, as I passed the field that America possesses no noble ruins. Europeans routinely accept, and live beside, the devastated shell of a tenth- or eleventh-century dwelling. We don't abide such things in America; we knock them down and clean them up. Land has to be in motion. The new must replace the old instantly. That is why, maybe, I had felt saddened at seeing the barn removed. Barns, alone among our buildings, are temporarily permitted the dignity of pleasant decay. It may not be fair to judge a barn by today's needs. We should see it for the lichen it has grown, and for the burled wood, weathered for centuries, that cannot be taken from it except by flame.

❀

We kept an annual bird list, noting visitors to our feeders from our kitchen window. Ironically, as we approached Thanksgiving, a flock of turkeys began clustering around the feeders first thing each dawn. In the cold gray morning, coffee in hand, we watched the turkeys peck and hunt around the feeders, their beaks plucking black beads of sunflowers like a surgeon's forceps removing a bullet from a cowboy's leg. Later, when they left, we went outside and studied their footprints—Mercedes automobile insignias, a thousand triangles with a tail—and tried to follow them to their denning yards. We made progress on the trail. We followed them as honey hunters follow bees: Each time the tracks vanished, we marked the spot and went from there the next time. Beeline. The tracks led us deep into the woods on a northeast course, but eventually we gave up. The turkeys took to the trees too often and slept through the night haunched in oaks and maples, vigilant in windless hollows.

But we heard them; and we heard about them. Turkeys, we were told, were making a healthy comeback in New England. Driving to work, we often spotted them in the bamboo forests of harvested corn. Black and definite, they moved against the white backdrop, black mercury dots in the surrounding quiet. Mornings we heard them clucking and cackling, feeding in sideways pecks, ready to be away at our approach.

The turkey tanks at the Plymouth Shop'N'Save filled with Butterballs. Pie, understandably, had difficulty reconciling the squawking, vital birds we saw in the wild with the yellow, goose-fleshed carcasses we prodded in their cooling bins. But the turkeys proved merely a symptom: Animals were on the move and we spotted their preparations everywhere. Underneath a forgotten bale of hay, Pie found the tunneled maze formed by a family of voles. Mice entered the barn and we kept traps set under the kitchen sink, the snap of their peanut-butter deaths going off late at night. Migrating birds spooled around the yard, waiting for a wind to set them moving south. A pair of northern cardinals settled into serious feeding on our sunflower seeds and cracked corn, the male as bright as a brake light.

Ten days before Thanksgiving, in a move that bordered on craziness, Wendy and I decided to renovate the kitchen. The renovation had been on our list, but it had required the quieter season, the slow push inside, to start us. Besides, we had people visiting for Thanksgiving. Wendy's mother, Sherry, was due in from Florida. Her sister Shea planned to arrive from Boston, along with her husband, Ben. Wendy's friend Jude, and Jude's children, Parker and Ian. Dave, the ex-Navy sergeant, from the séance. And more. Plans swirled around and the telephone rang early in the morning and late at night with additions and subtractions. We needed a big bird, we agreed, probably around thirty pounds. Wendy started a shopping list on a roll of adding-machine paper. It grew longer every day,

But first the kitchen. Wendy's handiest sister, Sarah, agreed to come up early and help with the renovation. Her visit coincided with a neighbor's offer of a Vermont Castings Resolute stove. They had no use for it—did we want it? The stove had been manufactured in 1979, but it still burned beautifully. It had been in service up until the end of the summer, but now, heading into Thanksgiving, the neighbors wanted to clean out a guest bedroom. They had a new stove on order, a larger one that threw more heat, and they didn't want to store the stove. Come and get it, they said. If we didn't take it, they promised to put it on the street next to a FREE sign. Free stoves didn't last long in this part of New Hampshire.

Dave called and offered to come up early, too. He had tools, time, and a strong back. Suddenly the barn became a busy place.

Shortly after he arrived, we rented a hand truck from the Burning Bush, the local hardware store, and drove the Dodge pickup to our neighbors'. The Vermont Casting stove was cast iron and putty colored; it weighed somewhere around 500 pounds. We had little difficulty loading it onto the hand truck, but it provided the usual problems going through doors and down stairs. We backed the Dodge up so that the tailgate met the back porch. Dave tilted it way back on the hand truck, and we slid it into the Dodge.

Using six-inch insulated stovepipe, Wendy cut through a wall into the last thimble in the chimney. While Dave and I backed the stove into the main-floor guest bedroom, Wendy and Sarah cut fire shields out of aluminum and fit them into place. We propped the stove on flat fieldstone, leveled it, then checked everything over again. When we satisfied ourselves that our fittings worked to code, we used scraps of birch and started a fire in the stove. The firebox was not large—it was a Resolute, the smallest stove in the Vermont Casting line—but it threw a marvelous heat. In no time the guest bedroom heated to sixty, then seventy. We opened the stove doors—it could double as a fireplace—and we discovered we could lie in bed and watch the birch hunks turn the color of raw pumpkin. Wendy's mom would stay here; as a mom and a thin-blooded Floridian, she had first dibs. That was resolved.

The success of the stove installation jazzed us all. Suddenly we wanted to turn on music, to stay up late, to finish projects. Transistor-radio nights, in other words. Sarah and Dave slept in the other two guest rooms—one above the kitchen, the other catty-cornered from Pie's room. Although we had hosted a crowd at Halloween, now the barn really seemed to show us what it could do. The large keeping room, the bubbling fireplace, kept us centered. The space was not static, as my architect friend, Jennifer, would have pointed out. People felt good being in such a large, uncluttered space. The French doors pushed out into the meadow, and we had the warmth of the fireplace behind us as we looked out.

We yanked out the kitchen sink. We yanked out the flimsy counters, the rickety shelves. The basic structure of the kitchen was ideal, but it had always served merely as a summer preparation station. It had been carved out of an old stable, the beams rubbed shiny by cow rumps and horse necks. The floor, in its first transition to a living space, had been painted red and cream in alternating squares. The windows, original casement windows, opened onto the garden and the hydrangea bushes. Hook-and-eye closures kept them in place. Someone along the way had built a breakfast bar on the northern end of the kitchen, and this we decided to enhance by hanging a miniature track-lighting strip above it. Everything else went. Wendy and Sarah gutted the interior, then made a huge list of things to buy from Home Depot. They disappeared on a sister run while Dave and I, still energized, headed to the Baker River to collect rocks for a fire pit.

The Baker River ran so cold that to step into the current, as we were forced to do, made you feel a simple knock on your ankle bone would shatter it like a piece of Turkish taffy. I stood in the water for a while and handed up rocks the size of Jack Russell terriers to Dave. He lugged them to the truck, then we switched positions. The river had a billion rocks and we were selective about which one we chose. We wanted a uniform fire ring; we wanted one around which cowboys might gladly congregate.

We drove back to the barn with thirty rocks knocking around the flatbed. We selected a spot halfway to the sheep fence and backed the truck into position. We rolled the rocks into a circle, the diameter five feet across, and situated maple stumps like elf stools around the fire. A fairy ring. As we worked, John Lester's sheep peered at us. They regarded the rocks with placid faces, their jaws working sideways, their bellies as brown as pencil shavings. We piled brush on the fire ring for a bonfire. The sheep scattered when we dragged the brush too close to their enclosure. But they returned as soon as we passed, curious to discover the meaning of the branches.

Dave and I built a horseshoe pit next. We had time; we were in the mood; it was easy. Pie came home from school and helped us. We measured the distance between the poles, then framed out two pits with scraps of lumber left over from Wendy's insulating job. While Dave and Pie raked the pits into shape, I drove to the town yard and filled up four buckets with road sand. We spooned the sand around the poles. As we played the first game, a wind came up and began tripping the treetops. The pines bent and shook and we looked up when the hardest winds blew. Clouds moved across the barn roof; the weather vane cut the clouds like pinking shears passing through batting. It was autumn and everything was in motion.

Wendy and Sarah returned at sunset. We unloaded on the back porch, arranging everything according to Wendy's specifications. Hardware: PVC piping, clamps, nails, screws, drill bits, a welding torch, three tanks of propane. Lumber: a dozen two-by-four-by-eights; two twelve-foot lengths of black countertop material, complete with splashboard; pine shelving; glue; a nail set. Wendy had bought white cotton work gloves for all of us. She passed them around and supervised us as we wrote our names on the fists. She also passed around chicken-breast sandwiches, chips, and pickles so sharply dill they fought a duel with our tongues. We ate next to the fire, gazing at the lazy heat. Then we went to work.

Wendy and Sarah built a frame. Wendy knew, from working with her dad, the appropriate heights. A standard counter, she said, is one yard high. A kick board, in most instances, is four inches. She pounded nails into the floor, sawed, pounded more nails. By ten o'clock, lights bright, we had the skeleton of the counters. I proposed stopping, but Wendy and Sarah wouldn't hear it. They pulled the countertop into place, sank the sink into a cutout rectangle, and began running flexible piping up through the floor. Dave ran a bead of grout under the lip of the sink. I went downstairs and yelled up when they twisted this pipe, that one, the one over there. We connected the dishwasher, the hot water, cold water, hose spray. At midnight Wendy strapped a pair of safety glasses on and struck up the gas torch. Bending close, she soldered shut the sink connections. Water restored.

We yelped outside and grabbed beer from the porch. A Wednesday in November. A friend had sent an asteroid warning via E-mail, and for a while we circled around the back meadow, eyes up. Wendy saw a shooting star. So did Sarah. Dave and I lit some brush in the fire pit and got a good flame going. Coyotes began calling at the moon, or at the fire, or at the black tree boughs that now made the night darker. Or maybe, Sarah said, they howled at the shooting stars.

In bed that night, Wendy told me about the big cut. The big cut was coming. It was the cut, done on the reverse, where one portion of the counter must meet, at an exact angle, with the other portion of the counter. No fudging. They either fit or they didn't, and because the countertops cost seventy-five dollars a slab, she wanted it right. The trouble was, she said, she had been turning the cut over and over in her mind. Doing the insulation, she had been forced to scribe the boards next to the chimney stones. Scribing is trying to cut wood to meet the variations of an uneven surface. The stones had been impossible, the scribing so painful as to be nearly maddening, but that was nothing, *nothing*, Wendy said, compared to the big cut. She had to cut the second piece to match the piece under the sink. She couldn't blow it.

I comforted her as much as I could. I promised her coffee first thing in the morning. I told her we had done a day's work, a day and a half's work, and we were right on schedule. Wendy said she had already begun to have turkey dreams. What if she forgot to turn on the oven? What if the turkey burned? What if it came back to life, sprang up on its basted legs, and began wandering around the barn, searching for its head? Then we lay for a long time staring out the window, trying to see an asteroid streak across our sky.

In the morning we drove to White River Junction, Vermont, and visited the Vermont Salvage store there. Vermont Salvage is a huge, abandoned railroad warehouse, in which someone had conceived the clever idea of collecting salvage from old buildings. Walking in the unheated space, coffee and bagels gripped in our mittens, we wandered around the crowded aisles, marveling at the sights in each direction. A thousand doorknobs. Finger locks for ancient doors. Fifty door chimes, all antique. Church pews, spiral staircases, claw-foot tubs, toilets, steam tables, confession booths, glass cigarette stands, barn doors, hayracks, freight elevator fencing, skylights, radiators, bricks, bowling lanes, slate, pedestals, casters, marble balustrades, window mullions, elf statuary, andirons, wainscoting, stacks of school desks thirty feet high. The owner, a broad fellow who sat in the one heated section near the front of the store, told us to call him if we needed anything. A few young guys lugged fresh wares into various corners of the building, all of them wearing Vermont-green sweatshirts, hoods up, eyes down. Two employees carried in a section of wrought-iron fencing, the border of a graveyard or vestry lawn, stored against future use.

We were after windows. Wendy wanted old windows instead of cupboard doors. We rode a freight elevator to a basement level, and there, stacked against framed two-by-fours, were all the windows the world had ever known. Conceive of a window, and it was there. Wendy had exact measurements, so we were able to ignore countless piles, but that still left a hundred, two hundred racks of windows. Dave and Sarah wandered off; Wendy and I, coffee handed back and forth by whomever tended the pile, lifted windows up as if exhibiting the results of a corporate flow chart. Finding one—which we did after a few minutes—meant nothing, because we couldn't count on finding a mate. We needed six windows to be on the safe side in case one broke during installation.

Truly, this was the haunt of the Count of Monte Cristo, of Quasimodo. The enormous wooden beams of the basement—a basement built to support a factory—made our barn beams appear modest twigs in comparison. Steam lifted from the water pipes. One could imagine cannons here, or draught horses mashing oats and pulling engine turbines down engineering rip lines. AMERICA AT WORK would be the motto beneath such a picture. One could imagine progress, industry, as easily as metal shackles hammered into the wall, a dungeon of cruel waiting and despair.

We found the windows before we had finished our coffees. Wendy actually shrieked when I held up a likely bunch near the middle of the dreary basement. She whipped out the tape measure and did a series of calculations more rapidly than I had thought possible. Perfect, she said. We counted the windows. Seven in all. They were eight-paned windows, once used, we guessed, in a summer cottage somewhere. The cordovan paint showed signs of wear and the window caulking was shot, but Wendy promised they were the windows she wanted.

We bought them for $28, four bucks a window. Dave and Sarah commented that it was one of the strangest, most interesting places they had ever visited. We drove home, stopping to pick up silver hinges for the windows. Then we went back to the kitchen.

Things moved even faster now. Wendy and Sarah hung the windows as cupboard doors. Wendy had been correct. They fit perfectly. The cordovan paint even matched the maroon squares on the floor. Finally it was time for the big cut. I tried to make sense of the problem, but it was the sort of three-dimensional

conception that perplexes me immediately. Wendy used a pro-
tractor and charted the forty-five-degree angle on the first
piece. Then she used a pencil and scribed the reverse angle on
the final countertop, narrating as she went. She flipped it and
examined the potential angle. Then she flipped it again. Back
and forth, back and forth, all of us watching. No one had the
courage to speak.

Wendy cut the countertop freehand with a power saw. She
shook her head as she finished it. She didn't like it. When we flipped
it over, it matched beautifully. She still shook her head. Naturally
we would apply caulking to bring the two pieces together.
But Wendy sputtered and complained that she had messed up the
cut. We didn't see it. She took a break and went outside.

The kitchen, remarkably, had reached a stopping point.
Wendy wanted to do more sometime, but not now. Not today or
the next day or anytime before Thanksgiving. We had improved
the space dramatically, while the good bones of the room
remained. Because it had been a stable, the overhead beams lay
exposed across bigger, more solid beams. A barn inside a barn,
sort of. We had installed a dishwasher, cleaned the oven, made
sure everything worked. When Wendy came back inside, she ran
her hands up and down the matching cuts. No one, really, would
notice any separation between the two top pieces. I hugged her
and told her it looked great.

We spent the afternoon organizing the kitchen. Now that
she had the kitchen design at least moving in the direction she
wanted, she felt comfortable pulling out the odds and ends she
had purchased at auctions and yard sales. A red bread box. A
drink set, complete with martini glasses. Wooden molding,
nailed above the breakfast bar, for wine glasses. A nutcracker
and a bowl of walnuts. Months earlier she had finished a piece of
furniture—a jelly cabinet, we guessed—that fit perfectly in one
corner of the kitchen. A red-trimmed baking table with metal
wings that opened if one needed to roll out particularly large

crusts. A dozen spatulas, wire whisks, a butcher's cleaver. Now we had a kitchen. I could tell Wendy was happy. She didn't leave the kitchen for the entire afternoon. She wanted to cook.

I brought out a present I had been saving: twenty oversize plates from Mesa. They looked to be double the size of standard plates. The plates were mismatched, either rowboat blue or pale sage, and they had a pottery feeling that seemed right for a country home. They struck me as appropriately large, useful, and plain. I gave them to Wendy in a huge brown box that I set on the breakfast table. She opened them slowly, as happy as I had ever seen her. She leaned across the breakfast counter and kissed me. Now we had a table. Now we had dishes. Thanksgiving was here.

The night before Thanksgiving, I poured Wendy a glass of merlot and we sat together in the kitchen playing backgammon. Dave and Sarah had taken Pie off to see *Toy Story 2*. The turkey, a thirty-one-pound Butterball, lay on the baking table, white as winter slush. Wendy had spent the day preparing food while I cleaned house and ran errands, brought in wood, and swept the outside porch. Around the kitchen, stacked like brown nickels, pie crusts stood ready to receive their fillings—apple, pumpkin, mince. A beaver-size hump of stuffing bread rested next to the pie crusts, and next to that Wendy had arranged cans of cranberries, creamed onions, and chicken broth.

A wind pushed the barn and now and then we heard the weather vane turn its tired arrow. Branches from the hydrangea clicked against the casement windows. The woodstove adjusted logs to the flame, letting them sink into coals. We felt heat pushing across the room and over the breakfast bar. The house smelled of winter and the cold scent of boots and gloves and plastic shovels. Besides the wind and the occasional log shift in the woodstove, the house was silent.

As we played, Wendy talked a little about Thanksgivings growing up. One of the things, she said, she had loved about her mother's and father's Thanksgivings was the open invitation to anyone who looked to be sitting alone on that day. They had invited everyone—strangers, bag boys from the grocery store, the man who fixed their cars, exchange students—and made room for them around the table. Thanksgiving, she said, had always been the best holiday. No presents to mar it, no rush to get things wrapped, no balance to maintain about who gave what to whom. It was easier to stretch a turkey, she said, than to stretch Christmas presents.

For my part, I remembered the last Thanksgiving my mother had been alive. Late at night in the kitchen, she enlisted me to yank the entrails out of the turkey. They had been placed inside the body cavity by the butcher and I suppose they had partially frozen there. I pulled them free—the giblets, the heart, the inverted neck—like a man delivering sheep. My mother put them together in a baking pan, then poured salt in my hands and told me to massage the turkey all around. I liked working with her. I liked being of some use to her, never guessing that her hands had become too weak to trust. I felt aware, too, that I had become substantially larger than she. She struck me as a mother out of a book or a poem, a mom of gray hair and anxious cardigans.

After backgammon Wendy and I took advantage of the temporary orderliness we had imposed on the barn in preparation for Thanksgiving and we made rounds to come up with a punch list. Item by item we wanted to check off what remained to be done. We had entered the middle of the tunnel where it was hard to know if we were heading backward or forward. The list, we figured, would give us an idea. Wendy carried a yellow legal pad and wrote down suggestions. We went top to bottom. In no particular order, we made the following list:

1. Finish kitchen renovation
2. Get chimney pointed; repair cement cap
3. Septic: check in spring
4. Paint southern side of the barn; get bids for the rest of the structure
5. Get estimates about heating systems in case the coal gets to be too much
6. Paint garden fence
7. Ask about replacement windows? Would they fit with the interior?
8. Wainscoting for the walls?
9. Sink clothesline; laundry chute?
10. Do a water test
11. Check beams for insects
12. Get and install fire extinguishers
13. Smoke detectors
14. Find out cost of grapple load of cordwood: roughly nine cords worth
15. Cut three cherry trees that obscure view of mountains
16. Put orange tape around fence struts to warn snowmobilers
17. Prune apple tree
18. Plant forsythia and lilac

We stopped ourselves short of twenty. Happily, most of the list did not strike us as urgent. One of the luxuries of taking up permanent residence was the hope that we would have a long, long time to complete the renovations we planned. On the same yellow pad we wrote down a list of recreational things we wanted to do outside.

1. Climb Mount Moosilauke
2. Kayak the Baker River from our house to Plymouth
3. Kayak the Connecticut River from First Connecticut Lake to ocean

4. Sleep out more
5. Walk the Appalachian Trail from Hanover to Warren
6. Attend more auctions
7. Buy a piece of land way up in the mountains, someplace without road access
8. Build a log structure or a stone house for the hell of it
9. Winter camp once or twice

By the time we finished, Pie and Dave and Sarah had returned. Dave made a fire and we moved everything over there. Pie got ready for bed. He gave everyone a hug good night and I went with Wendy to tuck him into bed. I liked thinking of him deep under his covers, listening to us play Trivial Pursuit next to the fire. I wondered if he would remember this Thanksgiving, remember the barn as it looked on our first Thanksgiving, or whether his Thanksgivings would run together as one block of time. It struck me again—as it had at Halloween—that we were in the business of constructing his past.

In the morning I rose early and immediately set a fire going. We had learned the trick of banking a fire. In Colonial times, they had heated exclusively with fireplaces, so they had become masters at forwarding heat from night to morning. We buried the fire in its own ashes now, uncovering the egg-shaped hunks of charcoal first thing in the morning. When I scraped the ashes free and added birch sticks, the fire nibbled, then ate. With the light barely pushing over Carr Mountain, I got the flames lifting waist high.

Wendy clambered out by the time the coffeepot finished wheezing through its morning routine. The phone rang almost immediately. Wendy's sister. What could they bring? Anything last-minute that we needed? Then Wendy spoke for a few minutes with her mom, who had spent the night outside of Boston. When Wendy hung up, she looked at me, dazed, and said we had a lot of people coming. She went to shower.

I brought in more wood, let D Dog take care of business, then did the rounds of bird feeders. The turkeys hadn't shown up, apparently, because I couldn't spot their tracks. By the time I returned to the kitchen, Wendy handed me tablecloths and sheets and asked me to take them out and start shaking. I stood on the back porch fluffing the sheets and tablecloths into the air, then letting them drift down. I glanced at the thermometer: forty-four degrees. The Maine weather stick on the porch beam, an alder twig that rose in good weather and sank in poor, extended horizontally to the earth, calling for fair skies.

We stayed busy around the house, trying our best to help Wendy without getting in her way. She was the cook. Sarah woke and headed right into the kitchen, ready to chop and dice. The phone rang repeatedly. Wendy remained unflappable. Everything would work, she seemed to say. Nothing got to her. And soon the house smelled of roasting turkey, yams, stuffing. We baked cookies on the dry back of the enormous woodstove.

We heard the first car door around noon. Everyone in the house froze. So soon? But it was time; the invitations had been set for around noon, but we had lost track. Wendy caught my eye and sent me out to greet the newcomers. D Dog beat me to the door. She barked and then began wagging her tail. Company.

I stepped out onto the porch, realizing, as I did so, that this was the time of my hosting. For years I went to my mother's table, then to my sister, Cathy's, but now it was my time. Whatever I had, I knew, I would gladly share with the people pulling into the driveway. For just an instant I remembered my father stepping on his back porch, waving to me as I returned from college. Now I was the age he must have been in those memories.

Hello, hello, hello, I said, stupidly, inevitably. I raised my hand and waved while they backed out of their cars, stomping their legs alive from sleep, rubbing their eyes. Pie's Aunt Shea reached back inside for a plate, while Sherry, Wendy's mom, lifted a wreath carefully out of the back seat. She removed it like a life-saver from a difficult package. When it finally popped free, she turned and smiled at the barn, at the mountains beyond, at the sight, I suppose, of D Dog and me. But before they could say anything, Pie burst from the basement door and flung himself on his grandma. He had a thousand things to say, a thousand things to show everyone. "Mom," he yelled over his shoulder, "they're here, they're here."

✲

In the huddle, in the middle of the meadow, I called the Russian Polka. The Russian Polka was a pass pattern that, in my entire career as a amateur quarterback, had never failed. It required the two receivers to run square-ins, then, when they approached each other, to hook their arms through the arm of the other receiver and spin, heading off in a different direction. A Polka. When I called the pattern for Shea and Wendy, they immediately liked the idea. Just as quickly, they began to argue about which arm to use—right or left—but they headed to the line of scrimmage anyway. Ben, the six-foot-four captain of the other team and also Shea's husband, began to yell that we had something up our sleeves. Dave, also on Ben's team, shouted to Pie that he had to count, then rush us right away. Pie was designated pass rusher. He was getting tired of counting alligators and Mississippis.

The audience on the porch—Marion, a friend of the family's; Sherry; Jude; and a few of the smaller kids—cheered as we came out to the line of scrimmage. I called signals. Pie snapped the ball, because he snapped for both sides, and Wendy and Shea ran the pattern. They met in the middle of the field with a screech, began to laugh, then hooked their arms and spun around. Shea came open right away and I lofted a soft pass to her. She caught in, ran three feet, then dropped it. Game over, more or less.

Ben's team yabbered at us, calling us sissies and pansies and anything else they could think of. Someone on the porch asked who won. Wendy excused herself and headed back to the house. She was nervous about the turkey, although her mother, who had cooked a million birds over the years, had assured her it was okay to take time out for football. I watched her go, feeling at the same time the nice muscle roughness that comes from unaccustomed exercise. My hands felt cold; so did my neck and ears. I remembered playing pickup football at Tomaques Park when I was twelve. On a day like this one—chilly and gray—we had finished our game, then come together and howled. I don't know who started it, or why, but all of us boys, bony twelve-year-olds who typically believed themselves too mature to be howling like wolves, ringed in a dog circle and lifted our voices together. No reason, I suppose, except the cold, grass-stained knees of our jeans, the icy feeling inside our sweatshirts, the tundra sense of being out on a flat plain at nightfall. Boys being boys. Walking back to the barn now, the welcoming lights strong in the windows, the fire crisp in its hearth, I felt divided. I was here at the barn, certainly, but part of me had traveled back to Tomaques Park, felt that boy pleasure of loud noises and pack activity. When Pie came up to me, I threw a hand on his shoulder and told him he had been an expert pass rusher, that he had done a good job. He walked with me for a few paces, then darted ahead, and again, for an instant, I remembered the feeling of coming home on an early winter day such as this one, the stiffness of my fingers as I turned the doorknob and stepped inside.

What better feeling is there, in the end, than being outside and returning to a warm house and the smell of roasting food? The turkey smelled of a hundred holidays past. Sherry had turned on the lamps around the barn, so suddenly we were indisputably inside and the gray, solemn day had been pushed back outside. Time for drinks. Ben helped me as a bartender, while Sarah turned on a tape of Ella Fitzgerald & Louis Armstrong. We poured wine, a Scotch or two, soft drinks. Pie asked for hot chocolate and we put a teakettle to boil on the woodstove. Dave threw two more logs on the fire. Birch and ash, I thought. One bright, one hot.

At four, Wendy started enlisting us all to carry food to the table. She passed things through the breakfast bar and we set them in place. The table—the Irish wake table—stretched halfway across the room. Wendy had set the table with the large barn plates I had given her. They looked right for the table, properly sized for the space. Marion had set up the requisite card table for the children at the far end of the barn, closest to the meadow, and the kids clustered there, arguing quietly about who would sit next to whom. We opened five bottles of wine and set them at strategic intervals along the adult table. Shea lit the candles. We turned out extraneous lamps around the barn, then threw more wood into the fire.

Wendy carried the turkey out and everyone clapped. Then, still standing, I said that I welcomed them all, that we were happy to have everyone here. I said that though we were not religious people, there might be religious people in attendance, and maybe we could have a moment of silence for them to return thanks. Thanksgiving was, after all, a day that pushed us to such thoughts.

I held Wendy's hand while the moment passed, then someone, Ben, I think, toasted the table and we returned the toast. Then we all sat and dinner began.

Plates everywhere. Wendy carved. I poured wine and gave the nod to Ben to keep the wine flowing as well. He understood. Yams, mashed potatoes, creamed onions, stuffing with sausage, olives, pickles, celery, squash, turkey. Wendy sliced the turkey in white folds and passed the platter around. The kids' table called for drumsticks, for some reason a universal favorite of children. I filled my plate and ate like a drummer, my fork ticking around this edge first, then that edge. Delicious food. Often I caught

Wendy's eye. This was what we had hoped for. Here it was. The red wine shimmered in the glasses, rubies, prisms. The kids, loud and a little tired, popped up and down from the children's table. Noise everywhere. The barn, I saw, could be mildly formal while not stifling people. Ella Fitzgerald sang. The windows to the back meadow stood black as crows.

When the meal slowed, we handed out papers detailing a haiku contest. This had been my idea. We had all experienced Thanksgiving dinners where people had gobbled the food—in a nice way, naturally—and then felt compelled to push away from the table. Sleepy, folks sprawled out on the couch and cut short the dinner. Wendy and I had talked about keeping people at table, something not all Americans are easy about, and I had devised an exercise from my classrooms. We handed out the following challenge with assigned teams:

Haiku: A three-line poem, Japanese in origin, narrowly conceived of as a fixed form in which the lines contain respectively five, seven, and five syllables. Haiku are generally concerned with some aspect of nature and present a single image or two juxtaposed images without comment, relying on suggestion rather than on explicit statement to communicate meaning.

Though it didn't fit the syllabic count, we gave an example from Basho (1644-1694), the Japanese master:

The falling flower
I saw drift back to the branch
Was a butterfly.

The rules were simple. Each group of four people could submit one haiku. The group would be judged on the quality of the haiku and on the dramatic quality of the reading, so each group had to select a representative wisely. The winners would be chosen by the ancient and true method of a clap vote.

More wine. To my delight, our guests took up the challenge. Huddling in different sections of the table, they scribbled on the pads of paper I had set aside. The kids tried for a while, then asked to be excused. Meanwhile the adults counted syllables on their fingers. That was one of the rules—the syllabic count had to be exact. Or, at least, the group had to make the rest of the table believe that breaking the syllabic count was in the interest of great poetic feeling. That provision, Wendy and I hoped, would put the cat among the pigeons.

The kids wandered off downstairs. Then they came back and asked if they could go out. They wanted to play hide-and-seek. Jude took over and helped the littlest ones into their snowsuits. They filed out like Easter marshmallow ducks. Wendy called Pie over and told him he was responsible for everyone's safety. *Use your head*, which was a mantra we repeated to him a thousand times a week. He gave a chimp nod and headed off.

The haiku readings proved hilarious. We had imbibed just enough wine to make people jovial and critical at the same time. The runner-up went like this:

Black crow lights on fence
The only movement today
In a soft white field.

People shouted that it was too derivative, that Wallace Stevens had cornered the market on black birds in white fields years ago. The winner went like this:

Puddles shatter when
The gently falling raindrops
Bounce back to the sky.

Remarkably, people actually gave the haiku an appreciative silence after Marion had finished reading it. Then we called for a second reading.

We were still listening to the reading when the kids spilled back into the room. *Snow, snow, it's snowing,* they yelled. They were so excited we couldn't ignore them. Everyone pushed away from the table and headed out onto the porch. Snow fell in white puffs over the meadow. We all stood watching. It wasn't much of a snow—a deer snow, good for tracking deer back to their yards. A squall. But it was the first recognizable snow of the year and the kids leaped off the porch, shouting, happy. Out in the meadow the hiders waited for the seekers. We watched them running into the darkness, snow collecting on their shoulders and on their hats.

pine
fort

The first true snow arrived on a chicken-soup afternoon in December, twelve days before Christmas. It began as clouds covering the moon. For three days beforehand we had experienced Wolf Moons, the bright, crisp moons that come only in winter, under which wolves are said to gather in the rigid moonbeams and dance behind the pine glades. The local Pemigewassett tribes believed that by throwing sticks and spears at the moon it might be hastened from the sky, thereby hastening spring's approach. But I had no interest in having the moons gone. Each night they slid quietly onto the horizon and pushed a yellow triangle across the frost. I waited for them to appear nightly, then walked D Dog around our loop of land. Cold pushed through my lungs and bit at something inside. Winter had stopped fooling around now. Everywhere I saw signs of its presence. Lilacs cowered in icy clumps, and the goldenrod, afraid of nothing all autumn long, turned black and decrepit, its fall to the earth held by blank cold.

On the night before the snow, in the last Wolf Moon, we ice-skated on the fishpond. We did not know it well and could not fully trust it, but I took a shovel out and scraped up the hoar-frost from a small ring beside the shore. Then after dinner we took our skates out to the frozen bank and laced them up. It had been years since I had skated outdoors, but the memory of boyhood, of Ghost Pond decades ago, came back to me instantly. Pie was not a steady skater, but Wendy proved to be as good as she always was at winter sports. She skated backward with Pie's hands in hers. He performed the childish step-skate of all wobbly beginners. *Click, click, click* his skates tapped on the ice, like a teacher trying to get a classroom's attention. Wendy's skates made white, sweeping sounds. The moon stayed bright enough so that we might have read if we'd liked. D Dog followed from the edge of the pond, amazed that we could glide on water.

The weather report called for snow the next day, but I did not believe it. The Maine weather stick we had nailed to our porch beam stood exactly level with the earth. That meant a fair day. By noon, however, snow had become a taste in the air and I found myself drawn outside to finish errands I had not worried much about until then. We had already transported the wood inside, stacked the coal, placed the green True Value garbage cans under cover. In the dimming afternoon I hurried about with a wheelbarrow of pine boughs and laced them around winterberry bushes, around spindly crab apple trees, giving their roots what protection I could. I fed the birds and hung out suet. I rode the lone bicycle still remaining on the farmer's porch down the curve to the barn overhang, where it retired peacefully, finished for another summer. Then, to tempt fate, I started the snowblower. It clogged and sputtered but finally popped to life. I let it run a while to flex its muscles. When I shut it down it backfired at the last, notifying me that its cooperation was temporary at best.

Four o'clock is the winter hour. Light gives up on cold December days and pulls back away from the earth. Walking with D Dog, I watched it recede. By the time Pie climbed over the fence, returning from an after-school play session, we hardly saw his red jacket in the gloom. I yanked off my mittens and made an owl call to him. He answered back with a shout. D Dog galloped to greet him and they danced for a while in the mad way of boys and dogs, round and round, happy with each other. Then Pie chucked his backpack and ran out to meet me halfway around the loop, his cheeks red as flannel.

"It's going to snow," I told him.

"A lot?" he asked.

"Might be."

He did a conga dance, wiggling his hips and butt, singing in syncopation that *yes he would have no school, no school, yes he would have no school tomorrow*. He performed his dance roughly to the beat of "Yes, We Have No Bananas." He pretended to sit on D Dog and ride her around. He finished by furiously throwing the tennis balls we had found toward the school. *Snow, snow, snow,* he chanted at the sky.

Brueghel's painting of hunters returning to the village on a winter's evening has always been a favorite of mine. *Hunters in Snow.* Together with Pie and D Dog, we composed a scene not unlike the one Brueghel captured. Light tricked us by staying an instant too long, making us nearly regretful at relinquishing it. We wanted to be inside, true, but something kept us out. The light of the barn—and it was a good, soft light, coming from many windows—smiled to have us in, but the late afternoon would not let us depart. We did another loop, purposeless, not talking very much. The joy Pie had expressed a few moments earlier had been eclipsed by the gray moon that fought against the white clouds.

Ironically the snow appeared without our notice while we sat at dinner. Pie detected it first, probably because he was absolutely prayerful about it. Each glance to the window could mean a day free of school. When he finally spotted the flakes, he whispered as though afraid his voice could send the storm fleeing. We went outside, and D Dog went with us. The snow had started by brushing away the frost and dead grass. A fair wind blew from the northwest, bringing with it a soft moisture. The flakes fell large and hungry; I did not think it would last very long unless the flakes hardened and became smaller. The snow brought pause. Not only had we halted dinner, but everything in the meadow had become still and quiet. This was the great holiday season, our first Christmas at home, and the snow felt appropriate and long anticipated.

Pie finally gave out a whoop, shouted to the sky that it was snowing, then ran and did a small canter off the porch. Then he had to make a snowball—the last one had been in May, after all—and he waggled it by his side, promising to hit us if we did not dance. Wendy told him to put it down, but she didn't mean it. He lobbed it at us and we moved aside easily. When he saw D Dog eye the snowball, he began throwing loosely packed snowballs for her, letting her jump to catch them.

Pie went to bed that night hopeful. He kicked his legs under the blanket and settled in with difficulty. We let him read *Calvin & Hobbes* for a while to calm down. He asked a dozen times, before we kissed him good night, if we thought, really, he was being serious now, no fooling around, if he would have school tomorrow. We told him frogs decided about rain and snow. Frogs could ride in clouds, we said, and if they needed to go see their relatives, well, then they would let it snow a foot or more. If not, he was out of luck.

We tucked him in and then went out one last time to study the night. We left the porch light off so that the only light came from the swirl of snow toward us. I thought of Joyce's line from *The Dead* about the snow being general all over Ireland. This was a general snow. The pines stood as if being dressed for school and the fishpond became a white plain. The black spaces between flakes stood out as much as the snow itself; the sky sneaked closer to the ground than it could without snow. D Dog went out and did her duty and returned covered with a white fleece on her back, a dog in sheep's clothing. She shook and got the snow off.

For Pie's sake I hoped the snow came harder. I wanted it to snow all night, to bury us and keep us home.

Pie had school the following morning, but when he returned at three we built a pine fort. I had been taught to build one long ago when I was about Pie's age, and so I decided to show him. In the northern quarter of our land, someone had dug a foxhole, maybe to be used as an ash pit. It went three feet into the ground and held the shape of a gibbous moon. Working together, Pie and I dragged brush to circle the hole. We stacked oak and maple, pine and beech. Pine worked the best because it provided the most cover, but the hardwoods lent stability to the piles of brush we caved around the foxhole.

When we had a good U-shaped ring, the eastern end not quite closed to allow entrance and exit, we topped off the walls with wide branches of oak, leggy runners that formed rafters for our roof. Then, laying boughs crosswise, we cobbed a roof of spruce. The result, when we inspected it, turned out to be a woody cabin, a hut of fresh-cut twigs and limbs. A beaver lodge, I told Pie. I had to squat to enter the lodge, but once inside it provided a comfortable space at least as big as a tent. Immediately, Pie began thinking of ways to improve it. He wanted to bring out chairs, easy chairs, but I persuaded him that logs made more authentic seats. We rolled in five or six birch logs that I hadn't gotten around to splitting. Like white toadstools, they circled the interior of the lodge. Pie sat on each one, testing the balance and the flatness of individual stools. He liked the fit.

"When it snows," I said, "you'll have an igloo."

"Seriously?" he asked.

"Seriously. The snow will stack up against the sides. You may have to shovel off the top, but when you tighten up the sides, the roof will gain strength."

"Dude," he said.

Wendy came out and Pie asked her about various pieces of furniture around the house. She took him inside and came out a little later with a few odds and ends that wouldn't spoil in bad weather—a short, rickety coffee table, an old bread box that he could use as a refrigerator, and a steel bucket he could fill with snowball ammo. He squatted like a mountain troll inside the hut and set things up, arranging the small stick house to his liking. While he worked inside, we shoveled snow around the foundation of the fort. The snow did not pack well, but we kept at it and soon had a foot-high rampart. The snow gave the fort a solid footing.

Pie took us on a tour of the fort a few minutes later. He had set it up to accommodate his height. He had already stacked a half-dozen snowballs in the metal bucket. These, he declared, would be emergency snowballs. He would only use them under the most dire circumstances. We asked him what those circumstances might be and he said attack by sixth-graders. The Warren Elementary School went to sixth grade, so I knew this was as serious as an attack was likely to get in his world. It seemed a wise move to have emergency snowballs on hand.

"Fort Pieconderoga," Wendy said when we stepped out after our tour and that became its name.

Two days later, when we received more snow, the walls became milk. Pie and I climbed inside and saw that the sun drew from the structure a dull white light. The branchy ribs still pushed at the skin of the lodge, but now the walls had gained more permanence. We scooped snow from the inside of the hut and packed it against the foundation. Afterward we sat in a saucer of snow and looked up at the winter sky through branches and wattled pine.

On the day Pie went on Christmas break, we slept in Pieconderoga. Pie spent the afternoon loading it with niceties. After we spread a tarp to keep the moisture down, he arranged sleeping pads and candles. He filled the bread box with pretzels and chips. Fortunately the weather report called for mild temperatures for December, probably dropping only into the mid-thirties. I didn't anticipate that we would make it through the night. By midnight at the latest, I assumed, we would be scrambling for the house.

But Pieconderoga surprised us by being better insulated than we had anticipated. When we lay in it after dinner, it seemed comfortable, if not quite toasty. We had carried the sleeping bags out from inside—after propping them as close to the coal stove as we dared—and they provided sufficient residual heat to get us settled. Wendy showed up with hot chocolate and she joined us for a few minutes, rolling her eyes and letting us know that we were brave, hearty boys, who couldn't be goofier if we tried. Pie and I both wore wool hats and gloves; we wore wool trousers and heavy socks. I'm sure we looked like a pair of idiots, sleeping out in our yard when we might have had warm beds. But it was an adventure, we said, and Wendy groaned and went back inside. We ate pretzels out of Pie's icebox and gobbled a few chips. A few minutes later D Dog appeared and came to sleep with us. She curled into a heat ring at the bottom of the sleeping bags, both of us wiggling our toes to be under her.

We had a candle lantern for steady light. When we blew it out, the world became dark. Then little by little light filtered through the rooty ceiling, leaving us enough to see our hands or our curling breath. Pie asked for a story and I told him a looping account of how a polar bear first became white, but the story didn't hang together. Later we simply lay quietly and listened to the wind trying to find us. I felt like a boy again. I wondered where the blue heron that summered on our fishpond had gone, where it stood now, gray-legged and patient, studying new water.

As a Christmas project, something to do inside when the outdoors became inhospitable, we began tearing down interior walls in the basement. Probably a bad idea. We intended to tear down the walls eventually, of course, but we had enough going on in our everyday lives without beginning something new. One project at a time had been our motto, but it was a false motto. Mood has something to do with the project you tackle, and in the cold short days of December, we decided to be destructive.

This was the last great frontier in the barn. Someone, probably the Rogerses, had decided that the way to handle the basement was simply to board it up. They had strung pine boards vertically to make a sort of knotty-pine basement, cut some lovely stained glass into the walls, then closed their eyes to the darker corners of the building. They had fenced things off and with their old Franklin stove, they probably felt pretty warm when they visited for ski trips. On the other hand, we lived here year-round, so we ignored the dark corners of the building at our peril.

The work required pry bars and hammers and leather gloves thick enough to resist nail points. It was addicting work in the way that eating pistachios can be addicting—getting one board loose, you wanted another, and another, and another. We traded jobs on the work: First Wendy pulled down boards and I carried them away and placed them in piles according to their relative worthiness, then I yanked down boards and let Wendy carry. The work felt good. We could easily track our progress.

In two afternoons working on the basement, we cleared it of the pine planks. Portions of the job became ugly. We found mice nests in one wall, and in another, the planks had become so rotted as to be more closely related to medieval parchment than wood. We threw the scraps into the Bennington stove and kept ourselves warm. By taking down the walls, we also exposed the fieldstone basement walls. Now, instead of smaller rooms, we had one, large continuous space bordered by the basalt rocks that Farmer Gale had stacked there a century before.

On the last piece of two-by-four framing—the framing that had been nailed in place to accept the vertical planks—Wendy had to give a particularly hard tug. The board, nailed up and down beside the main support post, wouldn't give. Wendy yanked again. This time, amazed, she stopped in mid-pull.

The post had spun. The enormous, twelve-by-twelve center post had turned. It was so inconceivable that Wendy didn't mention it to me for a moment. If the post spun, she told me later, that meant the center of the house, the entire post column, sat on nothing. That could not be. She could not accept it. She gave the two-by-four stud another yank and this time, despite her desire to see the post as solid and serene, the post clearly turned a smidge to follow her pry bar.

"The post just turned," she said, her voice as horrified as it had been the moment we discovered the mice nests.

"What?" I asked. I had been carrying planks to the pile.

"It turned. The center post of the whole goddamned house just turned."

"What are you talking about?"

She showed me. Imagine, if you can, that you have four poles coming together to form a tepee. Imagine that the poles, instead of rising vertically to meet on an angle at the top, stick straight out, horizontal to the ground. Then imagine that each pole rests on a center post, each beam with a two-inch lip resting on the post. Finally, imagine that the post—the center pin of a helicopter rotor system, in other words—is standing free and clear and providing no support whatsoever.

We called Clarence. He arrived the next day, jacks in hand again, and whistled when he saw the problem. He liked this kind of thing. Foundation work, he called it. Nothing else like it. He poked a pencil into various spaces between the beams. He clucked. He had suspected this outcome. He blamed himself for not checking all the beams when he had fixed the exterior one.

"That whole thing could rupture," he said. "It could go at any time."

"The building could collapse?" I asked.

He nodded, and said, "Because in a post-and-beam, you have a post on top of a post, on top of a post. If the bottom post isn't doing its job, well, then you're dancing on air."

"Wonderful."

"And you see here? This beam that runs across the barn, end to end? In most cases, that's the first beam they lay in a foundation. A girder. This is the main carrying beam of the whole building. That's supposed to be held up by this girder post, but it isn't. It's just suspended in air. That post over there is gone, too. You have two posts to replace."

"Can you do it?"

"In a jiff," he said.

I worked with him. We repeated the process we had performed the last time we replaced a post, only this time, if possible, it was even more unnerving. This post was the stick under the juggler's spinning plate. If it slipped, the whole house went. Fortunately, though, it did not require the critical lifting the first post had needed. Working slowly, we jacked the weight off the center post. Then, rapidly, we lodged four eight-by-eights around the center post, surrendering the weight to the temporary reinforcements. We solidified the four eight-by-eight posts, then cut enough rot from the bottom of the post to make sufficient room for a decent cement footing. Clarence built the forms from the boards we had torn out and we filled them with a heavy mix of Portland cement. When we had finished, the remaining post sat on a fourteen-inch-tall cement block.

"You see what they did?" Clarence said when we had the job moving in the direction we wanted. "They knew the building was sinking. The footings were rotting. So they kept sticking shims under the top so that the beams sat on something. Fix the symptom, ignore the cause. Lazy way of doing things."

"You see a lot of that?"

"It's why I'm in business. People take the easy way and that makes it the hard way for someone down the line. When you skip on something, you pass it to someone else. It never goes away until you do it right."

We finished the second post a few days before Christmas. Clarence dropped the posts down on their new footings, then coffered the sides with old barn boards. He built soffits around them and left the beams decorated by soft, sweet wood. Suddenly the basement had a different feel. Clarence had set the barn right again. Now, when I looked at things carefully, I felt anew the substantialness of the barn. This was a large, solid building. It wasn't going anywhere. Not now, anyway.

Clarence had the rest of the week to fill, so he switched to electrical work. He yanked wires and reconfigured things, talking so fulsomely about the state of modern electricians, the hodgepodge work they left behind, that I wondered how he kept the connections straight. He installed a light outside the barn overhang so that we could turn on some illumination from inside the house. Then he consolidated the wiring that had run haphazardly across the basement beams. Now that we could see things, he whipped them into shape. At the end of the week, when he produced his bill, I paid it gladly and added a Christmas bonus. We would have been lost without Clarence. That was a simple fact.

On the last day Clarence worked, he took me around the barn and made recommendations. From sixty years of working on houses, he said, he knew that the enemy of all homeowners is moisture. New England weather is hard on houses. As he pointed to the beams he had installed to support the porch roof, he told me to sweep off the snow. Don't let it pile up, because snow eats wood as surely as beaver does. Follow water, he said. Water always goes in the path of least resistance, so give it ways to escape from the house. We talked for a little while about spring. We still had plenty of projects to do, but the barn was in reasonable shape. It had a good roof and a strong foundation. Everything else, he promised, would flow from that.

"Ten, fifteen years from now, people will show up and say, gee, how did you ever find a place like this," Clarence said when I offered him a beer at our breakfast bar. "They won't understand the work you put into it. To them, the barn just sprung out of the ground. They'll see the finished product and they'll think they could do the same thing. And they could, if they were willing to put some work into it. It's all about time."

"And money," I said.

"Yes, but time more than money. Most young people don't care to put the time into it. They have other things on their minds. You're at the right place in your life for this kind of project. You won't have to do another house."

"Tend your garden," I said. "That's what I'm trying to do."

"There you go," Clarence said, drinking hard from the beer. "That's the ticket."

On Tuesdays growing up I attended Catechism class at the local Catholic high school, Holy Trinity. I hated to go. I hated Tuesdays and hated the long, suffocating ride in my mother's car, the bushy-headed seminarians who taught us the Baltimore Catechism— *Who is God?*—and the scripted replies. I hated the sense, too, that we needed such instruction, that these folks at Holy Trinity had secrets to share with us that we desperately required. Homework on top of homework, it seemed to me, another thing to learn. Though I hated the classes, I loved the splendid emptiness of the buildings. For any possible excuse, I slipped out of the class and wandered the gray hallways. A funny thing to love, certainly, but

I craved the rhythmic ticking of the clocks, the lockers lining the hallways, the square pattern of cement, painted gray, under my feet. Holy Trinity had been built of yellow brick, like the path to Oz, and somehow that lent the structure an exotic quality my junior high did not possess. When I encountered the nuns and priests who often walked the halls, I nodded and continued on, persuaded that we understood the contemplative light, the solace of empty hallways.

But I feel that emotion each year when college classes end and the school empties in its quiet way. An afternoon arrives when suddenly everything is finished, classes are done, and the hallways become empty. On the December day the semester ended in our first barn year, classes closed on a raw, foggy day. It seemed fitting that fog covered us; we could not see the sun and night seemed close by. As I handed in my students' final grades, the dean's office stood nearly empty. The staff spoke in quiet tones and a few ate candy canes. The registrar's assistant, who accepted my grade forms, wore a Santa pin on her lapel. She pulled it for me and let me watch as the nose lighted. On, off, on, off. *Merry Christmas,* she said, as I walked down the empty hallway and left for home.

I climbed into my truck and threw my briefcase on the passenger's side. Pie and Wendy were waiting. During the late fall, when the leaves had fallen, we had hiked into the White Mountain National Forest to find our Christmas tree, marking it with orange tape. Now it was time to fetch it out. On the phone Wendy had promised to pack mulled cider and cookies. Everything was ready, she said.

Joy filled me as I pointed the truck home. Few places could be better suited to holding Christmas cheer than the barn. The tree we planned to cut stood fourteen feet tall. We knew the hollow where it grew.

Home and a month off. I felt giddy driving up Route 25. I played a tape of Tony Bennett's Christmas carols and sang along. The day lay white and moist around the road. The fog ate snow and pushed black holes against the tree boles. We would need a fire later. A fire and plenty to drink and eat.

Pie ran out to greet me, crazy to be going out for the tree. Then D Dog arrived, barking and fluffing herself up as if she had never seen me before. I calmed her down and followed Pie back to the house. Wendy joined us on the porch. She poured me a glass of mulled cider while I went in to change. Pie hung about, telling me he had the saw, the cutting permit, the compass. I nodded at everything he said. As always, the event had grown to gargantuan proportions in his mind. He told me about his class-mates and what kind of trees they had purchased. He said some kids in class thought reindeer ate pine, which was why you put a tree in your house. I told him it was more likely a pagan ritual, the green boughs adjuring the sun to return, but he pre-ferred the Christmas-tree-as-food explanation. I didn't push my interpretation.

We left the porch in great spirits, D Dog charging ahead of us, Pie pulling a sled for transport. We had tied a thermos onto the sled, along with a plastic tub full of cookies. The bell tower on the Warren Congregational Church struck four o'clock. Wind came from the north and began shoving the fog around. The temperature stood at thirty-one degrees.

It took a half hour to reach the tree. Snow had twisted some of its lower branches like a woman's skirt held in a twirl halfway around its body. The trunk rose straight, five inches across at the base, and the branches dripped off at half-foot intervals. Its orange tag, though, identified it as the one we had picked out earlier that fall. Now the tree appeared enormous. The white backdrop transformed it into a missile of sap, a greedy weed that had grown recklessly on the side of the mountain. We pulled the sled next to our tree and took out food and drink. The mulled cider tasted of apples and cinnamon. The cookies, oat-meal raisin, had grown cold on the walk to the tree. We stuck them inside our jackets and let them warm up against our bodies. When they regained their softness, we shared them with D Dog. She went through her paces: We made her give us a paw, saying "enchantez" each time she did it, then we threw snowballs into the air and let her catch them like a marlin coming free of blue water, her tail and body wriggling, released from the ground.

"Shouldn't we sing 'O Christmas Tree?'" Pie asked.

"You laugh, but it would be nice," Wendy said.

"It's a bit much," I said.

We compromised by singing scattered verses of "Grandma Got Run Over by a Reindeer." Pie could remember most of them. Then for D Dog we performed the dog rendition of "Jingle Bells" that consisted entirely of barks. That proved more successful. D Dog looked around. An echo sent our voices into the hills and D Dog suspected other dogs nearby.

We cut the tree down in a matter of minutes. Lying on my belly, I used a bow saw and hacked away. Pie shouted "timber" and we applauded the tumble. With a few pine boughs, we spanked Pie and then spanked everyone round in a circle, saying an old incantation for good health: "Fresh and green, pretty and fine, gingerbread and brandy-wine." Bad health, according to tradition, would remain in the forest and the health of the tree would enter our bones. Then we pointed the tree-butt down the hillside and walked it to the main path. The tree came reluctantly from the forest. Its branches grabbed saplings and pucker brush whenever they could. We struggled to get it out, but finally, as night settled in, we had it on the path.

Back at the barn, we carried the tree inside and hoisted it up into the southwest corner, the luckiest place to have a tree, we'd read. Pine scent filled the keeping room. The tree's top just brushed the rafters, which signified that it stood a bit more than fourteen feet. It grabbed the entire wall next to the bank of southern windows. Driving home, we would see the lights through the windows, Christmas lights reflected against the glass. The tree branches stretched as big around as a Volkswagen.

I made a fire in the hearth while Wendy tended the coal stove. Then we decorated for the rest of the night, marveling over each rediscovered set of lights, each fondly remembered ornament. Pie jumped around and nearly broke a thousand lights, but we managed to get him calmed enough to work with us. In time the tree began to glisten. Bright red and blue balls, green pyramids, bubble tubes, clothespin reindeer dangled from the boughs. The tree remained as fragrant as a forest. To reach inside it, to hang a bulb, reminded us of where the tree had been earlier in the evening. We found a nest in one of the branches, old and dried now, but we carried it carefully to our specimen case and placed it beside others we had found over the year.

Pie ran around and flicked off the lamps before we lit the tree for the first time. When we counted to three, Wendy plugged in the string of lights and our tree became a Christmas tree. Lights ran back and forth through the branches, all the way up to the ceiling. No tinsel. Bulbs—some from my childhood—dangled from the boughs. I had never dreamed of having such a large tree inside a house—it was twice, maybe three times the size of the largest tree I'd ever had. It rose to Pie's window, peeked inside it. We stared at it for a long time, first examining it, then letting it seep into our senses. My forty-fifth Christmas tree, I thought. Pie's paper angel, made in first grade, sat atop the peak.

We slipped into our boots and walked outside. It was December dark now, as dark as the year becomes. The moon had not appeared and fog choked everything black. The tree shown prettily through the windows and pressed light into the darkness. It wanted us back inside. We stood for only a short while. An excellent tree, Wendy said. The best ever. But the night felt too damp to remain outside for long and the fire flickered from the hearth. We hurried back inside. D Dog went directly to the tree and sniffed at the lowest branches.

Near midnight on Christmas Eve, Wendy and I climbed the stairs of the cupola with a Flexible Flyer in one hand and a bag of wood ash in the other. This was the last thing we needed to do for Christmas morning. I'm not sure who hit on it first, but one of us had realized that, with the existence of the cupola, it was possible to run a sleigh down the roof, complete with appropriate wood ash, to demonstrate that Santa had indeed visited our barn. We had already planned how we would bring it to Pie's attention. We would step outside on Christmas morning, long after the packages lay opened, and casually notice that *something, what, oh my gosh, look at that!* Maybe we'd spring it on our way out to burn the Christmas wrapping paper. The trick was not to make too much out of it. We promised to shrug a lot and keep turning the question back to Pie. *Well, what do you think?*

The cupola, in winter, had become a cold, icy box. I pushed up the trapdoor, pushed away the insulation, then climbed up. Wendy handed the Flexible Flyer through. Then she handed up the bag of cold wood ash. Finally she climbed through and took a seat catty-cornered from me. Her breath plumed in white fog. Her wool hat took away her hair.

The view ran for miles into the darkness and the high, humped mountains of snow that surrounded us. Moonlight filled the cupola and cobbled across the snowy meadow. Sitting so high, we could see smoke coming from our own chimney and from other chimneys around the village. Wind drifted the smoke to the east. With the wind at his back, Santa would be traveling east to west, following time zones and chasing darkness. Other than the wind, though, the scene was still. When we talked, our voices fell naturally to whispers.

It took some time, working by flashlight, to open the window on the meadow side of the cupola. Finally it popped open and the wind caught us and flapped around the interior. Cold. Wendy wondered if Pie had heard anything. If he did, he might mistake it for Santa up on the roof. Why not? How many houses had sounds coming from above a sleeping child? We had a funny moment then, thinking about what we would do if the sled did not get enough momentum to shoot off the porch. That wouldn't be an easy explanation. But the benefit, we calculated, was worth the risk. Then we debated about the best way to do it. A straight, perpendicular run would be the easiest to accomplish, but we doubted it would look persuasive. Did Santa really shoot off straight down the roof? No, it was more likely that he angled slightly to the north, so we propped the sled in the window and aimed it.

"Push it hard," Wendy told me.

By this time we were giggling. I lowered the sled onto the snowy roof, counted to three, and shoved it as forcefully as I could. The sled, to our astonishment, set off like a rocket. It dashed down the roof, paused not a bit, then took to the air off the porch roof. For a moment it hung in that kind of adventure-movie slow motion, then it began to arc down. Its nose tipped reluctantly, and gravity finally asserted itself. The pull rope whipped forward and down and the sled followed, landing in a crash on the lawn below. Two lovely runner tracks ran straight away from the cupola. Fortunately, Pie was eight. We doubted he would spend too much time analyzing the tracks or their origin in the cupola.

Wendy stretched out of the window to sprinkle the wood ash. She wanted it to drip over the west side of the roof—where the chimney stood—onto the east side. Authenticity. If Santa climbed out of the chimney, then hopped on his sled, he would leave wood ash on both sides of the peak.

We sneaked back down, covering our tracks as we went. I tucked the insulation into place again. Then we went to the catwalk overlooking the keeping room. In sappy movies and bad poems they talk about the magic of Christmas, but here it was, nevertheless. Standing on the small walkway looking down at the tree, the presents, the broad, hand-knitted stockings hanging from the blunt wood mantel, gave us to understand that this was as good a Christmas as we could imagine. The windows let in sufficient moon glow to illuminate the red couch, the dark beams running up like fingertips touching, the fireplace red and sweet-smelling and dying to coals. And Pie. Though we could not see him, we knew he lay in his trundle bed, Slam Fist and Archer and Reggie standing guard, his eyes closed, his excitement temporarily stilled. D Dog, far below, slept on her bed beside the fire, her tags clinking sometimes when she moved. Snow on the meadow. The tree, green and dark in the southwest corner, the forest represented in its scent.

I retrieved the sled, kicked snow over its landing spot, and went to bed. Pie woke us the next morning at five-thirty. He climbed into bed and told us, barely able to contain himself, that Santa had come, it was Christmas, we had to get up and see! The cookies he had set out for Santa were gone! And the carrots, too. I told him to wait a few minutes, just a few, and I would turn on the tree and get the woodstove heated up. Wendy pulled him under the covers, but that couldn't hold him long. After I had turned on the tree, but before I stirred the woodstove properly, he had flown out of our bedroom. He squatted next to the tree and examined each present, shouting out gleefully when a tag posted his name. His heart was kind enough to give us a sort of verbal pat on the back when a package happened to be for us, but he was at pains to be interested in our loot. He wanted his things and now. Wendy came out and fixed coffee while I threw wood in the stove, then went and built up a fire in the hearth. Pie remained transfixed beside the tree, his greed so open and pure as to be refreshing.

Finally the great moment arrived. Pie slashed through his gifts, shouting as he unveiled each one. He got a Game Boy! A Pokémon cartridge! Wendy persuaded him to slow down just a little and help hand out presents for us. He did, impatiently, but with a willing spirit that indicated he wanted our Christmases to be enjoyable, too, as long as they did not impede his own. Then he dove back at his presents.

Wendy and I exchanged tools and gift certificates from Home Depot. Our exchange had been prearranged, for the most part. But it pleased us both that each, independently, had selected dozens of seed packets: zinnias, marigolds, hollyhocks, daisies, bachelor's buttons, petunias, cosmos, violets, sunflowers, poppies. We had given each other vegetable seeds, too: tomato, corn, radishes, beans, peas, kale, zucchini, summer squash, pumpkins.

We ate cinnamon rolls for breakfast and drank coffee. The house began to warm. Pie roamed like a mad drummer who could not settle on one rhythm. Christmas, almost, was too much. By nine it felt like we had been up forever. The day was gray and cold and we had to resist the push back to bed. We enlisted Pie in collecting the discarded wrapping paper, and together slammed the paper into plastic bags, then told him we wanted him to join us burning the paper in the incinerator. He resisted for a moment—he wanted to stay inside—but we told him we should all get outside for a few minutes. D Dog led us out and we followed her to the fire ring Dave and I had built at Thanksgiving. Pie insisted on lighting the match. We let him do it under close supervision, our eyes meeting often to look at the roof. In the dim morning light, it did not look quite as convincing as we had hoped. But it was clearly a sled mark. We had succeeded to that degree. Wendy made a little shrug at me while Pie still bent close to the paper, match extended, and then she said, "Look at that!"

Pie immediately turned. He didn't see anything.

"On the roof," Wendy said. "Is that what I think it is?"

Pie caught on. He looked at it. I saw hope rise in him, then cool. It broke my heart a little to watch it. Cynicism had won a place in his world view. He studied the roof, the flames from the Christmas paper burning finally, and we waited. We did not want to lead him too baldly.

"Tracks?" he said.

"I don't know," I said, falling back on the old parents' trick of turning it onto the child, "what do you think?"

He regarded the crime scene with suspicion. He went along with it, I knew, as surely as I knew anything, for our sake. I had done the same thing myself at his age—believed so that my parents would not have to break the news to me. Gradually, as we stood and watched the paper burn, argument went to belief. Little by little he talked himself into believing that Santa had indeed left sled marks on our roof. He convinced himself of the fact, even as we realized that things go as they must, this would be the last Christmas he would believe in Santa anyway. In some part, he bought the evidence of the sled runners as a final gift to us. He didn't push hard. And we quickly dropped it.

burning
dinosaurs

C old. After Christmas, cold came through the hills and fell
out of the north. We listened to the weather reports and
heard, as if about a war, that a cold front would arrive
from the Canadian plains. A Yankee Clipper. When the weather
forecasters stood in front of their maps and pointed to this or
that cloud covering, we listened intently. Several times we had
dipped down to zero, once to minus ten, but we had yet to experience the great pull of winter. "Watch for the turn of the year,"
the old timers told us. And they were right.

Cold comes not as a force, but as an absence of all force. Like
Nosferatu, the great rat vampire, cold comes by stealth. At first
I noted it on the porch thermometer. By three in the afternoon,
right at the tail of the year, the temperature marked minus
twenty. When I went outside, the weather moved into my chest as
fast as I breathed. I had read in an almanac about methods to tell
the temperature by walking on snow. It revolved around the
amount of moisture colder snow contained or the shape of the
crystals. The colder the snow, the higher the squeak. Though I
couldn't recall the exact explanation, the snow now squeaked like
mice under my boots. I walked to the woodpile and brought back
an armload of loose kindling. By the time I pushed inside, my
nose had frozen and my cheeks had turned numb along my jaws.

We kept the coal stoves going full blast, but this proved to be the moment we had feared. The barn's insulation remained primitive. The roof was not insulated at all. Whatever heat roared out of the coal stove quickly filtered up and out into the atmosphere. *Heating the great outdoors*, my father used to say when we left a door open in our Jersey suburb. The cold, combined with our uninsulated roof, gave new meaning to the phrase.

That night our bedside water froze solid. Later, when we told people about the water in our glasses turning to ice, they thought we meant a skim of ice over a tumbler of water. But our water glasses froze solid, like bright white bullets of ice. They thawed in our sink all day. In our bedroom the temperature dropped to thirty degrees. Outside the temperature turned to minus thirty.

And it stayed. It stayed through New Year's Eve and stayed for ten days afterward. We considered calling Wendy's father and asking if Pie could stay there for a time. We could not budge the interior temperature above fifty. Each day we woke and thought this would be the last cold day. Now it will break, we told one another. But it didn't. I remembered the Paul Bunyan stories about the great freezes in Minnesota, stories I had always taken as fanciful. Now I knew them to be true. All we needed was an iron skillet so big we could strap butter to our feet for skating.

Wendy and I became cautious with each other. How had we gotten into this? The great horselaugh had finally arrived; we had been foolish to ignore the comments and raised eyebrows concerning the barn. After all was said and done, the building remained an agricultural structure. That remained indisputable. All of the insulation, the careful work we had done, now seemed foolhardy.

"Are you worried?" Wendy asked one night after we had climbed beneath our electric blanket. Our bedroom air pushed so coldly at us that Wendy talked with the blanket over her mouth and nose, a Muslim woman in veil. It would have been funny if it hadn't been so pitiful.

"About the cold?" I asked, knowing perfectly well what she meant.

"Yes, of course about the cold."

"Is it cold?"

"Don't," she said.

"We'll be okay," I said. "As long as the pipes don't freeze and as long as we can stay by the stoves, we'll be fine. This is how people lived years ago."

"This is also why they invented central heating."

"That's right," I said. "You've got a point."

We wanted to be good-humored about it, but it didn't quite work. Each morning we woke with dueling hair dryers to thaw the pipes. Wendy took the bathroom while I took the kitchen. Fortunately the pipes did not freeze solid; they simply became wheezy and clunky and we chased the ice back to mush with the hair dryers. But our hands grew numb as we worked and the cold settled deep in our bones. We wore hats indoors and never took off our heaviest sweaters. Pie, always good-spirited, spent hours seated next to the fire. Whether he knew our worries or not we couldn't tell. Certainly the house felt like a rubber band being twisted or stretched too tight to fit a package it shouldn't accept; we felt it must snap eventually, but we could not guess when.

The coal stoves, too, tried us. Coal is different from wood. Once a wood fire is going, it's an easy matter to keep it going. If you add wood, presto, the new fuel catches. The only sin with a wood fire is letting it burn too low. When it smolders, it creates creosote, the black, chalky kindling for chimney fires. Coal, on the other hand, creates no creosote. But it also requires art rather than casual attention in order to work properly. You begin all coal fires by getting a hot wood fire going, then, gradually, you ladle coal on top. Coal is cousin to stone. It sits amid the flames and merely promises to burn. After a time, when the wood fire begins to slow, you shake down the coal grates—metal jaws at the bottom of the stove—and the grate eats the dead ash. You shovel out the ash, put the ash in a metal container, then you add more coal. The balance, then, is extreme: You must get the coal to ignite more coal, and to do so requires a precise combination of heat, air, and patience. Coal can smother coal, even the hottest embers, so you also must dig a hole in the coal bed so that air can flow through at least one gap in the overriding new coal. Then you wait. If you open the door of the stove too quickly, gases can explode in a blue flame that will lick the eyebrows off your forehead. If you smother the gases too tightly, then expose them to air, the stove can erupt with a backfire, literally knocking the stovepipe free from the thimble. The ideal is to get a lawn of blue flame working over the new coal, a bright, barbecue burn, then tighten down the stove air ducts. You need a true heart, though, because at that point the stove temperatures begin to back off. The fire actually appears to be dying, and if you attempt this, as we did, in a cold, cold house without backup heat of any kind, then the stakes are considerable. And even if the stove works correctly, and the heat begins to build, the blue flame can ignite and pour out of the stovepipe until it glimmers in the chimney like a swaying aurora borealis. You wait and listen as the blue flame cauterizes the chimney, and you pray that nothing catches, nothing turns into a train noise riding up and down your flue.

This was the art we had to learn. No one we knew could help us. Like many people of a certain vintage, Clarence had burned coal as a child, but his memory of it was imperfect. In short order we knew more about it than he did. But Wendy and I often had different ideas about the stoves and it frequently made us terse with each other. Turn it down, look out, blue flame, make sure it gets hotter, and so on. Beneath each comment rested the comprehension that we had no room for error. If the stoves went out, if we fumbled it, then the barn would turn into a cold brick of anguish and recrimination.

The house held us. We could not leave it for more than eight hours at a time for fear that the stoves would go out. We could ask no one to watch the house, because who could we teach to run the coal stoves? On the other hand, we never lacked for an excuse to escape a social engagement. *Sorry, we can't make it, the stoves, you know. We must get going, I'm afraid, the stoves, we have to feed them.*

When they worked properly, as they did finally when we got the hang of them, they produced magnificent heat. Eighty thousand BTUs the manufacturer said of each stove, and that seemed right. Standing beside them, heat saturated our clothes. Wendy and I made Pie absorb the heat next to them, then come over and sit on our laps. He felt like a warm loaf of bread. When it was going properly, the coal fire lay four inches deep at the bottom of the stove, glowing a red the color of sunsets. Down in the basement, where the Rogerses had once heated with their Franklin stove, we now collected around the Home Heater. The temperatures, in reasonable weather, reached seventy-five or eighty degrees. When the outside temperature dropped below zero, though, even the basement stove failed to heat us.

A thin margin. That's what it felt like. Most of us take heat as a given, but of course it isn't. When we visited restaurants, or sat through a movie, we marveled at the luxuriousness of the heat. The winter stretched out long and dark. Rarely had I been more conscious of time passing—or stalling and lingering. Pie, when he learned that coal was a carbon substance pressed during the earth's glacial ages, said we were burning dinosaurs. The idea that this rock-like material had been a tree or a fern when dinosaurs roamed America fascinated him. Trees were coal, he said, pushing the point. Roses were coal. He enjoyed reciting that fact to people.

Finally the weather broke. "Altitude Lou," the Portland, Maine, weatherman, came on television one evening and informed us all that relief lay just to our west. The mid-January thaw, he called it. He had a jovial laugh and he bantered casually with his on-air sidekicks.

When the weather broke the next afternoon we went outside and took a walk. Pieconderoga had become a white cake. A yellow birch had exploded with the cold, almost as if its paper skin had grown too tight for it. A milkweed stalk had simply frozen where it stood and then tumbled to the ground in disjointed sections, jack straws thrown by winter. A late apple on our lone tree hung like a red ball, its sides punctured by nuthatches and a strident blue jay. The hunger that the cold had brought seemed eased somewhat. Birds flew as if making up for lost time. We found one cottontail track running up and under a fan of raspberry bushes. A deer had passed through the yard and left without pausing at the fence. It had jumped into the corral, eaten what it liked, then jumped out.

The temperature chugged above freezing at last. We sledded in the afternoon, then returned and made another healthy fire in the hearth. Wendy and I passed looks back and forth as we watched the birch twigs take on heat. The looks said the same thing every time: *We had made it.* If we had been honest, we would have admitted that we hadn't been certain we would. I told her that in the spring, when we had made it through the worst of the weather, I would dance a jig on the porch. She promised to hold me to it.

Then one morning the sun returned to our southern-facing bank of windows. It had passed too far south to see for several days—probably for the length of the cold snap—but now it popped up in the transom above the doors. It meant that the sun again approached the northern hemisphere. Our barn worked as a sundial; we could determine the change of seasons by the slant of sun breaking through our windows.

We marked the anniversary of our first visit to the barn by snowshoeing into the woods to watch the maple syrup flow. In Rumney, New Hampshire, we knew of a net of silver tubes a farmer friend had strung to collect syrup. He told us the syrup had begun to spill, though not in great quantities yet. Tapping tubes replaced the old-fashioned sap buckets long ago, all of the tubes emptying into a large lidded wash bucket. The three of us wandered around a bit to watch the sap's slow progress down the tubes. Sun struck the lines everywhere and we observed white bubbles throwing prism lights on the hard snow. The prisms traveled with the sap, so that, for a moment or two, we watched the primary colors raking across the ground and smashing against trees. Pie made the prisms walk over his foot. He pretended for a while, as always, that the prism gleams represented death rays and he dove around on the ground escaping them. We told him when the gleams got him and when they didn't. He kept the game going long after we had lost interest. To change his focus, I told him a story about the native peoples of northern Canada, how they divide themselves into ptarmigans and ducks. The ptarmigans represent the people born in winter; the ducks are comprised of people born in summer. The village lines up and stages a tug of war between the two groups. They haul on ropes made of sealskins and try to yank the opposing group over a prescribed line. If the ptarmigans win, winter continues. If the ducks win, however, spring and summer are not long off.

Pie naturally proposed a tug of war. That wasn't quite the point, I told him, but that was the point to him. Wendy and I, both born in October after the autumn equinox, decided we were ptarmigans. Pie, an April baby, was a duck. We found a stick and on the count of three tugged him all over the place. Winter must remain now, we told him. We dragged him past maples and past the birch grove that marked the beginning of the sugar bush. He leaned back and yelped whenever we got him going too fast. Ptarmigans rule, ducks drool, we told him. We pulled him back to winter and the cold that still turned the sap lines to white icicles each night.

On a Friday night in February, the Warren Fire Department flooded the town common to make an ice rink for a winter carnival. The night before we had gone with a group of volunteers to shovel a ring of snow around the common. The Fire Department tapped into the municipal well and sprayed water with incredible force into the ring, and by the next morning, the rink was complete. John Lester, the owner of the sheep, proved a capable foreman for the job. In the space of a night, the town common went from being an indistinguishable field of snow to a Currier & Ives skating scene. The town gazebo, a pretty white structure also built by John Lester, stood at its center. On the day of the winter carnival, it became the headquarters for parents supervising the events. A boom box played skating music while the kids performed skating routines and played broom hockey. The PTO provided a large thermos of hot chocolate. Snowsuited children staggered by with brown moustaches and double-bladed skates.

We attended, but my attention was elsewhere. I had two projects under way. I had read in a homesteading book that the best time to cut firewood was in February. The sap is deepest in February, which makes the cordwood dry that much faster come summer. To speed the cutting, I had built a sawhorse from spare two-by-fours, and now I had a sturdy log holder nearly sternum high. I went out each afternoon, selected one of the trees I had marked in autumn, felled it, then sawed it into stove lengths. I specialized in cherry. For some reason cherry grew all through the north hedgerow, and I cut its scaly wood in long draws, pleased with the soda-fountain fragrance that sprang from its cambium layer. I piled the logs in a plastic sled and pulled them to a mounting wood stack. The black bark stood out against the snow. The trees, I remembered thinking, constituted banks of sunshine.

I also collected stones from the Baker River. Years before we had taken over the barn, the basement floor had been composed of large flat stone. Over time, the barn's owners cemented portions of the floor, so that now three quarters of it had become a standard basement floor, complete with a gray indoor-outdoor carpet. But one large section remained simple dirt, and this, to keep me busy during the winter, I had decided to lay with stone.

Working with a pick and shovel, a collection of buckets, and a wheelbarrow, I removed dirt for a week before I managed to level the floor. It was not an easy task. Then, walking sometimes with Pie and always with D Dog, we scoured the river for flat rocks along the bank. I carried a hammer and tapped the rocks until they shook free of any ice that held them, then I loaded them into a backpack. At most I could handle three stones. Then I walked back to the truck, emptied them, and repeated the process. It became, in short order, an addictive hobby—a strange form of prospecting. I felt, ridiculously perhaps, the rise of eureka pleasure when I saw a particularly handsome, flat stone. Pie rolled his eyes. D Dog sniffed the imprint of the rock when I yanked it free.

I also came to love the ice. Ice on a still body of water is one thing, but the ice beside the Baker River flowed and snapped and stalled in remarkable variety. Like a great staircase, the river descended in stages, the unfrozen water a tongue under each riser. Perhaps the loveliest discoveries were the instances of spray that froze like lace around the rocks. Here the water had pushed free, leaped for a second, then stilled. I knew the water must have frozen in increments, yet I failed to see how the water had built against the rocks. Instead I liked to picture one single splash—on a perfect night, at the perfect temperature—rising out of the body of water below it and relinquishing its liquid state in a fatal instant.

I had never laid a floor before, so I spent many pleasant hours reading about how to do it. Opinions varied. Some suggested using wet mortar; others recommended filling the rocks with dry mortar mix, then carefully spraying the rocks until the dry mortar took on moisture and began to set. But my first order of business was to completely rake the space—an eight-by-twelve rectangle in the southwest corner of the basement—and make sure I had everything ready. That took another day. Then I spent a day sprinkling sand and raking that smooth. At last I had a level bed of sand and a hundred rocks ready to fit into place.

One by one I lay the stones in position, frequently setting a level on top to make sure the rocks presented a reasonably uniform surface. I did not expect the floor to be perfectly smooth, but neither did I want it to stub every toe that crossed it. Fortunately, I remembered the stones, and to my surprise I could often recall, with improbable accuracy, which rock might fit here, which one over there. I pressed the stones close, leaving approximately one-eighth inch around the borders. In places where the stones did not naturally fit—not every pair of stones were Vermont and New Hampshire, one making up in its northern section what the other pushes forward in its southern section—I chipped triangular pieces to fill gaps.

A stone floor. By noon my knees ached and I felt I couldn't continue, but I enjoyed the work so much I didn't want to stop. I rolled a towel and kneeled on it wherever I went. My hands, too, felt the stone work. But it went rapidly. At two o'clock the next day I set the last stone. I stepped back—as I had done a thousand times both days—and studied the pattern. I had used some large rocks as anchors and the rest of the stones played off these. It was far from perfect, about as level as a windblown beach, but it saved the price of cementing or hiring someone else to do it. Besides, Wendy and I had vague notions to build a wine rack on top of the stone floor, thereby establishing our own northern

New Hampshire's comic version of the lignite caves in Poe's "Cask of Amontillado."

The next day I sprinkled Portland mortar mix into the cracks between the stones, then used a watering can to moisten the mortar. The cement smelled like cement—a good, rock smell that conveyed solidity and permanence. When I was satisfied that the mortar had begun to set, I built a corral around the border of the floor, the better to keep out eight-year-olds and black Labs. I burned the coal stove hot, making sure the temperature of the room remained well above fifty degrees to help the mortar dry.

Wendy and I carried a glass of wine down that night and inspected the floor. We didn't walk on it, but Wendy nodded her approval. Not bad. I didn't dare think about how many hours I had put into it. Shining a work light on it, I recognized different rocks. I could recall where they had lifted out of the river bank, how they had looked with ice ringing them. I tried to imagine their journey, where they had come from, how long they had waited in the river, but now they were floor and not stone. I bent and put my finger on the mortar. My finger left no print at all.

In March we taped a dollar to the refrigerator for anyone who spotted the first robin. Another dollar went for the first green shoot and another dollar for the first duck to reappear in the fishpond. Before anyone had a chance to make a claim, snow piled us under one last time. March storms are often the worst in New Hampshire and also the most heartbreaking. Just when you think you may finally be gaining warm weather, snow comes from the west and covers you.

This was a big one. It began snowing early in the morning and snowed straight through the day. Businesses shut down early; the radio provided a constant bombardment of updates and cancellations. No Girl Scout meeting in Haverhill. No Knights of Columbus meeting in Bradford. The 4-H demonstration talk on shearing canceled for inclement weather. Fortunately Wendy and I made it home by early afternoon and we buttoned down the house one last time. When Pie got home we all climbed into the cupola and watched the flakes drift and scatter across our acres. Snow hung in the green pines. It settled on the fishpond and on the last of the woodpile. As we watched, a dog sled flew past out on the old railroad bed, the driver's calls to his team clear as apples from where we sat. We listened for a long time to the dogs barking as they made their way north. It was pretty to hear them, but I suspect all of us hoped they took winter with them when they went.

Snow came fiercely through the late afternoon and night. The next day icicles hung from the porch roof, great white pyramids of ice that dripped and sometimes shattered on the ground. I rose early and plowed out the driveway with the snowblower, although no one had plans to go anywhere. When I went back inside I made a fire and drank too much coffee sitting beside it. Wendy woke and we told each other that we didn't mind this last storm. Cabin fever, though, had found us at last.

At noon we hooked D Dog to a harness and let Pie cross-country ski behind her. D Dog proved a failure as a sled dog. She pulled only for the biscuits that I had to dangle in front of her. But several times we got her going pretty fast. She pulled Pie in bursts and starts, his weight negligible on the well-packed snow. We had read *Call of the Wild* together, so he shouted *Gee* and *Haw* to guide D Dog left and right. Unfortunately that only caused her to turn around and look at him, curious about what he wanted.

We walked to a ledge of rock that had been cut years ago. Dynamite lines ran down the striated stone. We unhooked D Dog, her work done, and let her roam. In a little while she nosed out some turkey tracks and we all gathered around them, trying to see what they ate. Juniper berries, we guessed, from the looks of the bushes around the tracks. The tracks poked peace signs in the snow, then disappeared, probably in flight. Pie suggested aliens had sucked the turkeys up in order to study them, then transported them back to Gaala-Gaala, a space station he had once visited himself. We checked his head for fever, then let him chase D Dog for a time.

We headed for home. Near the fishpond Wendy stopped us and made us listen. What we had taken before for the sound of snow melting now came clearly to us as water running. Something in the fishpond had given way. Ice had cracked or dived beneath the surface of the black pond and water had begun to move. We searched the landscape until finally we spotted a black rivulet cut through the white snow. It ran at the edge of the pond, a pry bar lifting the cap of ice. Around it we spotted the red of new growth held by the willow wands. One good rain would have it out; the ducks, the summer-born, had won after all.

When we rounded the last curve to the barn, Pie and D Dog sprinted ahead. They ran across the snowfields, two small creatures in a white glaze. We watched them make their way across the snow and finally push open the barn door. They went inside and we watched Pie shuck off his jacket and hang up his hat.

home

On the first genuinely warm spring day Wendy and I repaired the screen doors. We took all six screens off the French doors and carried them to a makeshift workshop beside the picnic table. The screens exhibited the usual signs of wear and tear: a few rips where the mesh had sprung, several bulges where dogs, over the years, had pawed to be let out. Because of their large size, the screens did not seem particularly sturdy; the openings demanded stout wood and good, biting nails. But we admired the old-fashioned shiver they gave off when you pushed them open. We liked, too, the windy slam of them when Pie scrambled through them.

Wendy set them one by one on the table, then attended to them like a doctor at triage. She tapped tacks in places, reinforced weakened wood with one-by-three stripping, and patched the screens with a kit we had purchased at the local hardware store. Black flies had not yet begun to be serious about their business—it was late April—but their approach was imminent. When she finished administering to each door's most pressing complaints, she passed it to me so that I could touch up the black paint that had been weathered over the years. I scraped and sanded, then dabbed paint where I could. I enjoyed putting on the black paint. It gave the doors a definite outline, a frame for the meadow beyond.

By evening, working pretty steadily, we finished. We carried the screens back to their various perches, getting them to hang on their hinges with a quivering hesitancy that spoke of summer. Wind blew back and forth from the house to the porch. We tried out the screens, moving them at various speeds until we satisfied ourselves that they worked. On the main door—the northern door we used most frequently—Wendy included two triangular strips of wood at waist level, a target for an elbow or a raised knee when one carried a tray of drinks onto the porch.

The next morning Clarence arrived. We had asked him to work on the southern sill. Wendy and I had noticed the rot on our initial house inspection, but we had not seen the dimension of the job until she had begun to take measurements for a two-step porch. The idea was to build a small porch off the side French doors, a place to step out and stand for a moment before proceeding to the fenced garden. When she knelt to see the job better, her eyes fixed on the measurements, she had pressed the tape measure to the sill and watched in horror as the wood splintered away. Crumbled, more accurately. Insects had paraded through the wood, and moisture, dripping for a century, had finally carried the day. With the claw of a hammer she pulled away wood as easily as one might remove pulp from a cantaloupe. She tapped the hammer up and down the sill. The knock of the hammer produced no sound louder than an oar against the submerged hull of a canoe. A thunk. We postponed construction on the porch.

Clarence arrived, as always, in a happy state. This, he said, would be a difficult job, but one that had to be done. Besides, he wanted to be outdoors in such glorious spring weather. He wore blue Dickie shorts and a hooded sweatshirt. He set up camp beside the fenced garden and immediately plugged his saws-all into the bathroom outlet. Before he began in earnest, he took a wood awl and went up and down the building, stabbing the sill. He clucked. The awl sank in over and over, stabbing deeply into the false wood. He relished the rot; his theory was confirmed. Water was the enemy. Here was yet another example.

"It's lasted a hundred years," I pointed out as I walked with him. "It doesn't owe us much. It did its job."

"True," he said, "but you want to keep the ground off the wood. You see how it's come up? The ground, I mean? Dirt tries to climb a building if you give it a chance. You watch that sheep fence of yours. In a few years, dirt will be up over the first few strands of wire. Don't ask me how it does it. It's just does."

He kept stabbing, hoping to find a section of the sill worth saving. But it was all shot. Clarence pointed out that the barn's animal ramp had once pressed up to the sill we were ready to repair. Cows had passed over it, doing what cows do, their urine and droppings contributing to the rot and drawing insects. He placed a level on the sloping ground. See, he said, here was the last vestige of the animal ramp. He handed me a shovel and asked me to level it off while he got to work on the sill. He wanted a flat surface, more or less, with perhaps the tiniest remnant of a grade away from the house. That way, he said, water would flow from the foundation, not to it.

Using a saws-all, he gutted the sill, slicing the exterior of the house with no difficulty whatsoever. An odd sensation, really, to see him cut for a moment, then step back and yank a piece of sill away. In an hour he had cut a grin in the building's foundation, a guilty, sly look that revealed the connection of building to stone. In various places he jammed rocks and wooden butts into the new opening to make sure the sidewall did not begin to think about sinking. He doubted that it would, he said, but you never knew. As always he worked at stupendous speed. His legs churned. Now and then he turned to me and asked if that was all I had done. I admitted that it was.

And I didn't get much accomplished. It was dull work, certainly, but it was also spring and I didn't have much of a mind for shoveling. At lunch, my job perhaps a third finished, I asked Clarence how he kept moving at such a rate. He always had, he said. His family had grown up poor, getting by trapping rabbits, fishing, hunting. His father had been part American Indian and Clarence's memory of him was watching his father eat small pieces of poison ivy. That way, his father claimed, he would never have susceptibility to the rash. His father had moved fast. It ran in the family.

After lunch Clarence and I drove to Carr Mountain Pine, a local logging yard, to see if the shop foreman had any unfinished timbers. The foreman, a fleshy fellow I had seen around town in the company of an enormous golden retriever, pointed to a stack of discard lumber. Huge beams, some with the bark still in place, lay stacked against a cement wall. Most of the wood had been cut as beams for various jobs, but one thing or another had gone wrong—some were too short, others not properly squared, and so on. Clarence couldn't have been happier. We would replace the rotted sill with three heavy lengths of hemlock, each about ten feet long, which we loaded in the back of the pickup.

I left my spadework and went into the basement. Standing on one side of the gap, I helped guide Clarence as he slid the beams in place. They did not fit precisely, not at all, but we glided them in and out, trying various arrangements, until, in an hour, we had them roughly where Clarence wanted them. They fit together with perhaps a foot between each section. These, he said, we could patch with pressure-treated lumber.

He called it a day around five, stretching a tarp over the opening in the foundation, tucking it up for the night. Wendy and Pie returned from visiting a friend. She examined the work, whistled, then walked with me out to the wild garden. We did this every night, content to check what had grown, what had taken shape. We weeded casually, but mostly we surveyed the day's growth.

Later, when the evening turned blue, we poured two glasses of wine and sat on the porch glider. Wendy did a crossword puzzle until it became too dark. We sat and watched the sunset. Light slid off the mountains and pulled back toward the sun. Bats flicked across the meadow and dipped over the fishpond, mowing insects. The last light went and I had the impression of the sun sinking below the horizon and pulling its rays after it like a sheet falling from a bed.

I wrapped up digging as Clarence finished nailing the pressure-treated facing onto the sill. He sank the last few nails with particular gusto, happy to have the work finished. A dreary rain had bothered us all day. I had replaced the torn-up sod to make a decent carpet outside the French doors. Now it rested in lumpy squares, the slope sufficiently pitched to run water away from the building.

When he stepped away and shot his hammer into its metal bracket at his hip, I knew he was pleased with the outcome. And he should have been. The pulpy, weakened sill now appeared resolute and permanent. A clean line. He walked up and down the building, checking his work. "Shipshape," he said. Together our work had given a new dimension to this side of the barn. Now instead of worry—is it rotted, how much will it cost to repair it, can it last a few more years—the pressure-treated lumber gave the wall a stiff collar. Combined with my lawn work, the building now appeared managed, the way homes do after you've raked the lawn or swept the walk. I told Clarence that it looked terrific. I also asked him to tell me if he knew of any more rotted wood that needed replacing. I said I had had enough.

"Well, an old building, you never know," he said. "But I think we've got it licked. You've got most of the work done. This old barn should last another century anyway."

"Anything else you're afraid to break to me?"

"Oh, a thing or two, but nothing dramatic. You've got the heft of it."

"We would have been lost without you."

He nodded. He knew. I wondered, watching him pack up, about the projects he had completed around the state. He couldn't drive anywhere in New Hampshire without seeing a roof he had replaced, a plumbing job he had completed, a chimney he had re-pointed. Sometimes he helped people do minor plumbing jobs by phone: *Do you see that valve? That stopcock? Now turn it a quarter spin to the left. Easy. Just a little bit. Yes, toward the lake. Go ahead.*

After Clarence left I brought the truck around and loaded the scrap wood into the flatbed. Then I drove out to the fire ring and worked a flame up. The rain gave us license to burn; state officials didn't care about a brush fire as long as rain fell. The old wood, despite the rot, burned crisply. I went inside and grabbed a beer. By the time I returned the fire threw good heat. I pulled a log up next to it and sat. Insects wandered past but didn't press the issue. The rain had stalled, although it threatened to return at any moment. The meadow had a sodden, muggy appearance.

I burned off all the old sill, odd bits of scrap wood, then worked, lazily, at the pile of brush we had been building near the hedgerow. Oak, birch, cherry. The fire burned through the grid of little branches, yellow pushing through a sieve of twigs. To burn properly the fire needed more cordwood, but I didn't want to waste the good stuff on an outdoor burn. I fed the flames twigs and let the ash burn in red caterpillars up the wood.

Wendy honked when she pulled into the driveway twenty minutes later. She had groceries. Pie, springing free of the back-seat, galloped out to meet me. They had taken D Dog with them and she, too, ran after Pie. Dog and boy. As soon as Pie reached the fire he showed me a new Lego dinosaur hunter he had bought with his own money. By slamming the front launching pin against a wall, a catapult tossed a net that would—in principle, anyway—ensnare a small Lego dinosaur. Another place at the back of the vehicle provided a transport platform so that the dinosaur, subdued in the net, could be loaded like cargo to be taken back for exhibit.

But the big news was that Parker, Pie's best friend, was coming to sleep over. Wendy arrived at the fire, glass of wine in hand. Parker was coming. Hot dogs and beans for dinner. A cookout, if we liked; just keep the campfire going.

"Can we sleep out in a tent?" Pie asked. "Please. We won't be scared."

"It will be cold," Wendy said. "Sleep down in the basement. You can sleep outside when summer really gets here."

Parker arrived a half hour later and the two boys dove into the basement, setting up blankets to form a tent and rolling out sleeping bags inside. Then they disappeared into two Game Boys, their conversation degenerating into grunts about the various powers of different creatures. I didn't know whether to be relieved or alarmed that they could amuse themselves so easily.

Wendy, meanwhile, began painting a section of dry wall on the northern wall willow-hedge green. She had fussed at the project for days and days, taping and mudding the drywall joints, so when I volunteered to feed the boys she went immediately to work. I got the woodstove going—the rain had made the barn damp—and cooked up dogs and beans. Wendy had the radio playing corny top-forty music and we listened to whatever came on. I yelled down to the boys when the food was ready. They came up, helped themselves to everything, and then retreated again to the basement. Wendy and I ate two hot dogs next to her half-painted wall.

Afterward we painted together. Listening to music, the boys' giggles sometimes reaching us from down below, we worked without stopping. It was a good night—one of those nights when you get things done and it doesn't seem to require much effort. The woodstove ticked and splashed up heat and steam rose out of the kettle on top. On the porch moths swirled around the overhead lights, electrons, their shadows chasing them. And when we looked up it was full darkness. Night had come. We hadn't noticed because a full moon shone in through the transom windows and set the prisms glistening. I had never seen that before. The sun regularly cracked light through the prisms, but never the moon. But here it was and I told Wendy to look. Up on her ladder, she stopped and held her brush straight up and down and stared. For a moment we didn't say anything. I noticed the dog's water bowl caught the full circle of the moon on its surface. The image of the moon dangled there as if someone had flipped a bright gold coin through the window and it had landed here, heads up, in this barn. Wendy shook her head. Then she drew a long straight line down the border of the drywall. Paint followed her brush like wind going over fresh grass.

ACKNOWLEDGMENTS

I am grateful to all those who read the manuscript of this book and generously gave their time and insight. I am particularly indebted to Jay Schaefer and Steve Mockus at Chronicle Books for helping to produce this work. Both demonstrated great patience with me and both made this a better book by their careful editing. I would also like to thank Nanci McCrackin, book lover and friend, who has always looked kindly on my writing. Thanks, too, to Clarence Maines, who has stood by us as we worked to reclaim this old barn. His devotion to his work and family and his never-ending enthusiasm for life have been an inspiration to everyone who comes in contact with him.

My research in writing this book has benefited enormously from the wonderful writings and illustrations of Eric Sloane. His many works on barns and woodcraft are a delight and treasure. I also learned from Phillip Ziegler's book on historic barns of the northeast and from two thoughtful books by Michael Pollan. Thanks, also, to all those people who patiently listened as I became barn crazy these last two years.

Finally, thanks to Wendy and Pie and D Dog. What a joy it is to hear you coming though the door.